The Art of
Ship Modeling

Written and Illustrated by
A. Richard Mansir

Foreword by
Cmdr. William D. Benson
Maritime Museum Association of San Diego

VNR

VAN NOSTRAND REINHOLD COMPANY
NEW YORK · CINCINNATI · TORONTO · LONDON · MELBOURNE

Copyright © 1982 by A. Richard Mansir.

Published 1982 in the United States of America by
Van Nostrand Reinhold Company Inc.
135 West 50th Street
New York, NY 10020

Moonraker Publications
24452-B Alta Vista,
Dana Point, California 92629, USA.

Published in Great Britain by
Arms and Armour Press,
2-6 Hampstead High Street
London NW3 1QQ,
and at 4-12 Tattersalls Lane,
Melbourne, Victoria 3000, Australia.

Library of Congress Catalog Number 81-83960

ISBN (U.S.): 0-940620-03-0
ISBN (U.K.): 0-85368-505-3

Printed and bound in the United States of America

TABLE OF CONTENTS

THE MAKERS OF THIS BOOK

Written and illustrated by A. Richard Mansir

Foreword by Cmdr. William D. Benson

Executive Administrator, D. J. Roberts

Ship Models

Ship Modelers Association of Southern California
> Henry Bridenbecker
> Clyde Chaffin
> Donald Dressel
> John Dupray
> Jack Elem
> Howard Judson
> Thomas Palen
> Arthur Robinson
> Richard Roos
> Joseph Seela
> Roger Van der Walker
> Alan Weiss
> Luther Whomsley
> William Wicks

Ship Modelers Guild of San Diego
> Robert Crawford
> John McDermott
> Robert Pranka
> Theodore Pugh

Unaffiliated Modeler
> Lloyd McCaffery

Dedicated to ship modelers everywhere, and to those who would seek out and preserve our maritime heritage.

Maritime Museum Association of San Diego
> Captain Carl C. Bowman, President
> Ralph L. Snow, Director
> David G. Brierly, Curator
> Cmdr. William D. Benson, Curator of Ship Models

Photography
> Photographic Illustrators, San Diego
> Michael Eich

Woods for Modeling
> Lloyd Warner

INDEX TO COLOR PLATES

Foreword

By

William D. Benson,
Commander, U.S.N. (ret)
Curator of Models
Maritime Museum Association of San Diego
San Diego, California

Commander Benson at work on a model of the
Queen Mary now at Long Beach, California.

It has been said that there is no more beautiful creation of the hand of man than a full-rigged ship under sail. If this is true, and I believe it is, a miniature of such a ship must be considered a true work of art. It is fortunate that this particular and unique art form can be appreciated by all, and created by many.

Any successful artist must have talent, time and a great deal of self-discipline. Other desirable attributes of an artist - and particularly of a model-maker - are reasonably good eyesight (perhaps augmented by a magnifier); a certain degree of manual dexterity; more than a little patience; and most important of all the determination to complete a task once embarked on it.

In building a model no mistake can be made that cannot be corrected by a small amount of additional effort, and the builder should recognize that time invested in re-doing an improperly made part will be a source of gratification for years to come. Although a model builder hardly ever is *satisfied* with his own work, he can be *pleased* with the result, and it is this pleasure of creation that makes model-making worth the effort. Dick Mansir's book reflects precisely the same sort of artistic effort.

There have been many books written on the subject of ship model building both in this country and abroad, some of which are widely regarded as authoritative and of great value to the modeler. However, many of the best deal with only one ship or ship type, and reflect only the authors' favorite methods of construction. Others, while containing plans and instructions for a number of different ships, are poorly organized and not too well written, and often show outdated tools, materials, and methods. There is thus a great need for a well-researched, well-organized and well-written book showing the most up-to-date information on model building available.

This need has been met in a most excellent fashion by Dick Mansir's "The Art of Ship Modeling". His research has been extensive and selective; sources used have included many of the great books on ships and the sea, as well as all the better ones on the subject of models.

For a modeler, time spent on research, while essential, is time away from actual work on the model, and it is hard to tell when to quit searching for additional data. Nautical books, plans, and photographs can be very expensive or unobtainable; to find so much accurate and relevant information in one volume is most economical in both time and money.

The organization of the book is also well designed to suit the needs of both the student of nautical lore and the model builder. Each of the chapters is complete within itself, covering the chapter subject clearly and completely. Though not directed to the construction of any one ship, there is a wealth of information on many ship types, and a great deal of technical data common to the ships of a certain specified era. The order of presentation of the chapters is logical and follows a rational pattern, proceeding from introductory material of general historical interest to detailed sections on the actual building of models. Dick is an excellent writer, lucid and entertaining, and his book is valuable as literature as well as a reference for modelers.

But excellent as is the text of "The Art of Ship Modeling", it is the illustrations that set the book apart from all its predecessors. With almost all of the pages containing one or more photographs and drawings, many in full color, it is an absolute delight to spend many hours just studying the pictures. Photographs of a wide assortment of models of superior quality are used to amplify the text; they are carefully selected and well arranged in the format of the book, and can only be an inspiration to other modelers. Photographs of the museum ship, the bark *Star of India* are used to enhance the value of the text. Built in 1869 as *Euterpe* on the Isle of Man, she is the oldest merchant ship afloat, and has been restored and is now maintained by the Maritime Museum Association of San Diego. Of the various ships of past centuries in existence -*Victory, Constitution, Cutty Sark*, and others - only the *Star of India* is still fully capable of sailing. Her sails are bent and usually set; thus her rigging and gear are absoutely authentic; she has a trained crew and her skipper, Captain Carl Bowman USCG (Ret) of the Maritime Museum Association is one of very few active seagoing Americans to hold a Coast Guard license as Master of Sail, Steam and Motor Vessels - (Unlimited). A reader of Dick Mansir's book can be assured that any information from the photographs or the text relating to the *Star of India* is accurate in every detail.

In addition to the photographs, both color and black and white, "The Art of Ship Modeling" contains what I look on as another complete collection of nautical art - Dick Mansir's superb drawings of an amazing variety of ships' structures, fittings, decorations, and rigging. These drawings are also well selected to supplement the text, with which they are most carefully integrated. Such well-researched, well-organized and well-drawn illustrations are of great utility - they tell their own story. Dick Mansir has provided those of us who love ships and enjoy their small recreations - either as builders, collectors, or observers - with a book filled with valuable and significant information, but even more, of lasting beauty.

INTRODUCTION

"Posted like sentinels all around the town, stand thousands of mortal men fixed in ocean reveries... Strange! Nothing will content them but the extremest limit of the land ... they must get just as nigh the water as they possibly can without falling in. And there they stand—miles of them—leagues... Tell me, does the magnetic virtue of the needles of the compasses of all those ships attract them thither?"

Moby Dick - Melville

These observations, posed by Herman Melville in the opening chapter of his *Moby Dick*, may account for man's age-old fascination with the art and craft of ship modeling. How else can we explain the presence of ship models in the tombs of the Egyptian pharoahs; the small replicas of catamarans made by the South Sea Islanders, and the exquisite tradition of miniature ships that dot the history of Europe, Asia, and the Americas?

To be sure, some of these models were made for religious and practical purposes, but even these seem to have been born partly of that other, peculiar mystique of a man's adventure at sea.

Ships are among the oldest and noblest of our technical achievements. Of late, model railroads and airplanes have occupied the imaginations of many hobbyists, but these machines are the product of but a single century, while shipbuilding was going on before the beginning of recorded history. The history of ships and ship modeling, therefore, engages us in the entire history of man's civil and technological evolution.

In recent years, more and more people have been caught up in this intriguing segment of the past, turning their eyes and hands to the intricate, special art of miniature shipbuilding. Manufacturers armed with new technologies and materials are offering hobbyists ship models of surprising accuracy and beauty, while a growing number of collectors are investing huge sums in ship models appraised into the hundreds of thousands of dollars.

Part of this renewed enthusiasm may be attributed to the recent dramatic discoveries by underwater archaeological teams, such as those of George Bass and Jacques Cousteau. Newspaper, magazine, and television articles about the uncovering of vast hordes of sunken Spanish treasure have no doubt contributed to popular excitement about our maritime past. However one accounts for it, one cannot deny the body of superb works of the ship modeler's art that is beginning to emerge from thousands of home workshops and studios across the land. This book, in part, is a tribute to some of these unsung artists, as well as a discussion of the subject in general.

It has been my good fortune to have become a member of the Ship Modeler's Association of Fullerton, California, and to be associated with the Ship Modeler's Guild of San Diego, California. The ship models pictured here are largely the work of these two memberships. All of them are the work of "amateurs" — hobbyists, who for the sheer love of it, have invested the thousands of hours necessary to their creation.

In this regard, one should be aware that the common distinction between "amateur" and "professional" ship modelers is often reversed. Few "professional" ship modelers, given that they must make a living wage from the craft, can afford to invest the time of the amateur without pricing themselves out of the market. Thus it follows that the work of hobbyists frequently outshines that of the "pros." Among ship modelers, the apellation "amateur" usually means the best there is.

That the ship modelers of Southern California have been singled out here is a happenstance largely of geographical convenience reinforced by the fact that they are perhaps the largest organized group of ship modelers in the United States.

We must acknowledge, however, that thousands more outstanding ship modelers exist in our country, and the world, whose work might just as well have graced the pages of this volume.

Our major purpose is to present the history of ships and shipbuilding from the modeler's viewpoint. Where other histories deal with the who and what of events, our concern is with the technical details of ship architecture as it was practiced through the years. The work, since some limit had to be placed on a limitless subject, is about sailing ships, particularly from the centuries between 1600 and 1900. Earlier sailing vessels have been dealt with in less detail, while the whole fascinating world of power driven ships has been left untouched.

One will find in these pages a description of the way the hulls of sailing ships were (and are) designed and constructed; the kinds of materials, fastenings, and paints that were used; the names and purposes of the lines and sails in a ship's rigging; the relative sizes and proportions of a ship's components; and other information not usually provided outside of the technical literature of marine architects.

The work, in a sense, is a primer of nautical lore designed to acquaint the uninitiated with the jargon of the sea as well as reveal some of the methods and secrets from the modern ship modeler's workshop. Aspiring modelers, together with involved collectors, we hope, will find our book a useful and stimulating springboard into the special fascinations of this unique and compelling craft.

It has been our intent to be technical without being burdensome — to offer functional information in an enjoyable format.

We asked Commander Bill Benson to write a brief foreword for our book because we knew that a man of his stature in maritime matters would not allow us to make many mistakes if his name appeared on the work. His review of our work as well as his kind words are much appreciated.

Bill has spent his life building ship models and driving ships at sea. He was graduated from Kings Point Merchant Marine Academy in 1944 with a degree in marine engineering. He joined the Navy in 1946 and served on submarines until 1962, with two years out to earn a Phi Beta Kappa key at the University of North Carolina. During these years, there was seldom a period when two or three ship models were not in progress.

He has completed hundreds of models, restored hundreds more, and today is one of the world's acknowledged professional experts in the field. Among his achievements were the towing tank models for Gerry Driscoll's 1974 America's Cup contender *Intrepid*, and other international racing yachts.

We could not have wished for a more knowledgeable testimonial than that offered by Commander Benson.

Special thanks is also due David G. Brierley, Curator of the Maritime Museum Association in San Diego. Dave went out of his way to provide us every assistance in the obtaining of photo material and reviewing our effort.

And, of course, the book would not exist but for my friends of the Ship Modelers' Association of Fullerton, and the Ship Modelers' Guild of San Diego, whose members so enthusiastically supported the project. Let them all be thanked in the persons of their elected directors. In Fullerton, Henry Bridenbecker, Craig Coleman, Don Dressel, Jack Elem, Jess Laughlin, Dick Roos, Bob Saddoris, and Bill Wicks make up the Board of Directors, while Tom Palen, the Logkeeper, has been a leading light of the organization for years. We may note that the Association itself has it roots in the person of Craig Coleman, who probably has done more to promote the art of ship modeling than any single individual in the area. Craig's expertise and willingness to teach are without peer.

In San Diego, Al L'heureux, Bob Crawford, Bill Kelly-Fleming, Doug McFarland, George Oliver, Bob Ross, and John Woodard lead the group. Thanks, too, to Lloyd Warner for his expert help in the preparation of the section on woods for ship modelers.

And finally, I have to thank my associates in Moonraker Publications: Dee Roberts, Jim Rahman, and Len Forman. It was Dee in particular who patiently bore the several years of creative stress behind the book, and who steadfastly defended me from my natural inclination toward folly.

ON THE QUESTION OF SCHOLARSHIP

The objective of this volume is to provide the reader a general view of the naval architectural ideas that have prevailed through history. The book is written in broad strokes, and as such is open to the legitimate criticism applicable to all broad generalization. If one accepts the idea that there is "an exception to prove every rule", the principle applies in spades to the subject of maritime history. Here one can say that for every "rule" there are at least a hundred exceptions to prove it. A strict scholastic presentation of this material would require an endless succession of *if's, but's, on the other hand's, nobody knows,* and confounding qualifications to a point of no return. We have chosen to slice this "Gordian Knot" in the interests of clarity but possibly at the risk of precision. The reader is then advised to consider the information given here with a grain or two of salt lest he be startled to find on further research that what we have declared to be *generally* true was certainly not true in every case, and, what we have declared as "fact" may be the subject of intensive controversy among the scholars.

Maritime history is as complex as it is long and many of the detailed facts concerning even the most recent periods are simply unknown and probably lost forever in time.

The ship modeler engaged in the creation of an authentic historical document is obliged to fill in certain details out of his historical imagination no less than more conventional historians are obliged to piece together a picture of the past from some scant remains. But where a written document might hold together with certain unknowns left out, a ship model, as a visual statement, simply cannot stand unless all of its many specifics are accounted for, whether by documented fact or intelligent guesswork. For example, a model of a ship known to have been a sailing ship would make no sense without a mast. So what would a modeler do if there were no documentation on the mast? Clearly he would have to guess if he were to make any statement at all and it would seem that *some* statement is better in every case than *no* statement. The quest for truth begins with an hypothesis.

What we think we may have accomplished is to provide a target for scholarly critics who in the act of proving us wrong will uncover the truth for the benefit of us all.

In any event, it is pleasant to believe that we shall provoke a more widespread inquiry into the story of men at sea.

Chapter One
An Introduction to Nautical Terminology

NAUTICAL TERMINOLOGY

Nautical terminology is a technical vocabulary that has evolved through the centuries of man's seagoing history. English nautical terms, I suspect, had their origins in the early English, Norse, and Celtic languages as they were spoken in the years before Christ. Each language of the world has a nautical vocabulary of similar antiquity.

Nautical terms are sometimes confusing to the initiate. Often the same word is used to denote several different things. The word *"tack"* is an example. Tack in one context means the side of the ship against which the wind is blowing; in another, a maneuver in which the ship steers a zig-zag course into the wind; in a third, a rigging line; and finally, the fore corner of a fore and aft sail. The key to meaning is context.

Spelling is sometimes confusing, too. Through most of history, the seaman's lingo was almost exclusively a spoken language. When literate men took on the task of writing out the vocabulary, they were dependent on the sailor's pronunciations, which could vary substantially, depending on the inclination of the moment. For example, the word *"trennel"* was also pronounced *"trunnel."* Literally, a trennel was a *"tree nail,"* a hardwood dowel used to pin a ship's planks to its frames. The phonetic spelling "trennel" reflects the casual, foreshortened pronunciation one might expect from an unlettered man of the sea. Fo'c'sle for forecastle is another example. There are many terms that reflect similar foundations.

This chapter is intended to give the landlubber a fundamental nautical vocabulary sufficient to follow the explanations offered in the later chapters. It does no good to describe, for example, an *athwartship* member, if one is not acquainted with the term "athwartship."

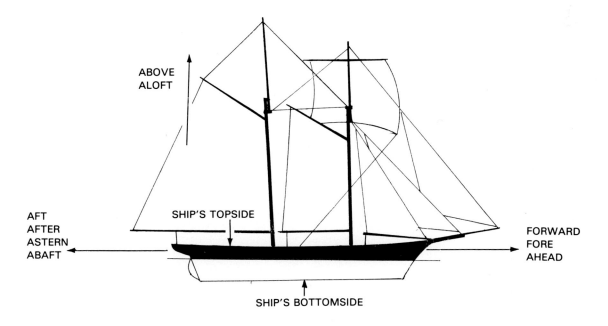

ABOVE
ALOFT

AFT
AFTER
ASTERN
ABAFT

SHIP'S TOPSIDE

FORWARD
FORE
AHEAD

SHIP'S BOTTOMSIDE

DIRECTIONAL TERMS

Ashore we say that things are "to the left," "to the right," "behind us" or "in front of us." At sea a different set of terms are used to convey these ideas. Generally the sea terms are more precise in meaning than their onshore equivalents because of the mariner's need to know fast and exactly where to look. For example, if a boat was attempting to rendezvous with a ship, it would not be enough for the helmsman to know that the approaching boat was "off to the left." He must know exactly where "off-to-the-left" so he can maneuver his ship into a meeting with the boat short of catastrophe.

Directions of this kind on shipboard are given with respect to the ship's head and are known as relative bearings. Relative bearings in turn reflect the nomenclature of the ship itself. The front of a ship is the bow; the back is the stern; the left-hand side looking toward the bow is the portside; the right-hand side, the starboard side. Anything either directly to port or starboard is said to be abeam because to see it one must look in a line across the width of the ship. A ship's width is its beam.

Thus, a sailor lookout, reporting the position of an approaching boat sings out, "she bears fine on the port bow!" And the helmsman understands that the boat is just a little off to the left of where his ship is heading.

The larboard side of a ship is the old term for port or left side of a ship. The official designation changed from larboard to port in 1844 to avoid further confusion in helm orders which arose from the similar sounding starboard and larboard.

A further refinement of relative bearings on shipboard derives from the points of the mariner's compass. Today we are more accustomed to compass bearings given in degrees where the circle of the card is divided into 360 parts. Sailing ships, however, subject to the vagaries of wind and sea would not hold to a course so precisely defined. Navigators specified their course in terms of 32 "points" of the compass, each point equal to a little over 11 degrees.

Thus, an old captain's log might record his course on a given day as "North East by East (NE by E)." Later as ships and helmsmen became more efficient, the points were subdivided into halves and quarters. Captains then could enter a course of "NE by E by ½ N." (One half a point closer to north than the coefficient.)

Sailors learned to live and breathe the points of the compass, the concept of "point" itself drilled into their mentalities through endless hours at the helm. It became second nature to explain that such and such was "two points off the larboard bow," and a regular occurrence to hear a lookout aloft cry, "Sail ho! Three points abaft the larboard beam!"

POINTS OF RELATIVE BEARING

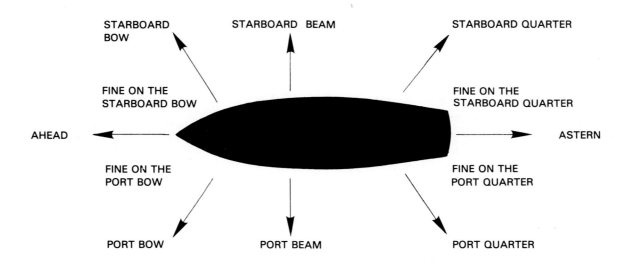

STARBOARD BOW   STARBOARD BEAM   STARBOARD QUARTER

FINE ON THE STARBOARD BOW   FINE ON THE STARBOARD QUARTER

AHEAD   ASTERN

FINE ON THE PORT BOW   FINE ON THE PORT QUARTER

PORT BOW   PORT BEAM   PORT QUARTER

TERMS ABOUT THE WIND

Sailing ships lived on the wind and much of the sailor's vocabulary had to do with how the wind was effecting his ship.

No ship, of course, could sail directly into the wind, meaning that the wind had to blow from some quarter of relative bearing other than dead ahead.

If the wind were blowing from either of the bow quarters, the ship was "on a beat" or "beating up." With "wind abeam," the ship is on a broad reach. When the wind blows from the stern quarters, the ship is said to be running before the wind or simply, running. Captains and sailors came to evaluate ships by their sailing characteristics at these various points of sail. A captain could nurse extra miles per day out of his ship by knowing that her "best point of sail" was with the wind two points abaft her beam.

The side of the ship against which the wind blows decides the tack she is on. If the wind is blowing from the starboard side, the ship is said to be on a starboard tack; if blowing from port she is on a port tack.

The tack side of a ship was also her windward side. The opposite was the lee side. The terms windward and lee have similar meanings ashore. One speaks, for example, of finding shelter from a storm in the lee of a barn or, in other words, on the protected side, opposite to the windward one against which the storm is beating.

Changing a ship's course changes her relationship to the wind direction. If the ship steers so that the wind moves from one side of the ship to the other she is said to "change her tack."

To "come about" means to change the ship's tack by steering first into the wind and then "falling off" again on the new tack. To "jibe" the ship means to change the ship's tack by steering first downwind. Wearing, or waring, a ship is the same maneuver as a jibe but applies to square-riggers.

POINTS OF SAIL

On the **Port Tack** the wind blows over the port rail.

On the **Starboard Tack** the wind blows over the starboard rail.

WIND DIRECTION

WIND DIRECTION

Beating - Beating up: ship sails as much into the wind as possible. Square riggers could beat up no closer than five or six points off the wind (see page 17).

Reaching - On a Reach - Reaching Off: ship sails with the wind blowing against her side. In other words, with wind abeam.

WIND DIRECTION

Running - Running Before the Wind - Broad Off: ship sails with the wind dead behind her, or wind astern.

Hove to - Sails Aback - Wind on the Luff: ship stopped with her head straight into the wind.

DARCY LEVER, Esq.

Among the classic works in the lore of the sea is Darcy Lever's *The Young Sea Officer's Sheet Anchor or a Key to the Leading of Rigging and to Practical Seamanship* originally published in London in the early 1800's.

His work was written primarily for the accommodation of the young Gentlemen of the Royal Navy, and as such became an almost standard text for all the young sea officers of the time.

While Mr. Lever's archaic style might seem a bit awkward to our modern mentalities, his words catch the flavor of the sea as the mariners of his day understood it. Where it has seemed appropriate, we have let Mr. Lever explain certain points here and there throughout our text in his own inimitable way. What better authority could we quote but one who has earned the approval of this distinguished list of naval worthies?

THE UNDER-MENTIONED OFFICERS OF HIS MAJESTY'S ROYAL NAVY

Have been pleased to give their Signatures of Approval to this Work, as worthy the Attention of young Officers and others The Names are placed in the order and manner they were signed in the two first pages of the manuscript:—

J. Holloway, Vice-Admiral;
Keith, Admiral;
Robert Jackson, Captain H.M.S. Edgar;
E.W.C.R. Owen, Captain H.M.S. Clyde;
John Laugharne, Captain H.M.S. Isis;
Joshua Sydney Horton, Captain
        H.M.S. Princess of Orange;
Henry Bazely, Captain H.M.S. Antelope
A.C. Dickson, Captain H.M.S. Orion;
Charles Ekins, Captain H.M.S. Defence;
George Montague, Admiral;
Isaac Coffin, Rear-Admiral;
William Young, Admiral;
E. Gower, Vice-Admiral;
B.S. Rowley, Vice-Admiral;
H.E. Stanhope, Vice-Admiral;
J. Vashon, Rear-Admiral
Philip Patton, Admiral;
George Grey, Captain R.N.
Thomas Dundas, Captain R.N.
Loftus Otway Bland, Captain R.N.
C.P. Hamilton, Vice-Admiral;
Walter Lock, Captain R.N.
P. Somerville, Captain H.M.S. Nemesis;

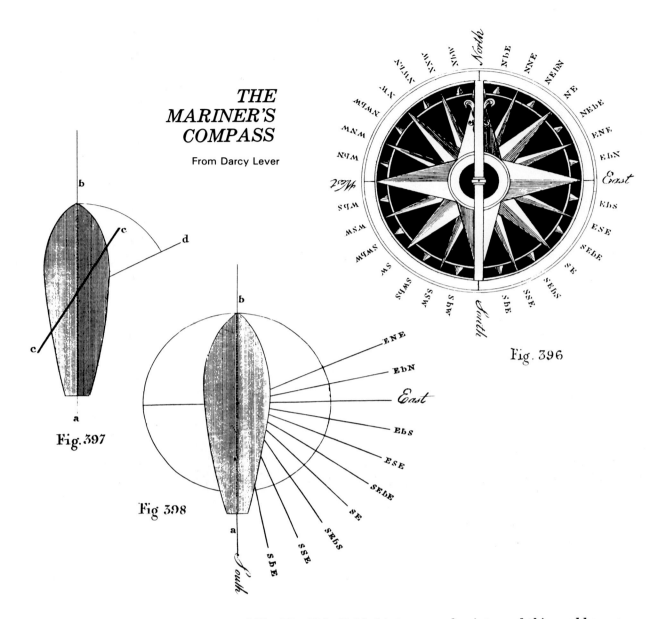

THE MARINER'S COMPASS

From Darcy Lever

Fig. 397

Fig 398

Fig. 396

The Compass is described on a card like Fig. 396, divided into several points; and this card being fixed on a piece of steele called the needle, which has been touched by a loadstone, acquires the property when resting on a pivot fixed vertically in the compass box, of pointing to the North. The North point of the compass then pointing to the North, the others will of course point to their respective parts of the horizon. The variation of the compass is not here noticed, as it may be referred to in any book of navigation.

The compass has eight points in each quarter, equal to ninety degrees, making in the whole thirty-two, equal to three hundred and sixty degrees of the horizon. A square rigged ship, when close-hauled (as before mentioned), can lie no nearer to the wind than six points: therefore, if a ship be close-hauled on the starboard tack, and her head at North, count six points from thence to the right hand, or towards the East, and you will find the wind must be at E.N.E. The wind then forms an angle with the keel of six points, or sixty-three degrees forty-five minutes: so that if the line (a. b.) Fig. 397, represent the ship's keel, (c) will be the yard when braced up, and (d) the direction of the wind. In practice the yard is braced up sharper, to make the sail stand to the most advantage.

TACKING A SQUARE RIGGER

To bring a ship *about* is to change her tack by steering her up into the wind then letting her *fall off* on the new tack. Coming about in an old square rigger required some tricky seamanship. Darcy Lever explains how it was done.

"Suppose (the word 'Helm's alee' has been given) in the Ship, Fig. 399, which had her Head North, as per Compass, and that in consequence she was coming around gradually to the Eastward, and approaching the wind: when she arrived at the position of the Ship, Fig. 400, her Head would be N E by N (see compass), within three points of the wind, which blowing on the Leeches or Extremities of the after Sails, made them shake; at this moment the word was given, 'Off Tacks and Sheets!' when the Main Tack, Sheet, and all the Staysail Tacks and Sheets were let go, because they were of no farther use in bringing the Ship to the wind; it having no effect upon them but to make them shake. (At this time the Tacks and Sheets of the Staysails were shifted over the Stays, to be ready for the other Tack; and the Main Clew-Garnet hauled a little up, that the Yard might come about the easier."

Fig. 399   Fig. 400   Fig. 401   Fig. 402

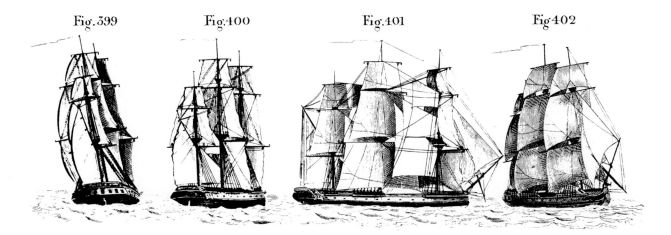

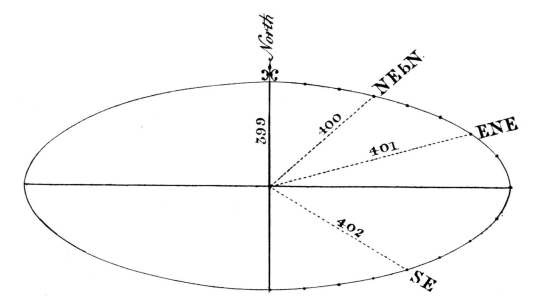

WARING A SQUARE RIGGER

To ware a ship is to change her tack by first steering downwind and then up again to the new tack.

"In the Compass, Fig. 415, which describes her Waring distance, the disadvantages of this movement is evident; for in the mere turning motion, she must go from S.E. to North, which is twenty points, being eight points (or one-fourth) of the Compass more than she had to go in tacking, but the principal defect is, that during this movement, whilst she is receding from the wind, she is forced rapidly through the water, and making all her way to leeward. However, in the present instance, all this is supposed to be necessary.

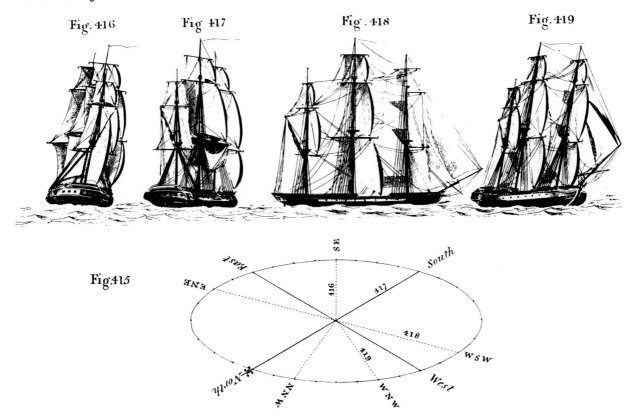

Fig. 416   Fig. 417   Fig. 418   Fig. 419

Fig. 415

The Ship, Fig 416, perceiving danger to windward, puts the Helm to port, (or a-weather) hauls up the Mizen, down the Mizen Staysail, and shivers the Mizen Topsail, (by letting go the Bowline and lee Brace, and hauling in the Weather one) and sometimes hauls up the Mainsail; but if not, the Main Sheet is eased off. (The Helm being a-weather, and the Power being taken from the Sails, which are at the after extremity of the Ship, effort is given to the Head Sails, which lie before the Center of Gravity, to pay her head off to leeward.) The Main, Main Top, and Main Top Gallant Bowlines are let go; and when her Head is South, (as per Compass) the wind being then two points abaft the Beam, like Fig. 417, the Main Tack is raised, and the Weather Braces are rounded in. When she has fallen off so as to bring her Head W.S.W. (as per Compass) she will be before the wind, and in the position of the Ship, Fig. 418: the Yards are then squared, and the starboard Main and Fore Tacks got on board: (the Head Sails, as may be seen in the Figure, will at this time be becalmed by the after ones) the Jib, and Staysail Sheets are shifted over the Stays, the Spritsail Yard topped up with the larboard Brace, and the Starboard Jib Guys set up. When her Head is W.N.W. (as per Compass) she will have the wind on the starboard quarter, at which time the Mizen is hauled out, the Mizen Staysail hoisted, and the Sheet hauled aft, like Fig. 419.

SHIP COMPONENTS

Out of the thousands of terms used to describe each part and bit of gear on a ship, a few terms may be useful as a basic orientation.

A ship's keel defines the centerline of her bottom. In addition to providing a structural backbone for the vessel, the keel is the major reference line for virtually everything else aboard. For example, the positions of masts are specified by distances measured along the keel; the width (beam) of the ship is expressed as a ratio of keel length, while mast lengths are expressed as a ratio of the beam.

The parts of a ship which occupy areas toward the bow are frequently prefixed "fore" or "forward." Thus we have foremast, forecastle, forward hatch, fore bitts, and so on. Similarly the parts toward the stern are often prefixed "after" or "aft." We hear then of the after companionway, or aft pin rail.

The term "fore and aft" means a direction parallel with the keel. So deck planks are said to be laid fore and aft, while sails that set along the center plane of the keel are called fore and aft sails.

Athwart means in a direction across the width of the ship. Skid beams used as racks to support boats and spare spars are examples of athwartship members. The yards of square-riggers are also set athwartship.

The suffix "side" occurs commonly also. A ship is said to have a bottom side, a topside, and shipsides.

Ashore when we describe the room of a house we refer to walls, floor and ceiling. On shipboard, walls are bulkheads, unless a wall happens to be also the side of the ship, in which case it is called the shipside. The "floor" is called the deck, while the "ceiling" is called the overhead. Now in fact ships do have floors and ceiling, but the terms have a completely different meaning from the way they are used ashore. The floors of a ship are the lower parts of her frames mounted on the keel. Ceiling refers to inside planking.

The term "port" plays a common role, referring generally to any opening in the ship's sides. Entry port, loading port, gunport and porthole are among this array.

A ship may have one or several decks which can run either the whole length of the ship or just part of it. A common deck arrangement consisted of a main deck running full length; a quarterdeck above the main, running from about midships aft; a foredeck at the same level as the quarterdeck but covering only a small section of the bow; and a poop deck covering a short length of the quarterdeck.

Larger ships might have several more decks, in which case the lowest deck was called the orlop deck.

In the old sailing navies, ships were designated by the number of full length gundecks they had. Thus a three-decker might have, from the bottom up, an orlop deck, lower gundeck, main gundeck, upper gundeck, spar deck, quarterdeck and poop deck.

The area of main deck left uncovered by the fore and quarterdecks was called the waist. The waist was a ship's work center. The main hatch to the hold was here. Burtons and winding tackle were rigged to service the area. Carpentry, sail mending, repair of rope and cable, and dozens of other tasks concentrated crewmen at sea around this crossroads.

The quarterdeck was "officer country." Ordinary seamen never stepped upon it except in the strictest line of duty, and most preferred not to. Mizzenmast hands, while their work was lighter than the rest, spent their hours aft in awesome proximity to authority. So, too, the helmsman. Relief from tension came only when the sailor went forward to the hearty comradery of the forecastle away from the steely eyes of captain and mates.

R.H. Dana in his *Two Years Before the Mast* explains a sailor's point of view, *"While there (living further aft in the steerage area of the ship)... you are but a mongrel — a sort of afterguard and 'ship's cousin.' You are immediately under the eye of the officers, cannot dance, sing, play, smoke, make a noise, or growl, or take any other sailor's pleasure...and the crew never feel as though you were one of them. But if you live in the forecastle, you are as independent as a 'wood-sawyer's clerk,' and are a sailor."*

PARTS OF A SHIP'S HULL

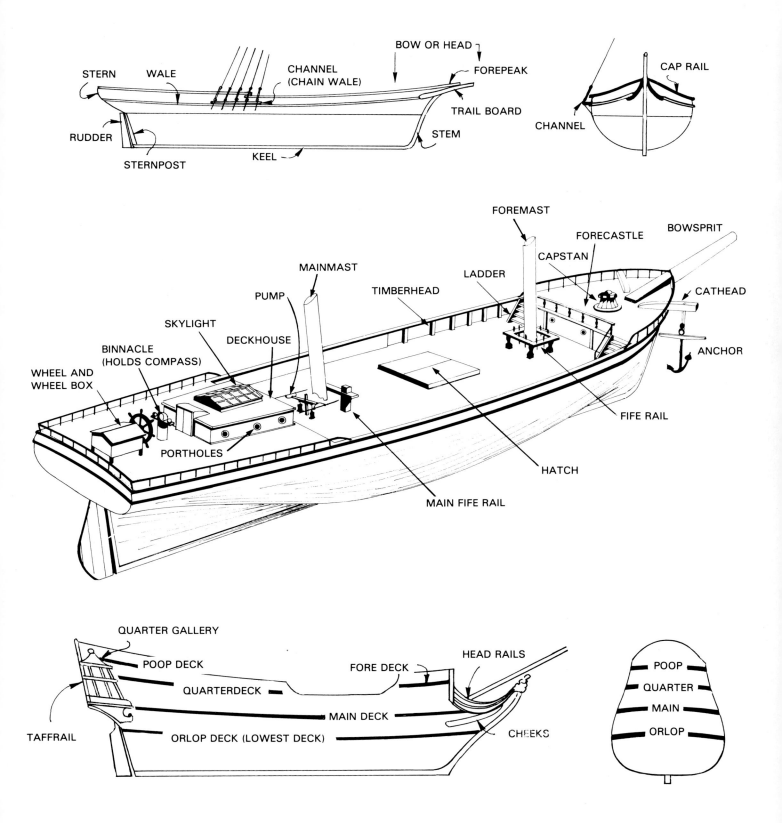

STERN
WALE
CHANNEL (CHAIN WALE)
BOW OR HEAD
FOREPEAK
CAP RAIL
CHANNEL
RUDDER
TRAIL BOARD
STEM
STERNPOST
KEEL

FOREMAST
FORECASTLE
BOWSPRIT
MAINMAST
CAPSTAN
PUMP
LADDER
CATHEAD
SKYLIGHT
TIMBERHEAD
DECKHOUSE
ANCHOR
BINNACLE (HOLDS COMPASS)
WHEEL AND WHEEL BOX
FIFE RAIL
PORTHOLES
HATCH
MAIN FIFE RAIL

QUARTER GALLERY
POOP DECK
HEAD RAILS
POOP
FORE DECK
QUARTER
QUARTERDECK
MAIN
MAIN DECK
ORLOP
TAFFRAIL
ORLOP DECK (LOWEST DECK)
CHEEKS

OTHER TERMS AND EXPRESSIONS

Beside the technical terms of the sailor's vocabulary, lie a rich store of colorful turns of phrase.

Sailors do not "go" places, they "lay" aloft, "lay" aft, or "lay" below.

When we say we are "between the devil and the deep blue sea," we refer to a precarious place aboard ship. The "devil" is the seam between the outermost edge of the deck and the side of the ship, and is a "devil" of a seam to caulk properly. Another "devil" is the seam between the keel and the first plank (garboard) of the ship's bottom.

Johnny's "lolling around" is borrowed from the state of a ship when water sloshing around inside her is causing her to roll and pitch.

To "whistle in the wind" is to recall the old sailors' superstition that one can whistle up a wind in a calm, but to whistle in the wind is to whistle up a gale.

And how many times have we heard "son of a gun!" The expression was born in the early 1800's when seamen's wives lived aboard naval vessels while in port. These wives gave birth to their children in the same place they and their husbands slept — in hammocks strung between the guns on the gundeck. Hence, the children were born as "sons of guns." The old saying had it, "Begotten in the galley and born under a gun. Every hair a rope yarn, every tooth a marlin spike, every finger a fishhook, and his blood right good Stockholm tar."

And, of course, many of us have come home "pooped" occasionally. The term comes from the predicament of a ship being chased by a following sea so large and fast that the rudder will not work. If the ship is "pooped," the great sea will break over her stern and probably turn her broadside to the waves. Being "pooped" at sea is a dangerous experience.

Then, too, many of us have stayed at a party to "the bitter end." Few realize that the "bitter end" is the unused end of a ship's anchor cable. A ship anchored to the bitter end therefore is in deep water.

One could, of course, go on for volumes exploring this intriguing estuary of etymology. However, we must give way to our larger purpose, trusting that the few tastes of salt provided so far will suffice to steer the reader off soundings in his quest for nautical learning.

Broaching to in a heavy sea is a dangerous matter

Chapter Two
Principles of
Marine Architecture

PRINCIPLES OF NAVAL ARCHITECTURE

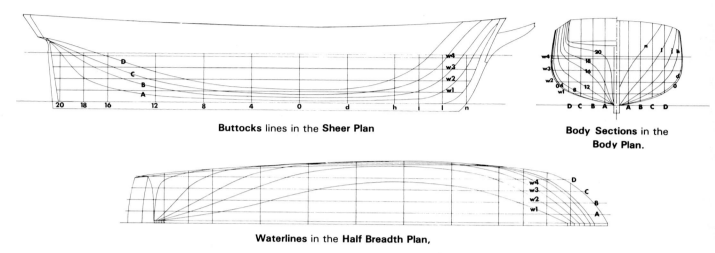

Buttocks lines in the **Sheer Plan**

Body Sections in the
Body Plan.

Waterlines in the **Half Breadth Plan,**

A ship's hull is described by the lines drawings.

Modern naval architecture relies on a body of scientific thought and technology which modern model builders bring into play primarily in the development and reading of plans. Historians and archaeologists record and expand upon the remains of ancient ships in the terms of contemporary ship designers as a way of coming to understand what the old ships looked like, how they must have performed, and how they were built.

Prior to 1550, very little of the shipwright's craft was set to paper. Plans, at least in the modern sense, were non-existent. Shipbuilders were hard-handed craftsmen whose closely guarded skills were passed down through generations by word-of-mouth and practical experience. Few of these men were literate.

Ship design followed traditional principles. Upon acceptance of a commission to build a ship, a shipwright would set to work on his lofting floor, laying out, full scale, the frames and other components with straight edge and compasses, according to the arcane "rules" he learned from his father, and his father before him.

As one might expect, some of these old ships were catastrophic failures, but more surprising is the fact that so many succeeded. Our unsophisticated ancestors were far from lacking insight into the "way of a ship in the sea." We may appreciate their achievements better in the light of our present knowledge.

THE DRAFTING OF HULL LINES

BACKGROUND

Mathew Baker, Henry the Eighth's "Master Shipwright" believed a ship should "go in like a Cod and out like a Mackeral."

During the 1500's, the Italian city states of Florence, Genoa and Venice harbored the genius of Renaissance Europe and, among other artists, spawned the leading shipwrights of the day.

When Henry VIII became King of England in 1509, he perceived a need for warships able to mount "stone gonnes of yron upon trotill wheles," and "great bumberdes of brasse upon trotill wheles." Initially, his perception led to the creation of the *Henry Grace a Dieu*, the first of a line of great ships which eventually established England as mistress of the seas. But for all that , though the *Henry Grace a Dieu* was a great ship for her day, she was designed and built by traditional technologies. She proved cumbersome and unwieldly as a gun platform.

Henry hired some Italians steeped in the intellectual and artistic ferment that had nourished Leonardo da Vinci, among others. They brought to England the newly evolved methods of technical illustration, which the great master himself had pioneered together with Filippo Brunelleschi, Leon Battista Alberti, and other maestri of quattrocento Italy. The Italians set to work to solve Henry's problem, and in 1546 the first four truly functional gun ships were launched.

At the same time, Henry established a new school of naval architecture in England, taught by the Italians, and created the office of His Majesty's "Master Shipwright." Mathew Baker became the first to wear the title in 1572. His sketches and drafts are the earliest known technical drawings of the lines of a vessel, though we must presume that he learned to make them from his Italian tutors.

Baker's drafting skills, however, were exceptional among shipwrights, even long after his death. While the practice gained some in popularity and technique, shipwrights continued to rely on their old methods. Baker, as the King's top man, after all, represented the best of the elite in matters of shipbuilding, as did his sucessors.

Baker died in 1613, having served Henry, witnessing the defeat of the Spanish Armada in 1588, and seeing the passing of the great age of Elizabeth the First. James I reigned in England when Baker's duties were assumed by Phineas Pett and William Burrell.

Pett and Burrell, no doubt, were competent draftsmen in the manner of Baker, but Pett impressed King James with his design for the *Prince Royal*, not with his drawings, but with a model. After Pett, models served shipwrights as much as drawings right up to our day and, often as not, were the only plans the builders in the yard had to go by.

Burrell died in 1630, and Pett became "Principal Officer and Commissioner" for the Navy. Shortly thereafter, the rest of his shipbuilding family were happily employed under fat government contracts. Peter senior, a nephew, became master at Deptford. Peter junior, his son, became Navy Commissioner at Chatham. Christopher, his second son, set up shop at Woolwich and Deptford, and last, his grandson, Phineas, finally took over at Chatham. The dynasty ended in 1678 upon the death of Phineas, the younger.

The prevailing influence of the Petts through the century did little to promote ship design on paper. Their contribution to ship architecture (which was considerable, as we shall see) lay elsewhere.

Their reign, however, gave rise to a new star, Anthony Deane. His *Doctrine of Naval Architecture* appeared about 1675, and for the first time, we see the subject of English shipbuilding treated with an academic rigor and clarity.

Deane's work not only established naval architectural drafting as a norm, but applied mathematics and the new methods of scientific inquiry to the business of shipbuilding.

MODERN DRAFTING OF HULL LINES

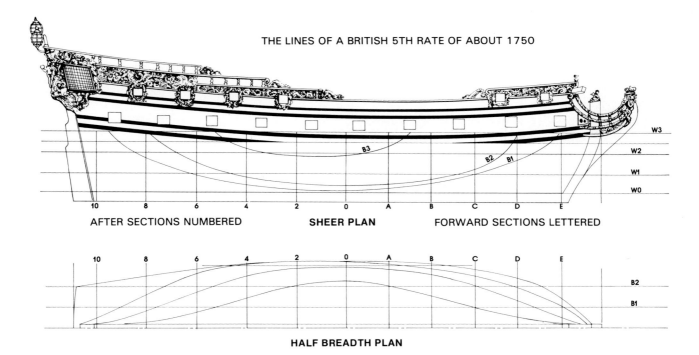

THE LINES OF A BRITISH 5TH RATE OF ABOUT 1750

AFTER SECTIONS NUMBERED   **SHEER PLAN**   FORWARD SECTIONS LETTERED

HALF BREADTH PLAN

From Deane's time to the present, marine architects have employed a more or less standard technique for the depiction of a three-dimensional hull form on paper. The delineations include a side view called the "sheer plan"; one-half of the top view called the "half breadth plan"; and an end view which shows one-half of each end in the same drawing called the "body plan."

The hull is visualized within a three-dimensional coordinate grid system referenced to a base line under the keel, a vertical line at the midship section, and the longitudinal centerline.

The lines of the sheer plan are called "buttocks." They represent the hull as if sliced vertically and longitudinally at increments measured out from the longitudinal centerline.

The half breadth plan delineates the "waterlines." They show the hull sliced horizontally at increments measured up from the keel base line.

The end view shows the "body sections," transverse vertical slices spaced fore and aft from the midship section. The midship section defines the widest section in the hull and does not

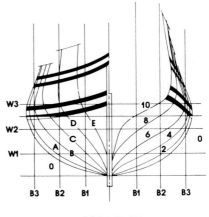

BODY PLAN

necessarily lie at the geometric center of the design.

Independent of the three sets of lines above, one may find one or more "diagonals" which represent the hull sliced longitudinally on a plane diagonal to the rest.

Finally, there may be a "displacement" curve which represents the distribution of the ship's underwater volume.

DISPLACEMENT

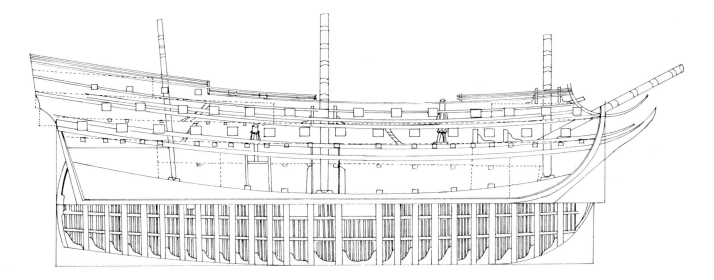

Sir Anthony Deane laid the foundation for modern architectural drafting. This longitudinal section drawing of a seventeenth century 3rd rate appeared in his *Doctrine of Naval Architecture* published in 1670.

Ships through most of history have been designated, taxed, and hired out by some measurement of their carrying capacities. Where other dimensions such as length, beam or depth of hold are ignored, a ship's "burthen" or tonnage is given as the key indicator of her size.

Originally a "tun" referred to a cask of wine of a dimension roughly equivalent in weight to a modern ton. A ship's "tunnage" therefore indicated the number of such tuns of wine she could carry. Later the "tun" became "ton" which referred not to a specific cargo, but to the actual total weight of the ship when loaded to her maximum. The total actual weight of a ship is designated by her displacement tonnage, since the weight of an object is exactly equal to the weight of the water it can "displace" or move aside when emersed.

Since a ton of water occupies about 35 cubic feet of space, knowledge of a ship's tonnage also gives us a rough idea of her other dimensions. For example, as we know that a 50-ton ship must displace 1750 cubic feet of space below the waterline, we must assign her a length, breadth and depth sufficient to accommodate such a volume. Hence, we can visualize a nicely proportioned vessel of perhaps 45 feet in length, 11 feet in beam with a draft of 5½ or 6 feet depending on the shape of her bottom.

Today the computation of a ship's displacement on the drawing board is a matter of course. But before the seventeenth century the mathematics for the computation were unknown. A ship's displacement was a matter to be settled after she was afloat.

As long as ships were built by the old conventions, the shipwrights could somewhat predict how a hull would float. He depended on the "school of hard knocks."

Trouble ensued, however, with Henry VIII's huge experimental vessels. Floating high out of the water and round as a log below water, many of the early gun ships sailed as cranky as corks. The problem was partially rectified by "girdling and firring," the practice of adding extra layers of planking around the waterline, but this was makeshift at best. Naval architecture required a new approach.

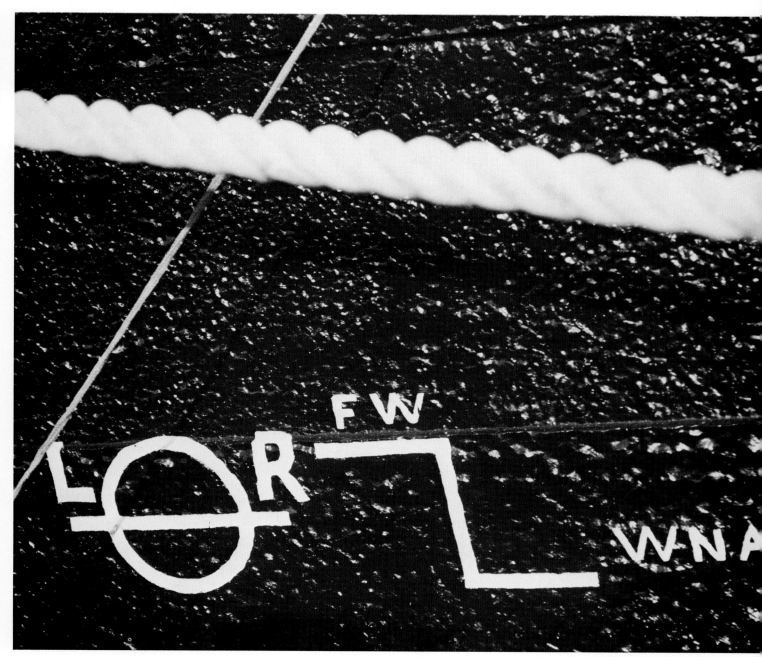

Plimsoll marks on the side of a vessel indicate her safe loading levels. They were mandatory markings for all merchant ships insured by Lloyds of London after 1876. The LR means Lloyd's Register. The line marked by FW indicated the fresh water load limit; WNA means the load limit for "winter North Atlantic." Twentieth Century Plimsoll marks include several more levels: W (winter seawater), S (summer seawater), T (tropical seawater), and TF (tropical fresh water). The different safe loading levels are specified because ships are buoyant depending on the kind of water that supports them. A ship floats highest in cold salt water (WNA), and the lowest in warm fresh water (TF).

In 1598, across the Thames from the naval base at Deptford (East Greenwich), Gresham College was founded under the terms of the will of Sir Thomas Gresham, Queen Elizabeth's famous financial advisor. The new college soon became the meeting ground and clearing house for a new breed of scientific scholar committed to mathematics and experiment. A half century later in 1662, the "Royal Society of London" was incorporated on the foundation laid by the Gresham College scholars and professors. Among the lights who participated here early in the 1600's were William Gilbert, the famous experimenter with magnets; Henry Briggs, who computed the Briggsian tables of logarithms; William Oughtred, the inventor of the slide rule; and Edmund Gunter, who computed the logarithms of the trigonometric functions. Also included in this group were John Wells, keeper of His Majesty's Naval Stores at Deptford; and the master shipwrights, Phineas Pett, Edward Stevens, Hugh Lydiard, and Henry Goddard.

Gresham College may rightly be called the nursery of modern science. Within it the ideas of Francis Bacon and Rene Descarte bloomed into those of Leibniz and Isaac Newton. And right in the midst of this towering ferment, spurring it on, were the navigators and shipbuilders seeking, among other things, an answer to the displacement problem.

Given that old Phineas Pett himself was engaged in Gresham College investigations, it is perhaps surprising that the first to solve the displacement question was none of the Petts, but again Anthony Deane. Deane's successful prediction of the waterline of a ship was what earned him his promotion to the top of his profession.

The exact computation of a ship's displacement tonnage is a subtle piece of mathematics, which at bottom is a problem in calculus. We may be duly impressed with Deane's accomplishment in 1666 when we realize that Leibniz did not publish his invention of the calculus until 1684 nor Newton his until 1687. We cannot, of course, credit Deane with having outdone either of these two mathematical geniuses, but we may suppose that he employed methods that set the stage for them.

REGISTER TONNAGE

Calculus, though, however valuable it became to the likes of physical scientists and engineers, remained an enigma to practical men of business as well as less recondite seamen. A more accessible computation of a ship's size was required for their purposes. Before Deane, a ship's tonnage was roughly computed by a formula. A ship's length in feet times her maximum beam in feet times her depth of hold (bottom of main deck to top of keel) all divided by 100 equaled her tonnage for taxing purposes.

$$\frac{L \times B \times D}{100} = \text{tonnage}$$

After Deane, in 1694, the formula was revised. Instead of dividing the product L x B x D by 100, one now divided by 94.

This rough and ready formula held standard until 1773 when the British Parliament enacted a new one, which thereafter became known as the "Builder's Old Measurement" (BOM). The BOM took the length of keel from the foreside of the stem to the afterside of the sternpost as the starting number and declared a ship's tonnage to be:

$$\frac{L - 3/5\ B \times B \times 1/2\ B}{94}$$

None of these figures bore resemblance to actual displacement tonnage but rather sought to describe a ship's carrying capacity. The formulas provided the businessmen what they recognized as a ship's "register tonnage."

Later the formula for register tonnage was revised again eventually coming down to a matter of dividing all the load carrying space in a ship (expressed in cubic feet) by 100. The last was called deadweight tonnage.

Each of the nations of the world employ their own formulas for register tonnage. Thus a ship of a given tonnage from the U.S. would find itself assigned a different number while going through the Panama Canal and still another upon arrival at Le Havre. The complexities of the issue derive from the prevailing economic conditions of international trade.

THE CENTER OF BUOYANCY

The laws of buoyancy and gravity play an extremely important role in the design of a ship. The laws of gravity, of course, account for the ship's weight and her displacement tonnage as discussed above. A ship's buoyancy, on the other hand, has to do with the counter force that keeps the vessel afloat.

In the simplest terms, a ship is buoyant so long as the total weight of her hull is less than the weight of the water she displaces. As long as this condition holds the ship is said to have "positive buoyancy." When the total weight of the ship exceeds the weight of water displaced, we have "negative buoyancy," and the ship sinks.

Submarines are vessels equipped to vary their buoyancy between positive and negative. When the water is allowed into the ballast tanks its weight is added to the rest of the ship until neutral or negative buoyancy is achieved and the sub dives. In surfacing, the ballast tanks are pumped out and positive buoyancy returns.

It is not enough, however, to simply make a ship "float." "How" it floats is as important to her performance as the fact itself. We may come to appreciate the marine architect's concern with the question through some elementary illustrations.

If we throw a beach ball into a swimming pool it certainly floats, but it also bobs and spins about without regard for which side is up. A beach ball, even though it floats, makes a poor ship.

We could improve the situation a little if we fastened a weight to one side of the ball. Doing this would move the center of gravity more to one side than the other, and the heavier side would sink giving us an 'up' side. The heavier we make the weight, the less is the likelihood that the ball will roll over. If we fasten the weight to the ball by a string, the system becomes even more stable.

Now the center of buoyancy in the beach ball is the very center of it, and as long as we have attached no weights to it, that point is also its center of gravity. So it is clear that a vessel whose center of gravity coincides with its center of buoyancy is a highly unstable affair.

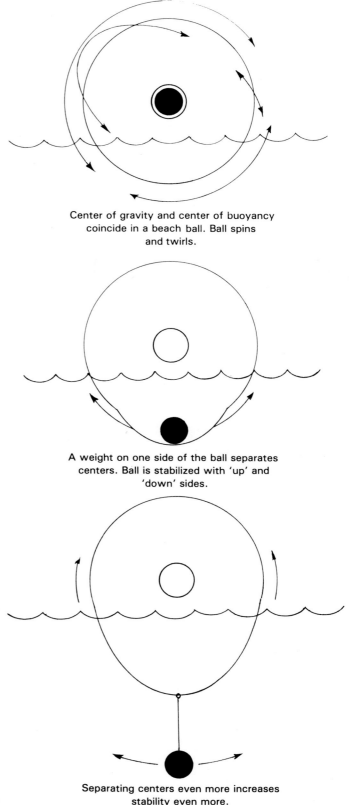

Center of gravity and center of buoyancy coincide in a beach ball. Ball spins and twirls.

A weight on one side of the ball separates centers. Ball is stabilized with 'up' and 'down' sides.

Separating centers even more increases stability even more.

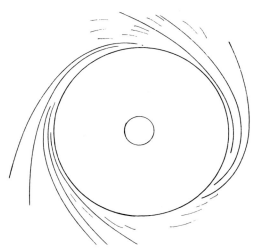

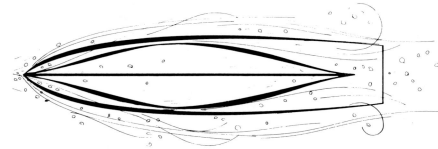

A ship needs to be longer one way than the other to reduce drag in the fore and aft direction while increasing the resistance of her sides.

A beach ball makes a poor ship also because it spins like a top and cannot be steered.

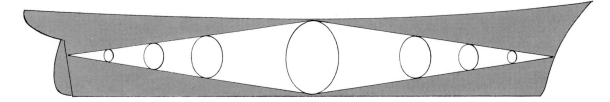

A ship is more buoyant amidships than at either of her ends because of the difference in the volume of air in these various locales. Structural strength is required to keep the two ends from sagging or "hogging."

As we add weight, first to one side of the ball and then to the end of an attached string, we progressively add to the distance between the two centers, and thereby make it more and more difficult to force the up side down.

Thus, the hull of a ship becomes more and more stable as its center of gravity is removed from the center of buoyancy.

A beach ball, even if ballasted, makes a poor ship for another reason. It has no bow and no stern. A ship, on the other hand, is required to go somewhere and must be designed to accomodate this requirement. For this reason, ships are longer than they are wide, have pointed, wedge-shaped bows, and long keels which cut the water one way, and offer solid resistance to it the other. We shall deal with these shapes in more detail later, but for the moment, we must consider how they affect the questions of buoyancy and weight.

If we were to float a vessel shaped like an ice cream cone, we would find that it would tend to float with the point end down. This would happen because the greater displacement volume, and hence the center of buoyancy, would lie in the larger end.

The hull of a ship corresponds to the shape of two ice cream cones set end to end, with the big ends facing each other. The center of buoyancy is midships, but the two point ends, like the ice cream cones, are inclined to sink, and they would if the ship were not structurally solid enough to prevent it.

Those intimate with ships recognize the structural failure associated with this principle as "hogging." As an old ship approaches the end of her days, her structure weakens and her bow and stern droop lower in the water, and she is evermore condemned as "hog backed" or "floating on a broken back."

THE CENTER OF GRAVITY

As we have said, the farther apart we can separate the center of gravity from the center of buoyancy in the vertical plane, the more stable is the ship. But where do we place it in the fore and aft direction? The answer depends for the most part on the means of propulsion, which, in our inquiry, is limited to sails.

If we have a weight to move we have the choice of either pushing it from behind or pulling it from ahead. Either way can work depending on circumstances. But if we have a situation in which our objective is to push a long stick through the water on a straight course it will be seen that trying to push it from astern becomes something of a

balancing act, while dragging it presents fewer problems. So it is with sailing ships. A ship whose concentration of sail area is aft of her center of gravity is nigh impossible to steer (though there are circumstances when sails would be so set). The effect is rather like trying to push a strand of spaghetti through a keyhole. So one is not surprised to find that the center of gravity on a sailing ship is invariably aft of the center of effort of her sails.

Other than this, the location of a ship's center of gravity is a matter of maintaining her trim. Some ships trim "down by the head"; others "down by the stern," often at the inclination of the skipper who loads and stows ballast or cargo.

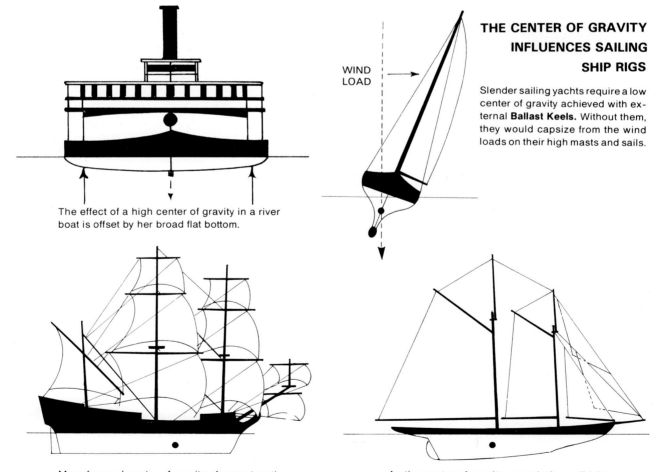

The effect of a high center of gravity in a river boat is offset by her broad flat bottom.

WIND LOAD

THE CENTER OF GRAVITY INFLUENCES SAILING SHIP RIGS

Slender sailing yachts require a low center of gravity achieved with external **Ballast Keels.** Without them, they would capsize from the wind loads on their high masts and sails.

More forward center of gravity of seventeenth century ships required more forward placement of sails.

As the center of gravity moved aft, so did the center of effort of the sails.

LATERAL RESISTANCE

The area of lateral resistance is the portion of the hull's surface which is vertical and broadside below water. Lateral resistance is provided by the keel plus the portion of the ship sides below the waterline. A larger area of lateral resistance reduces the tendency of a ship to be blown sideways.

A sailing ship requires a larger area of lateral resistance to offset the effect of winds blowing against her high sails.

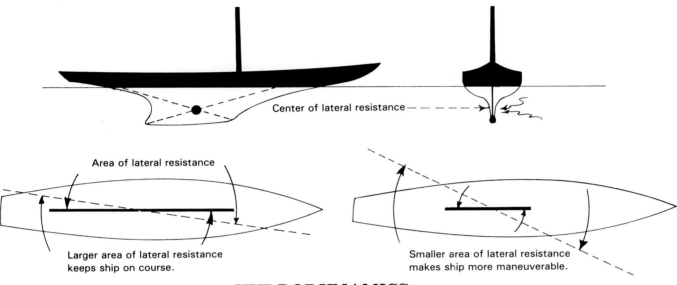

Center of lateral resistance

Area of lateral resistance

Larger area of lateral resistance keeps ship on course.

Smaller area of lateral resistance makes ship more maneuverable.

HYDRODYNAMICS

The hull of a ship is designed not only to float on water but to move through it. And therein lies the subtlest quest of the marine architect whose objective is to describe a hull that will slide through the water with optimum efficiency while satisfying the ship's other operating requirements.

Today hull design relies on a sophisticated body of theoretical and experimental science, but for many centuries the shipwrights depended on tradition, and intuition to come up with the shapes for their ships.

Among the most popular of intuitions about the "correct" shape for a ship grew from the observation of fish. It was easy to recognize that fish had the problems of hydrodynamic efficiency well worked out so what could be more logical than to copy their design into ships?

Mathew Baker in 1575 expressed this traditional intuition when he declared that a ship should "go in like cod, and out like a mackeral." Later, Sir Isaac Newton himself, through his investigations into hydrodynamics, demonstrated scientifically that indeed a fish shape was an optimal one for a body moving in a fluid. Thus, the "fish theory" dominated the shipwrights' thinking until 1800, giving rise to the large fleets of bluff bowed vessels that roamed the oceans during the early years of world-wide commerce. Yet the fish theory was flawed.

Isaac Newton's hydrodynamics described the physics of a moving body completely **immersed** in a fluid. He showed correctly that a teardrop shape would indeed be the ideal configuration for a hull if the ship were totally underwater. He had designed a submarine, while failing to account for the fact that a surface ship was only partially submerged. We now know that the hydrodynamics surrounding a surface vessel are substantially more complex than Sir Isaac imagined.

In any event practical shipwrights started to challenge the correctness of the bluff bowed tradition around 1800 as the demand for speedy ships began to be felt. The demand for speed was particularly acute in America where smuggling, blockade running, and slaving were big business. Around this time the idea of the "sharp ship" was born and found its best expression in the renowned Baltimore clippers. Sharp hulls were **characterized** by slender entries and runs, more steeply rising floors, and keels that sloped downward from the stem to a deep stern post.

Such vessels astounded the traditionalists with their speed, but they had drawbacks. Their steep floors limited their cargo space as well as giving them a tendency to be quite "tender" in strong winds. (A "tender" ship is one that will heel over or capsize easily).

The fast hull designs evolved rapidly through the first half of the nineteenth century and the problems of the first sharp ships disappeared. By 1850 the great, true clipper ships were setting the as yet unbeaten sailing ship speed records. The hulls of the true clippers were honed as fine as needles at entry and run, the lines flowing out to full, box-like midship sections. The flat floors of the midship section added stiffness, buoyancy, and cargo space to hulls that sliced water like shark fins.

The great clippers were designed by practical shipwrights and experienced mariners who depended less on academic science than their own "gut feelings" about what would make a fast ship. Rigorous science only began to play a leading roll in ship design after 1868, past the heyday of the clippers.

It was around 1868 that William Froude undertook experiments with ship models in a towing tank. Through these experiments Froude was able to work out mathematical correlations between the behavior of the models and their full scale counterparts, and then to develop what has since become a central tenet of modern marine architecture—wave line theory.

Froude considered that for a hull to be driven through the water its power plant must overcome certain resistances. He determined these resistances to consist of two components—skin friction and wave-making resistance. At low speeds most all of the hull's resistance is taken up with skin friction. At higher speeds, energy is taken up in the creation of waves which become fewer and larger the faster the ship goes. Thus an observation of the number of waves a model makes in the tank at a given speed provides a measure of the amount of drag or resistance present in the hull design.

With the theory marine architects predict optimal hull designs, power requirements, screw sizes, and a multitude of other variables.

WAVE LINE THEORY

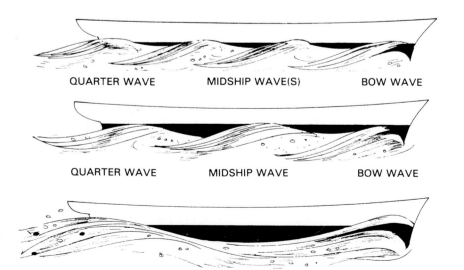

QUARTER WAVE   MIDSHIP WAVE(S)   BOW WAVE

QUARTER WAVE   MIDSHIP WAVE   BOW WAVE

4 WAVES UTILIZE
40% OF SHIP'S POWER

3 WAVES UTILIZE
60% OF SHIP'S POWER

2 WAVES UTILIZE POWER
BEYOND OPTIMUM LIMITS
FOR DISPLACEMENT HULLS

THE SIX COMPONENTS OF SHIP MOTION

At sea, a ship is tossed and turned by waves, wind, and currents. The naval architect views these effects in terms of six kinds of movement and takes them into account when seeking the most efficient hull shape for a given seagoing task. For example, the hull of an aircraft carrier is designed for maximum stability at the expense of speed and maneuverability, while that of a destroyer is just the opposite.

The prescriptions given below for minimizing roll, pitch and so on are anything but absolute. They simply suggest the kind of trade-offs that enter the thoughts of the architect during the preliminary stages of hull design.

The final design of a hull evolves through a series of tests using models in a towing task in a manner directly parallel to Froude's early experiments.

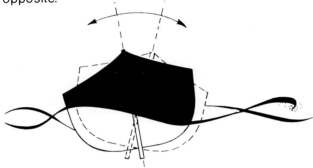

ROLL

Ship tips side to side. Roll may be minimized by increasing beam; increasing the area of lateral resistance; designing a more square body section, or lowering the center of gravity.

SURGE

Ship lifts up and forward. Surge may be minimized by distributing the underwater bulk of the ship along its length.

PITCH

Ship tips up and down like a seasaw in the fore and aft direction. Pitching may be minimized by concentrating the underwater bulk of the ship around the C.G., and increasing the buoyancy of the higher portions of bow and stern.

HEAVE

Ship lifts up and down parallel with the water. Heaving may be minimized by narrowing the beam, softening the chines, or spreading out the underwater bulk of the ship along its length. Minimizing heave could increase the tendency to pitch.

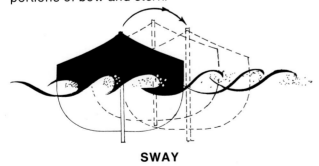

SWAY

Ship lifts up and to the side. Sway may be minimized by lowering the C.G., increasing the area of lateral resistance, or decreasing beam.

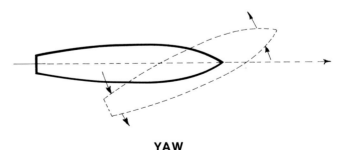

YAW

Ship pivots sideways to the line of her course. Yaw may be minimized by increasing the length-to-beam ratio and/or the area of lateral resistance.

DESCRIPTIVE TERMS

The naval architect uses a certain vocabulary to distinguish characteristic features and locales within a hull design.

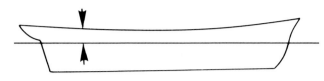

FREEBOARD

The height of a ship's sides above the waterline.

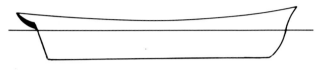

COUNTER

The underpart of the stern, above water, between the sternpost and the taffrail.

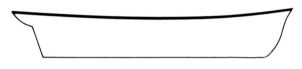

SHEER

The line of the deck or upper edge of the sheer strake as seen in profile. A strong or steep sheer line sweeps up in a curve fore and aft from a point midships. A flat sheer describes a more level deck line.

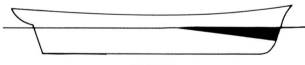

ENTRY

The shape of bow and forward part of the hull at, and below, the waterline. A fine entry is a long, slender wedge gradually curving out to the full width of the ship. The old, bluff-bowed ships had "rough" or "hard" entries.

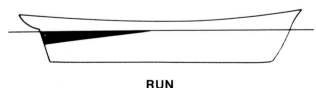

RUN

The shape of the afterbody below the waterline. A fine run tapers aft much as the entry does forward. A ship with a fine entry and run slides through the water with a minimum of turbulence.

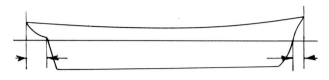

OVERHANG

The distance a ship's bow or stern hangs out over the water above the waterline.

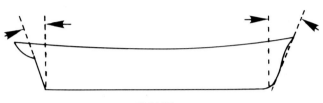

RAKE

The angle the stem or sternpost makes with the keel when viewed in profile. Also applied to masts, funnels and the like.

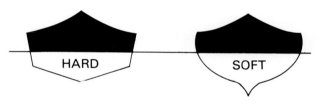

CHINE

The line of transition between the upper sides of the hull and its bottom. When sides and bottom come together at a sharp angle, the vessel is said to be "hard chined." If the transition is curved, the chines are "soft." Chines become softer as the radius of curve increases.

RISE OF FLOORS

The angle at which the floor timbers rise from the keel toward the sided. An acute "v-bottomed" hull is said to have strongly rising floors, while a more flat-bottomed vessel will have slowly rising ones.

ANTHONY DEANE'S DRAFTING PROCEDURE

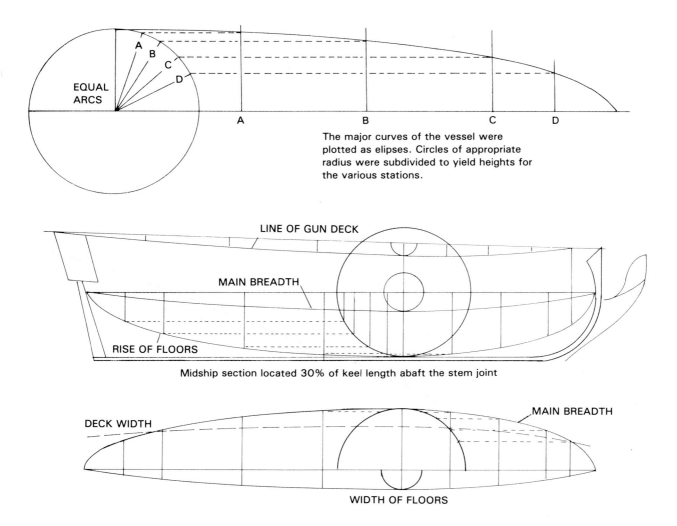

The major curves of the vessel were plotted as elipses. Circles of appropriate radius were subdivided to yield heights for the various stations.

Midship section located 30% of keel length abaft the stem joint

Anthony Deane plotted the basic curves of the sheer and half breadth plans from circles drawn to appropriate sizes. Ninety degree arcs of the circles were subdivided into four or so smaller arcs yielding as many heights above the reference line. These heights then were projected to the body section lines to provide a point plot for the eliptical curves in question. The lines so plotted included the sheer line, rise of floors, and main deck line in the sheer plan; and the maximum breadth line, and width of floors line in the half breadth plan.

The body sections were located by first locating the midship section at a point about 30% of the keel length abaft of the joint between the keel and the stem. Then each of the fore and after sections were subdivided into four equal parts and the most forward and aft of these parts divided in two again.

The sizes of the circles from which the eliptical curves were plotted were in some cases defined by the ship's primary specifications (main breadth, for example), but otherwise were simply "eye balled" so as to yield curves that looked right to the designer.

With this much of the ship defined, Deane was ready to proceed to the drafting of the body sections which we will allow him to explain in his own words.

"Now all the lines are prepared for sweeping out the Midship Bend, I take from my scale one fourth part of my whole Breadth of my Shipp which is 9 foot and set one leg of my compasses in ye flower line at K and sweep it from H to L, this sweepe is called ye Flower Sweepe, haveing don with that I take 7/9 of the flower sweepe and sticke it under the Breadth line downeward from E to N and the Center M . . .

"Haveing prepared those two sweepes above mentioned I take of 20/36 of my breadth setting one leg of my compasses in O and strike the line. From L to N the sweepe is the sweepe with which maketh the upper and lower futtucke moulldes as you will peceave ere you have don . . .

"Haveing don all my sweepes under ye breadth I come unto my top timber; for which I take 17/18 of the half breadth which is seaventene foot setting one leg of my compasses in P and stricke ye sweepe from E to R, haveing don that I take the same sweepe and stricke a hollow for the head of the top timber, by the same radious the last was strucke by and sweepe out the hollow sweepe from S to R which sweepe compleates the bends of timber by which you are to make the moulds for two gradiate all the rest of the bends of timbers and for the whoulle Frame . . .

"One of the last place you were showne how ye half bends of timbers were swept out by wch you were to make your Moulds and being made with a good scarfe for every timber you are to proceed in yet sweeping out yet remaining parts of the ship afte as you find out one within another where ye shipp is compleated, but for feare raiseing them may be to dark for ye understanding I will show you one example more to make you p-fit and shall suppose I were to raise ye bend of timbers it is where I do thus. I look at my draft and take ye riseing from ye pole to ye line where it stands on ye draft wch I set of from ye line A, B and is ye line C, C, haveing done that, I take allso from my draft ye narrowing of my flower wch I set of ye line D. E and is yet line F. G this is ye

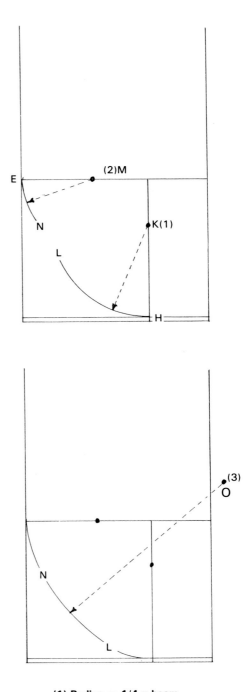

(1) Radius = 1/4 x beam
(2) Radius = 7/9 x (1)
(3) Radius = 20/36 x beam

narrowing of flower, haveing done that I take from my draft ye Height of Breadth at 15 wch 1 set of from ye line A, B, and is the line H, I, haveing done that I take from my draft ye narrowing of greatest breadth at 15 which I set of from I to H and yet like narrowing and riseing from ye top timber head which is ye line K, L, now haveing set of all ye narrowings and hights in every place I proced to swepe ye flower sweepe 9 foot as ye former setting one leg of my compasses in P and sweeping under breadth from Q to R haveing don that I take the same 20 foot swepe of my Midship Bend and set one leg in S and sweepe from R to O, haveing don that I keep my center all for ye top timbers as in ye Midships, setting one leg at T and sweepe from Q to W and from that ye follow sweepe as in ye other observing to fetch out ye hollow at ye stearne, all ye sweepes being thus struck you have ye 1/2 bends of timbers compleated at 15 in like mang and all the other . . .

"This latter is noe other than ye former for its nature of workeing onely as ye last was ye bend of timbers aftward on marked 15 this shall be a bend of timbers forward named N which is set of by ye narrowings and riseings as ye other onely as ye one is worked afte on the starboard side ye other is wrought on ye larboard side that one suite of moulds may serve your turne to builld by, as for example I look on ye drafte and take ye true riseing from N where it stands on ye keele to ye riseing line and set it of from ye line A, B which is ye line C, D, and this is ye riseing line, then I take from my drafte ye narrowing and set from ye line A, E which is the line F, G ye riseing and narrowing or ye breadth is the same as is often shewen, haveing thus done I proceed to sweepe by the same sweepes as above sweepeing out from H to I ye flower sweepe and from K to L under ye breadth from K to M above ye breadth and from M to N the top of the side, which I hope by this you see perfect the riseing of the whole ship's boddy in every part onely as you have these single ye other be one within as other as you will find in ye next place you come at as appear to your better sattisfaction . . ."

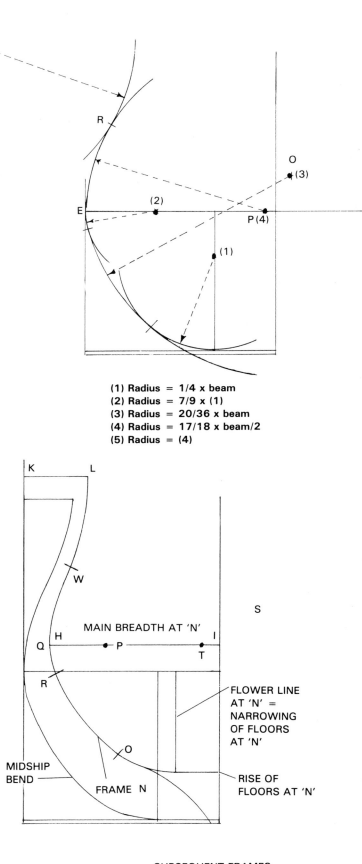

(1) Radius = 1/4 x beam
(2) Radius = 7/9 x (1)
(3) Radius = 20/36 x beam
(4) Radius = 17/18 x beam/2
(5) Radius = (4)

MAIN BREADTH AT 'N'

FLOWER LINE AT 'N' = NARROWING OF FLOORS AT 'N'

RISE OF FLOORS AT 'N'

MIDSHIP BEND

FRAME N

SUBSEQUENT FRAMES FOLLOW PROPORTIONALLY

COMPARISON OF MIDSHIP SECTIONS

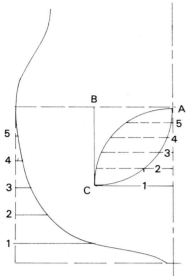

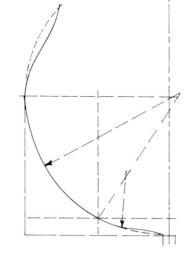

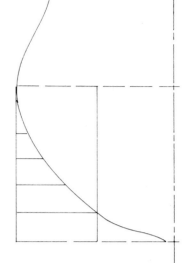

Full Built Ship in 1750
A-B was the key dimension in determining the fullness of a ship's body. An arc AC of smaller radius yields shorter lengths for the point plots of the body (distances 1, 2, 3, etc.) and produces a fuller ship. As AB increases, the distances 1, 2, 3,... become longer and a sharper ship results.

Round Bodied Ship 1750
This method of laying out the bends derives from Deane except that the flower sweep has a shorter radius. The narrowing of these ships above their maximum breadth was called *tumblehome*. Tumblehome was built into hulls to bring topsides more parallel with the run of the mast shrouds, to reduce the amount of deck exposed to boarding seas, and to make attack by boarding difficult.

Very Sharp Ship
A sharp vessel rode low in the water with a comparatively low center of gravity. Consequently she could carry a heavy press of sail with a hull that could "bite" the water and hold a course when other ships would drift to leeward. Among such sharp vessels as shown here were the famous American Baltimore clippers of the early 1800's.

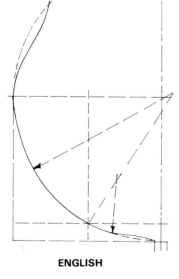

ENGLISH

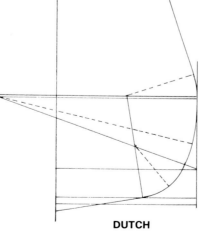

DUTCH

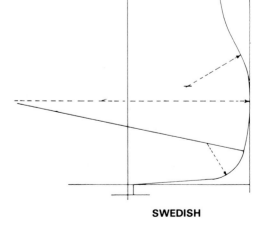

SWEDISH

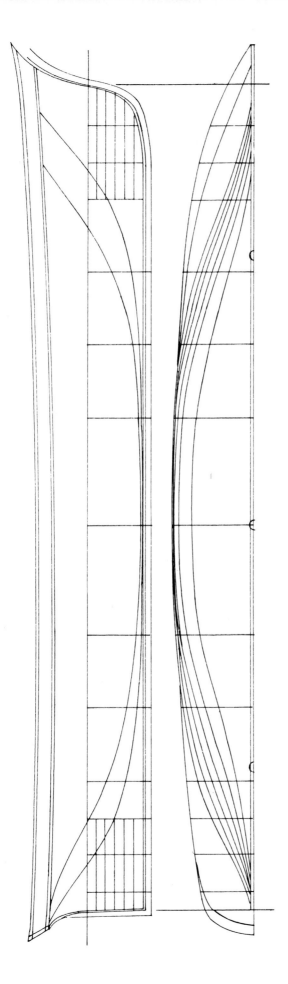

A SHIP WITH SHARP ENTRY AND RUN — A CLIPPER SHIP

Lines of the American clipper **LIGHTNING** 1854 East Boston, 2084 tons 243 feet x 43 feet beam x 23 feet depth of hold. Designed and built by Donald Mackay.

The lines of the *Lightning* reveal the thinking of a later day when sailing ships reached their maximum levels of performance. Full, flat floors amidships provided a solid buoyancy and stability for a ship that otherwise was needle sharp at bow and stern. The *Lightning* once covered 436 miles in 24 hours averaging 18 knots per hour, a dramatic contrast to the ships of Deane's day that averaged three or four knots per hour and caused a sensation if they made six.

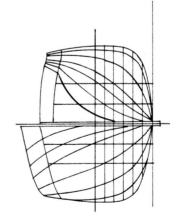

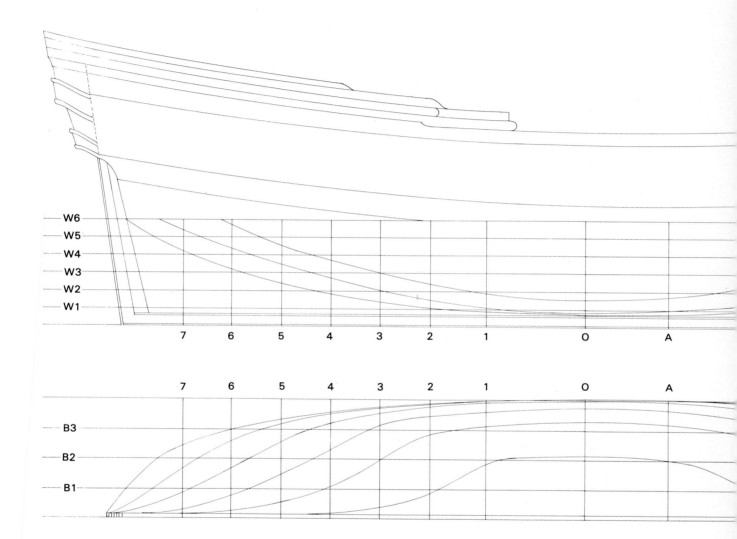

W6
W5
W4
W3
W2
W1

7 6 5 4 3 2 1 O A

7 6 5 4 3 2 1 O A

B3

B2

B1

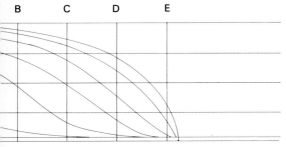

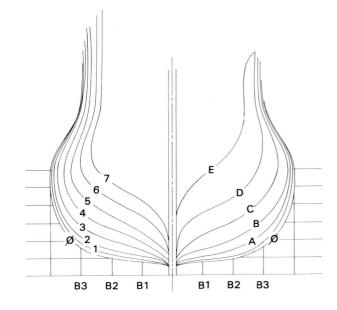

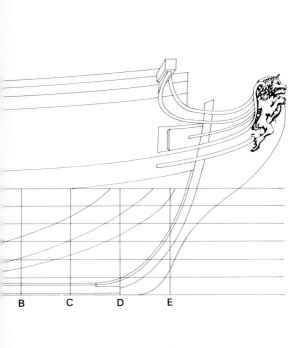

LINES OF HMS CENTURION
Launched Portsmouth, England 1732
A 4th Rate ship of 50 guns, Centurion sailed around the world in 1740-44 under the command of Commodore George Anson. The voyage, among the earlier of English circumnavigations around Cape Horn into the Pacific, cost 1300 lives out of Anson's squadron of six ships. Only four were combat casualties. The rest died of disease. Centurion brought home 500,000 pounds in prize money taken from a Spanish treasure ship in the Philippines.

43

Chapter Three
Shipbuilding Before 1600

THE BEGINNINGS

No one can say with certainty when man launched the first ship of his own contrivance. The date is lost in pre-history coincident with the times he discovered the use of fire and the making of stone tools. But there is reason to suppose that man was a practiced navigator as much as one hundred thousand years ago. Perhaps even earlier.

We know that the continent of Australia drifted away from mainland Asia some 75 million years ago carrying with it its own primeval plants and animals, none of which were of the class of the higher mammals. Fossil remains in Australia show nothing of man or other mammal until the comparatively recent date of 100,000 years ago when, quite suddenly, man and his earliest companions in the chase, the dingo dogs, show up. Where did they come from?

It would appear that men crossed the Straits of Timor to Australia from Java bringing with them their packs of tame dogs in ships, or watercraft of some kind. One might assume that they reached Australia at this time by a land bridge formed by the receding waters of the Ice Age. But the geologists declare that the water there and then only decreased in depth some 300 feet while the Straits of Timor are ten times as deep. Furthermore, had there been a land bridge, more creatures than men and their dogs would have crossed over. There is no evidence that any did.

A swim across the Straits would have been clearly impossible, so the only alternative left is to assume some form of navigable craft, invented by primitive peoples, on the very threshold of human achievement—in the days of the early Stone Age Java and Neanderthal man.

The fossil evidence from other parts of the world is less conclusive concerning other early navigational experience, but if man was able to sail the Straits of Timor so long ago, it is highly likely he was sailing other waters as well.

The glaciers of the Last Ice Age began to melt and recede about 25,000 years ago. The world became warmer, the waters increased, and men began to wander far and wide in pursuit of game. By this time, the Cro-Magnon race of men had gained ascendancy all over Northern Europe, to Spain, and through the length of Africa. The same Cro-Magnon people also populated

North and South America crossing the land bridge of the Bering Strait between Siberia and Alaska. Many of the travels of the Cro-Magnons were on foot, but they also settled the Canary Islands 60 miles across the sea from mainland Africa. Without question they made the trip to the Canaries by ship, and like the first migrants to Australia, brought their dogs with them. The Canaries are named from the Latin *canis*, dog, because when the Romans first visited the islands wild, vicious dogs are what they found there in company with the Cro-Magnon's descendents, the Guanche people.

Pre-historians refer to the years between 20 and 10,000 years ago as the Middle and Late Stone Ages. During these millenia man laid the cultural and technical foundations upon which all of his later civilizations were built.

The period, a bare instant in the context of the previous eons of evolution, witnessed an almost explosive transformation from man the primitive animal to man the creative, cultured intellectual—toolmaker, artist, engineer, farmer, and priest. And as man himself evolved so also did his most precious of tools, his weapons and his ships.

What were man's earliest ships like? Thor Heyerdahl's investigations of the question persuades us that they were built of reeds at least in the Mesopotamian areas where the earliest known true civilizations emerged around 6,000 years ago.

The oldest boat illustrations yet discovered in rock carvings and paintings represent ships as sickle-shaped craft curved from bow to stern. The design echoes and re-echoes in the surviving art from all over the Mediterranean, some representations having been found deep in the Algerian Sahara desert. The earliest Sumerian heiroglyph for "ship" dating from around 3,000 BC is a sickle-shaped boat. The illustrations clearly represent vessels built to the lines of reed ships known to have been in use in the area even up to our own time.

These early representations of ships come from the period just before and after the dawn of recorded history around 3,000 BC. They show that by this time men had formed a powerfully fixed notion of what a proper ship should look like.

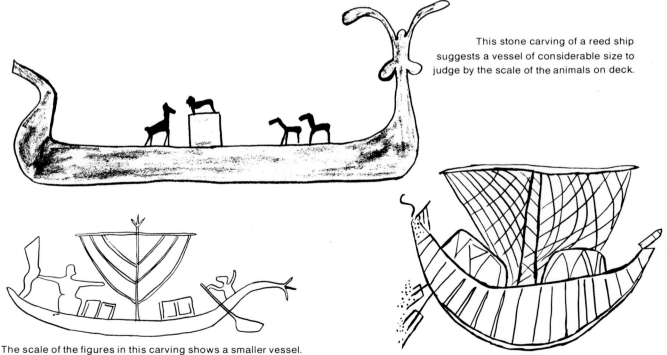

This stone carving of a reed ship suggests a vessel of considerable size to judge by the scale of the animals on deck.

The scale of the figures in this carving shows a smaller vessel. The central mast suggests an early departure from the forward stepped bipod mast.

Reed ship stone carving from a cave in Israel.

Thor Heyerdahl's *Ra II* successfully crossed the Atlantic Ocean in the Canary Current proving that early Egyptians could have migrated to America in reed vessels. *Ra II* was built using construction principles common to ancient Egyptians and contemporary natives of the Lake Titicaca region in Peru..

That the sickle-shaped vessel should be adopted as the written symbol for "ship", as it was in old Sumer, implies a deeply felt and widely held conception of "ship" which could only have been born of a very old tradition. One may also observe that by this time, men were starting to build wooden ships, but so fixed was the idea of the sickle-shape, that they forced the wood to conform to it. The curved configuration, so natural to the flexible reed ship, was not nearly so natural to a craft built of rigid, straight planks.

One thousand years earlier than the beginnings of recorded history, there were already advanced island trading centers at Bahrain in the Arabian Gulf; at Malta in the Mediterranean; and in the islands around Great Britain. The reed ships that served these centers carried cargos of 100 tons or more, and were voyaging far and wide to India, Africa, and probably to China. How long had it taken before this date to develop the reed ship to this level? One must suppose some thousands of years, and, if so, then one might set the date of invention of the reed ship in the Neolithic period perhaps 12 or 15,000 years ago.

But then what sort of ship did the Cro-Magnons use on their voyage to the Canary Islands? Perhaps the reed ship was born still earlier, a reflection of the increase in the waters of the earth as the glaciers of the Ice Age melted away. By this reasoning, and recognizing that "necessity is the mother of invention", the reed ship might be as much as 20,000 years old. But whatever birth date one might assign to the reed ships, the certainty is that such ships are among the oldest, continuously used contrivances ever invented, as well as the oldest known representatives of the ship builder's art.

The reed ships were not only ancient, they were also efficient. Heyerdahl's experiments with his Ra I and Ra II proved that these vessels possessed all of the characteristics necessary for long distance ocean voyaging. In fact, it was Heyerdahl's purpose to demonstrate the likelihood that men from the eastern side of the Atlantic migrated to the Americas in reed ships around 3100 BC to set up the great Mayan and Olmec civilizations. The evidence that they did just that is compelling.

The year 3113 BC is important. It is the

zero year of the Mayan calendar, the date which the amazingly keen Mayan timekeepers set as a beginning point for themselves. Almost simultaneous with this date a titanic natural disaster occurred which virtually annihilated the budding civilizations of Asia Minor. The theory today is that a gigantic volcanic explosion went off, similar in kind but much larger, to the eruption of Krakatoa in 1883. The Krakatoa explosion killed 36,000 people, blackened the skies around the world for months, and set loose tidal waves over vast areas of the Pacific and Indian Oceans. The power of the explosion of 3100 was such that the island of Iceland in the North Atlantic split in two.

The event was recorded and vividly remembered in the legends of Sumer, Egypt, and Babylon. The Hebrew Bible reflects the event in the story of the flood from which Noah escaped in his ark. The event not only terrified people but imposed on them the necessity to voyage out to new lands. Some of them went as far as America.

Aside from this astonishing coincidence of time between events on either side of the Atlantic are the similarities in art, religion, racial characteristics, and legends between the peoples of the East and West. The trip from the Canary Islands to America is no longer than the trip to the Canaries from the eastern end of the Mediterranean, while the Canary current provides an easy ocean highway flowing straight into the sites of the old Meso-American culture areas.

Finally, one finds the natives of the Lake Titicaca region of Peru still today sailing reed ships precisely of the sort common in old Sumer, and of the sort the culture bringers of Meso-America used to ride westward across the sea from Africa.

THE WOODEN SHIP

The catastrophe of 3100 BC interrupted the period during which the first experiments with displacement hulls were taking place. The reed ship was essentially a raft depending on the natural buoyancy of the building material to stay afloat. Displacement hulls depended for buoyancy on a watertight shell which would displace water with air.

The first displacement hulls were also made of reeds laid up in mats and payed over with pitch. The mats were held in shape by wooden interior framing. Noah, in the Book of Genesis (6:14-16), receives the command, "make yourself an ark with ribs of cypress; cover it with reeds and coat it, inside and out with pitch." Noah's ark was of considerable size with three decks, showing that just before 3100 BC considerable progress had been made in this new form of shipbuilding.

Wood replaced reeds as a shipbuilding material at first in Lebanon where the famous "Cedars of Lebanon" thrived. Then rapidly, wood became the favored material for ships everywhere and big business grew up around Lebanon's timber industry.

Egypt became a major customer for Lebanon timber for the building of ships that served the great dynasties of the pharoahs. The early Egyptian wooden ships retained the forms of the earlier sickle-shaped reed vessels, but since most of them were built for the quiet waters of the Nile, the shipwrights seem to have forgotten the original reason for the shape. They only knew that the form was the only proper one for a ship as we can observe from the earliest surviving ship discovered by archaeologists, the funeral ship of the pharoah Cheops who reigned in Egypt around 2600 BC.

CHEOP'S SHIP

Archaeologists opened Cheop's tomb and found the makings of a ship fully preserved after 4400 years by the dry desert atmosphere. It had been buried with the pharoah for his voyages in the afterlife.

When the 600 cedar planks were reassembled, a handsome vessel 147 feet long emerged. Indeed she exhibited elegant, **seagoing lines worthy of the best Viking ship** built 4000 years later. But the ship lacked a keel as well as the structural strength to withstand any sort of a sea. The shipwrights remembered the shape but built a vessel suitable only for the placid waters of the Nile.

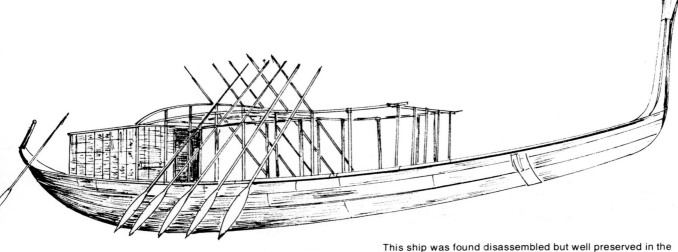

This ship was found disassembled but well preserved in the tomb of the Pharoah Cheops, dating from about 2600 B.C. She was 147 feet long, and was built of 600 individual cedar planks sewn and dovetailed together.

CRETE

In the aftermath of the disaster of 3100 BC, new communities gradually took root. In these years Egypt bloomed to its great cultural heights along the landlocked Nile, but left dominion over the seas to the island people of Crete. The Cretans founded the greatest maritime empire of the era. With Egypt as its major customer, the Cretans cruised the ancient world in quest of copper, tin, and gold, feeding the incessant demands of the age of bronze. Over a millenium and a half, their civilization grew to a magnificence unmatched even by Egypt herself.

The legendary King of Crete was named Minos and from him the civilization he represented has been called Minoan, while the **great deity of the kingdom was a bullheaded monster, the Minotaur.** The Greek hero Theseus was said to have slain the Minotaur after penetrating the labyrinth in which he lived.

The Cretans developed a large fleet of **magnificent merchant and warships. They refined the art of sailing, equipping their vessels with masts stepped midships. The** innovation made it possible to sail with wind abeam. **They also invented ramrod bows for their warships which was the first departure from the pure sickle-shape tradition.**

These vessels are drawn after the representations of Cretan ships in mural frescoes found in the buried city of Akrotiri on the Island of Thera. Dating from about 1500 B.C., these pictures testify to a highly advanced maritime culture, with ships capable of long distance trading voyages. Though made of wood, the ships are shaped like their more ancient reed ancestors.

But then, around 1450 BC when Crete had reached the zenith of her power, she ceased to exist. The second great catastrophe of the ancient world occurred. The volcanic island of Thera, 60 miles north of Crete and one of her important outposts, blew up. The city of Akrotiri on Thera was utterly buried in ash, and tidal waves drowned Crete to extinction while once more raising havoc throughout the Mediterranean area.

Recently archaeologists have disinterred Akrotiri from its volcanic grave, bringing to light mural illustrations of Cretan ships from which most of our present knowledge about them has derived.

PHOENICIA

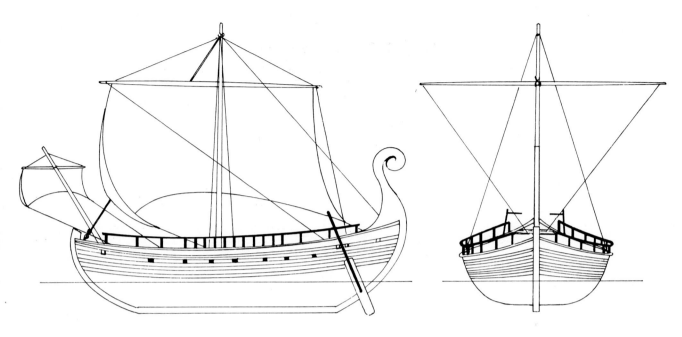

PHOENICIAN HIPPO
Hippos or *Tarshish* ships were the larger of the Phoenician's trading vessels. *Hippos* sailed the Indian and Atlantic Oceans around Africa, and at least to the British Isles.

The vacuum created by the devastation of Crete gave rise to new sea powers in the Mediterranean world. The name by which most of them have been designated is Phoenicia. In contrast to the close-knit civilization of Crete, the Phoenicians were unified by little more than their name and the proximity of their two major city states, Tyre and Sidon, in present day Lebanon. The distinctive feature of the Phoenicians was that they inherited the maritime traditions of Crete becoming the "sea people" of the time. It is likely that to have been known as "Phoenician" then was simply to have been a member of the "sailor's union" without reference to any particular geographical homeland.

In any event, the Phoenicians monopolized maritime trade from the death of Crete until Alexander the Great sacked their city of Tyre in 333 BC.

The Phoenicians sailed far and wide in their quest for trade goods. They circumnavigated Africa, traded in the British Isles, in India, Ceylon, and China.

As naval architects, the Phoenicians began with the designs handed down from Crete, the Cretans having just begun to depart from the traditional sickle-shaped hull when their culture ceased. From these beginnings the Phoenicians developed the ship designs and fittings that characterized sailing ships until well into the modern era. Their ships featured long, straight keels, multiple decks penetrated with hatches, life rails, two masted rigs, and stays and shrouds set up with deadeyes. But most important they built true sailing ships in which they confidently expected to voyage with a minimum use of oars. A relief carving on a sarcophagus at Sidon shows a ship without oar ports. Prior to the Phoenicians, navigators counted oars or paddles as a primary source of power. Such sailing as was done, was a downwind proposition, and, at best, considered a supplementary mode of propulsion.

The Phoenicians built ships of several distinct classes. Their largest merchantmen, called Tarshish ships, underwent an evolution from a single masted version, called a *hippo*, to a sophisticated "oar-less" version as described above. The earlier *hippo* featured a single square sail stretched between an upper and lower yard.

A smaller class of merchantmen, the *gaulus*, was reserved for shorter trading voyages near home.

Finally, the Phoenicians introduced what must have been the most frightening innovation in ship design to date—the war galley. The Phoenician war galley represented the most radical departure from the traditional ship design yet tried. With a length to beam ratio of 5 or 6 to 1 compared with the 3 to 1 ratios of conventional ships, the galley was a long slender battering ram of a ship. Driven by two banks of oars, the galley, called a *bireme*, could knife through the water at unheard of speeds and impale an enemy ship with a bronze plated, spearhead bow.

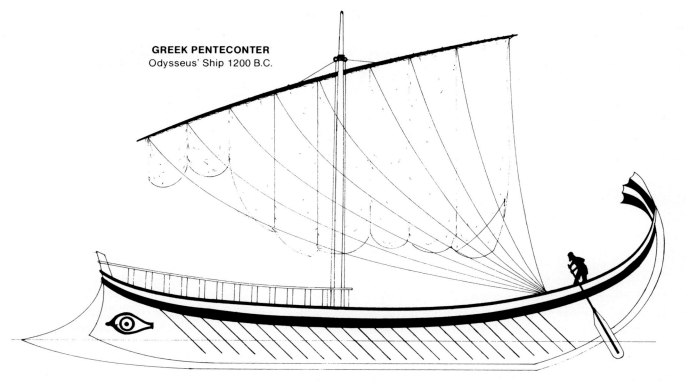

GREEK PENTECONTER
Odysseus' Ship 1200 B.C.

MYCENAE

The dislocation of the ancient peoples after the cataclysm of 3100 BC gave rise to migrations and resettlements all over the Mediterranean region. In this period a people who spoke Greek were set wandering from some devastated homeland, and made their way to the islands and peninsula that today bear their name. They displaced fragments of an earlier population and laid the foundation upon which grew the spectacular later civilizations of Athens and Sparta. But some of the Greek speaking people of this early time were in fact the builders of the Cretan civilization. At the time of the destruction of Crete the Greek people were divided into the poor of the North and the rich of the South. It was only after the death of Crete that the northerners were able to coalesce into organized groups sufficient to challenge the great powers of the south. The civilization that grew up there was called Mycenaen after its greatest city, Mycenae, located inland from the head of the Bay of Argo on the East coast of the Greek Peloponnesus.

After 1450 BC, the Mycenaens entered the competition for sea trade challenging the more sophisticated Phoenician groups some of whom, no doubt, were surviving Cretans. This competition reached a climax with the Trojan War immortalized in the great poems of Homer, "The Iliad" and "The Odyssey."

The City of Troy dominated one of the most important trade routes of the ancient world, guarding, as it did, the gateway to the Black Sea, and all the lands to the north and east. The Mycenaens knew that the capture of Troy would give them powerful leverage over the Phoenicians in their fight for maritime supremacy.

So the multiple city states of Greece organized a fleet to be led by the great King Agamemnon to attack the power of Troy.

Not surprisingly, the ships of the Trojan War are much like those of Crete and the Phoenicians. But it is interesting to hear Homer, himself, describe the shipbuilding practices of the day. His descriptions, although written 400 years after the close of the war, are no doubt close to the mark even if one assumes Homer is describing the practice of his own day. Technology progressed slowly in that era.

Homer declares that Agamemnon led the Achaens (Greeks) against the city of Troy with a fleet of more than a thousand ships. Variously he refers to them as "the curved ships"; "the black ships"; "hollow ships"; "decked ships"; "dark prowed ships"; "well timbered ships"; and "black beaked ships." An oarsmen's bench is said to be "seven feet long", while they " . . . raised the mast of pine tree and set it in the hold of the cross plank, and made it fast with forstays and hauled up the white sails with twisted ropes of oxhide."

At one point, the demi-goddess, Calypso, helps Odysseus build a sailing raft. This is how the project proceeds:

"Next she (Calypso) gave him a polished adze, and she led the way to the border of the isle where tall trees grew, alder and poplar and pine that reacheth unto heaven, seasoned long and sere, that might lightly float for him . . . and he set to cutting timber . . . twenty trees in all . . . (Calypso) brought him augers, so he bored each piece and jointed them together, and then made all fast with trenails and dowels . . . and therein he set a mast and a yard-arm fitted thereto and moreover he made a rudder to guide the craft . . . (Calypso) brought him a web of cloth to make his sails . . . and he made fast therein braces and halyards and sheets . . . "

Homer explains also that " . . . the vessel in full course ran ashore, half her keel's length high." He also describes Odysseus' fleet as " . . . one of vermilion prow." In another place, he tells us that one hero's ship rowed 50 oars.

Homer's hints confirm impressions from other data. The ships were decked or partially decked, oar driven craft, between 35 and 80 feet long. They were planked wooden ships with keels, treenailed together and fairly shallow of draft. The "beaked prow" refers to the ramrod we mentioned. They were waterproofed with pitch (black ships), and had a decorative painted bow. They carried a single mast with a square sail and the rigging was oxhide rope.

GREECE

After the Trojan War, which ended, says tradition, in 1183 BC, the Greeks gradually built-up a trading empire in the Aegean and northeast Mediterranean. The city states of Athens and Sparta finally reached their zenith in the fifth century BC.

The Greeks refined the warships conceived by the Phoenicians. In their hands, the *bireme* was built somewhat lighter. The keel was lengthened forward to better absorb the shock of ramming, and thick wales were added to the hull at the waterline as further reinforcement to the ram.

Finally the Greeks added a third bank of

GREEK TRIREME

Triremes, so called because they were powered by three banks of oars, were the devastating battleships of the days of Alexander the Great, around 300 B.C.

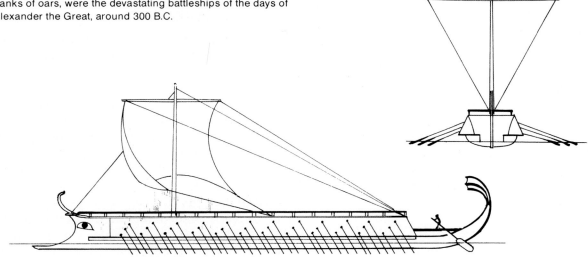

oars giving birth to the *trireme,* the most formidable capital warship of her day. Peter Kemp, in his *History of Ships* describes a *trireme* " . . . the waterline wales were brought up to a point with the keel to form a decorated sternpost. The stern rose from the keel at an angle of 70 degrees and curved backwards up to the level of the forecastle, or raised fighting bridge, then rose above it and curved forwards to finish in the *acrostolion* or ornamental decoration. The beak projected about 10 feet beyond the stem, reinforced by the thick wales, and formed a three toothed spur, with the center tooth longer than the others. This was covered in metal, usually bronze. Above it, but not so long, was a second beak, formed by the upper wales meeting in a point. This, too, was covered in metal, and frequently shaped like a ram's head . . . "

Triremes evidently were about 130 feet long and 16 feet in beam. A ship's company numbered 200 including 170 rowers divided into 62 *thranites,* 54 *zygites,* and 54 *thalamites,* each class corresponding to one of the three banks of oars. The top bank of *thranites* pulled 14 foot oars; the middle bank of *zygites* pulled 10½ foot oars; and the *thalamites* pulled 7½ footers.

Such were the *triremes* that fought in the famous battle between Athens and Syracuse in 412 BC. Thucydides in his "History of the Peloponnesian War" describes it.

"The Syracusans and their allies had already put out with about the same number of ships as before (about 76) a part of which kept guard at the outlet, and the remainder all round the rest of the harbour, in order to attack the Athenians on all sides at once: . . . When the rest of the Athenians came up to the barrier, with the first shock of their charge they overpowered the ships stationed there, and tried to undo the fastenings; after this, as the Syracusans . . . bore down upon them from all quarters, the action spread from the barrier over the whole harbour, . . . On either side the rowers showed great zeal in bringing up their vessels at the boatswain's orders, and the helmsmens great skill in maneuvering, . . . And as many ships were engaged in a small compass (. . ., being together little short of two hundred), the regular attacks with the beak were few, there being no opportunity of backing water or of breaking the line; while the collisions caused by one ship chancing to run foul of another, either in flying from or attacking a third, were more frequent. So long as a vessel was coming up to the charge the men on the decks rained darts and arrows and stones upon her; but once alongside, the heavy infantry tried to board each other's vessel, fighting hand to hand."

The Athenians finally lost this battle and entered into their period of declining empire.

THE POLYNESIAN MIGRATION

This map of the North Pacific shows the prevailing winds and currents the Americans sailed enroute to their new homes in Polynesia.

The explosion of 1450 BC unquestionably disrupted Middle East civilizations and once again set men in search of new habitats in that area. But curiously another important migration took place in the far Pacific about that time as well.

It is believed that about 1400 BC, Indians from the American Northwest set sail in twin hulled dugout canoes bound, in the grip of the southwestward flowing Japan current, to Hawaii. Subsequently these people came to settle in the rest of Polynesia merging with an earlier population which had come to the islands from Peru via Easter Island and the Galapagos.

It would seem that the famed Polynesian catamarans and outrigger dugout canoes originated in timber-rich Northwest America. For years it was accepted logic among students of maritime history that the earliest of primitive man's boats were dugout canoes, from which he gradually evolved planked hulls. Yet the logic fails when one considers the difficulty of making a log into a "sickle-shaped" boat and observing that the Polynesians never thought of building up the sides of their dugouts with more planks. The dugout, rather than representing the root of marine architecture, seems to have been a later experiment of a few scattered forest bound people. The experiment led to little development beyond its beginnings.

ROME

The Romans inherited Greek and Phoenician naval technology but did little to advance the art other than to increase the size of ships. They began by adding banks of oars to the Greek *triremes* and so introduced the *quadrireme* (4 banks) and the *quinquireme* (5 banks), though scholars have yet to figure out exactly how all these oars were manned. In fact some theorists argue that the terms *quadrireme* and *quinquireme* refer not to the banks of oars present, but to the number of men assigned to the oars of the more comprehensible *trireme*. In support of their theory, they point to Roman descriptions implying that some ships carried 16 or even 40 banks of oars, a patently impossible circumstance. Hence the terms *quadrireme*, etc. must refer to something beside the number of banks of oars present.

In any event, Roman ships as well as Carthaginian vessels were substantially larger than their Greek and Phoenician precedents. In 1934 the remains of two Roman ships were uncovered at the bottom of Lake di Nemi in the Alban Hills near Rome. One of them, a warship, measured 235 feet long and 110 feet in beam. The second, a merchant ship, measured 240 feet in length and 47 feet in beam.

To drive these large vessels, the Romans introduced some innovations in rig. Where the Phoenicians had sailed under a two-masted rig, the Romans added a third, mizzen mast, aft. They also set triangular topsails.

The dimensions of the Roman ships cited above draws our attention to an important consideration of naval architecture—the ratio of length to width in a vessel. We recall that the Greek *trireme* was shaped like a needle being 130 feet long by 16 wide, presenting a length to beam ratio of about 8 to 1. The Roman war galley presents a ratio of about 2 to 1, while the merchant ship is about 4 times as long as it is wide.

The slender Greek galley, while fast under oar power, was limited in sail carrying capacity. Too much sail aloft would have capsized her.

The Roman galley, on the other hand, was little more than a barge—a stable, broad bottomed floating platform able to carry a load of soldiers but which would have sailed about as well as an inner tube.

The merchant ship, however, exhibits the ratio of a sailing ship. She is broad enough to carry a good press of sail while narrow enough to slice the water and hold a course. Length to beam ratios in the area of 3½ or 4 to 1 are characteristic of sailing vessels up to the day of the great clippers.

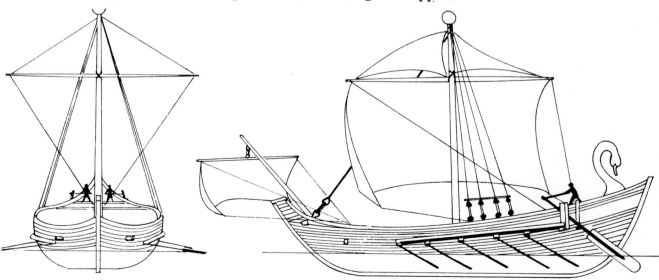

ROMAN GRAIN SHIP
The Romans around the time of Christ were obliged to import great quantities of 'corn' from Africa to feed the burgeoning Italian population.

ANCIENT ARMAMENTS

As Syracuse rose to power, in the years after the defeat of the Athenians, the city became one of the great centers of Hellenic culture. One of her most famous sons was the scientist, Archimedes. Perhaps no other thinker in history has contributed more than Archimedes to maritime technology. The list of his inventions is formidable. He, of course, was the first to expound the principle of specific gravity or "displacement." But he also declared the principles of the lever and pulley, claiming that if he "had a place to stand, he could move the earth." The last led him to the invention of the catapult. Under his direction the citizens of Syracuse defended themselves from Roman attack with catapults that bombarded the oncoming troops and ships with stones. Archimedes rigged cranes with cranks and pulleys capable of upending Roman ships and

dropping rocks on them.

From their embarrassing experience at Syracuse, the Romans learned and soon adopted Archimedes' catapults as heavy artillery in their army and navy.

Roman war galleys employed one sort of catapult that fire grappling arrows. Powerful bows were mounted on the gunwales, the bowstring drawn to the mast. The catapult was fired by chopping a trigger loop rove between the string and a hook in the mast.

The grappling arrow was perhaps six feet long with a heavy, barbed head. A doubled messenger line rove through a ring near the head so that once the barbed head was sunk fast in the side of an enemy ship, the messenger could be used to haul out a cable to make the enemy fast for boarding.

ROMAN CATAPULT
The Romans employed grappling catapults like this to make fast to a target ship.

The galleys also mounted stone throwing catapults. A throwing arm was sprung from a simple trigger mechanism on deck over a fulcrum to a "Spanish burton" sort of tensioning mechanism. A "Spanish burton" consists of several ropes rove back and forth between two members and a twisting bar poked between the rope lengths. As the ropes are twisted together, the distance between the members is shortened and a powerful tension created.

The "trigger" amounted to an 'E' shaped wooden latch that linked the throwing arm to a wooden link fastened to the deck. A hammer blow to the central bar of the latch fired the catapult.

The catapult remained the favorite siege engine until the coming of gunpowder 1400 or so years later. They used stone for ammunition but the Byzantines perfected "Greek fire" bombs. Greek fire, it is said, saved Europe from Moslem invasion in the seventh century. Supposedly it was invented by one Callinicus of Syria. The material was a mixture of naptha, quicklime, sulphur, and pitch. The highly flammable paste was strapped to iron balls with lengths of oil-soaked linen, set ablaze and catapulted at enemy ships or troops with devastating effect. Arrows, blowguns, and fire ships also served as carriers. Greek fire was the "atomic bomb" of the era and the most guarded military secret of the Byzantines for two hundred years. Finally, Saracen espionage cracked the secret and began to employ the weapon as "Saracen fire."

The earliest known reference to gunpowder in the western civilization is that of "Mark the Greek" who wrote a book in 1270 AD entitled "Book of Fires for Burning Enemies." In his volume he describes Greek fire, and then provides a recipe for gunpowder. He tells us that we make a fine powder of one pound of live sulphur, two pounds of charcoal from the lime or willow tree, and six pounds of saltpeter (potassium nitrate), then mix them together.

Roger Bacon, the great medieval philosopher, writing about the same time as Mark the Greek, recognized the explosive potential of gunpowder. He observes that certain toys, "crackers" are in use and, " . . .From the force of the salt called saltpeter so horrible a sound is produced at the bursting of so small a thing, namely, a small piece of parchment, that . . . it exceeds the roar of sharp thunder, and the flash exceeds the greatest brilliancy of the lightning accompanying the thunder."

One hundred or so years later the military potential of Bacon's fire cracker was put to the test and the history of gunnery was launched.

Archimedes developed the principle of the catapult, which the Romans employed in sea-going versions such as this one. Tensioning power was supplied by the twisted ropes.

BYZANTIUM

The Roman Empire reached her height in the first three centuries after Christ. Disintegration set in toward the end of the fourth century and in 410 AD the city of Rome fell to the Visigoths under Alaric.

Thereafter the remnants of Roman civilization centered on the city of Byzantium, later renamed Constantinople after the emperor who designated it as his capital in the fourth century.

The culture that grew from this foundation came to be called Byzantine. For nearly a thousand years the Byzantine Empire controlled the eastern Mediterranean in trade and maintained the traditions of advanced civilization while the rest of Europe languished in barbarism.

Through the centuries of Byzantine influence, connecting links with the west gradually reestablished themselves, witnessing the emergence of the Italian city states of Pisa, Venice, Genoa, and Florence. The maritime crafts advanced.

A most notable development of the early Byzantine period was that of plank-on-frame construction. Prior to this development, the procedure for building a ship was to first build up the sides then add reinforcing ribs, beams and other members as required. In plank-on-frame construction, the procedure is reversed. Internal frames are first constructed then mounted on the keel, after which outside planks are fastened over them. The method is that used to the present day.

The first hard evidence of plank-on-frame construction was recovered by George Bass off the island of Yassi Ada in the Aegean. Bass was able to bring up, in a remarkably good state of preservation, the hull of a small coastal freighter dating from the seventh century AD.

She was about 40 tons burthen, 70 feet long and about 21 feet in beam. She was a pure sailing vessel lacking row ports. She was fully decked, her sheer rising high in the stern. Right aft a cuddy with a tiled roof provided cooking facilities. Forward of the cuddy a steering platform provided the steersman level footing and a clear view. She contained virtually all the structural members of wooden ships built to this day while the sequence and method of their assembly seems to have conformed with our own familiar practice.

The Cathedral of Santa Sophia in Constantinople remains as the most triumphant monument of Byzantine culture. Santa Sophia was built by the Emperor Justinian in the Sixth Century A.D.

SCANDINAVIA

The earliest record of human habitation in Scandinavia dates from the Last Ice Age. As the ice of the glaciers melted, men followed their retreat in the pursuit of game pushing ever northward on the frozen tundra. Life was tough in these regions and the art these people left behind reflected the fact.

As Herbert Wendt observes, "Their art grew melancholy and froze into ornament. Then some of the great minds among them invented the ship and freed themselves from imprisonment on the ice and marshes, in the primeval forests, and among the mountains and fiords."

The sort of ship the Ice Age Norsemen seem to have invented were dugout boats such as the ones found in Amossen, Denmark dating from that period. The rock carvings depicting them show long slender hulls with upturned bow and stern but with a runner (or runners) along the keel suggesting an Eskimo dog sled. Could these early vehicles have been intended for travel on both ice and water? In any event, the Norsemen seem to have set in motion a distinctly separate boat building tradition from that of the south.

Archaeologists have uncovered the remains of actual Scandinavian vessels dating back to 300 BC which gives us a fairly clear idea of the evolution. The earliest of these preserved vessels is the *Hjortspring* boat. This boat is about 50 feet long and made of five long, thin boards. The boards overlap one another like shingles in the manner which has become the distinctive feature of northern shipbuilding—clinker planking. The central board extends beyond the others on both ends, and hollowed out end pieces are fastened to it. The side boards are sprung into the end caps, and internal reinforcing frames and thwarts added to make the whole sturdy. She had no keel nor sail. She was propelled by paddles and so in effect, was a large canoe. The planks were stitched together at the overlapping seams, while each board was carefully adzed to thickness leaving cleat-like protrusions for the attachment of the frames.

Boats of later period, such as that found at Nydam, Jutland, reflect the continuing refinement of the clinker building technique. Here we have a ship 75 feet long with upward curving stem and sternpost, but still no keel. The fastenings now include iron rivets, but the planks still run the whole length of the ship and are hewn down with cleats as before. She, too, was propelled by paddles.

As time passes, the boats become less canoe-like, true keels begin to appear, they are made broader, stem and sternposts rise higher, the lines exhibit the convex entry and run of the preeminently seaworthy Viking ships, and fulcrummed oars replace paddles.

The persistance of paddle driven canoe-like boats up to the Viking era testifies to the early Northerner's need to navigate the inland waterways, rivers and fjords rather than undertake long ocean voyages. While early

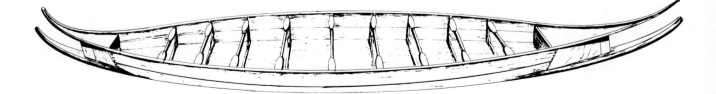

THE HJORTSPRING BOAT
50 feet long ca 300 B.C.
Paddle driven - no keel

Scandinavian traders went far abroad to Byzantium among other places, their routes were over land and down the rivers. Few ventured the open sea until around 750 AD when trade and war with the emerging kingdoms of England and France started looking profitable.

Sails do not appear on northern ships until the Viking era. But once the Vikings were attracted to the open sea, they soon proved themselves consummate masters of the sailing art.

Their triumphs of marine architecture were the famous *longships* which carried them on raiding voyages from one end of Europe to the other.

The *longships* were 90 to 130 feet long, built low to the water with shallow draft, and lightweight. They shipped 20 to 30 pairs of oars and a single square sail. They were the fastest ships in the world at the time. Howard LaFay in his book *The Vikings* observes, ". . . that no modern navy has been able to devise a landing craft as fast, effective, and seaworthy as a Viking ship-of-war."

The Vikings also worked out the problem of sailing to windward. They invented the *beitass*, which was a kind of "whisker pole" that could spar the windward tack of the sail hard forward. This Viking development was the first northern step toward the emancipation of ships from oar power and set the stage for the development of the great sailing ships of 1500 onward. The *beitass* eventually evolved into the permanently fixed spar, renamed the bowsprit, which originally had no other function than that of its predecessor.

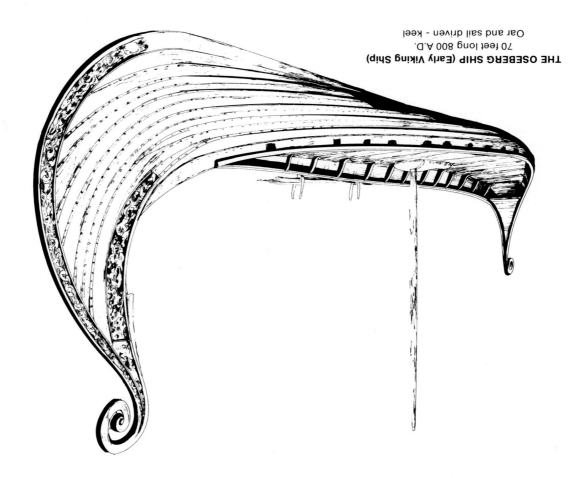

THE OSEBERG SHIP (Early Viking Ship)
70 feet long 800 A.D.
Oar and sail driven - keel

Muhammad entered the world toward the end of the sixth century. In the seventh century the foundation of the Arab Empire was laid on the points of the Koran and the spears of the Prophet's believers. In the eighth century, the rising sea of Islam became a tidal wave that swept the southern Mediterranean from Spain to India, and ships played their role. Among Arabian contributions to naval architecture in this period was the lateen rigged dhow still to be seen in the eastern Mediterranean today. The Arabs also contributed dozens of insights into the art of celestial navigation.

The Italian city States of Venice, Genoa and Pisa emerged in these centuries also, and, among other things, invented the legendary gondola.

While the Arabs and Byzantines pursued the virtue and vice of advanced civilizations, western Europe wallowed in the trough of the dark ages. It took 500 years, but by the year 1000 the westerners were becoming aware of the goods, commerce and culture of the East. The crusades were organized to rescue the Holy Land from the infidel Muhammadans. Thousands of zealous but ignorant Christian soldiers set out for the mysterious East, and returned often beaten, sometimes enlightened, but generally athirst for the gold and other riches of the faraway lands. Trading ventures followed and shipbuilding technology increased accordingly.

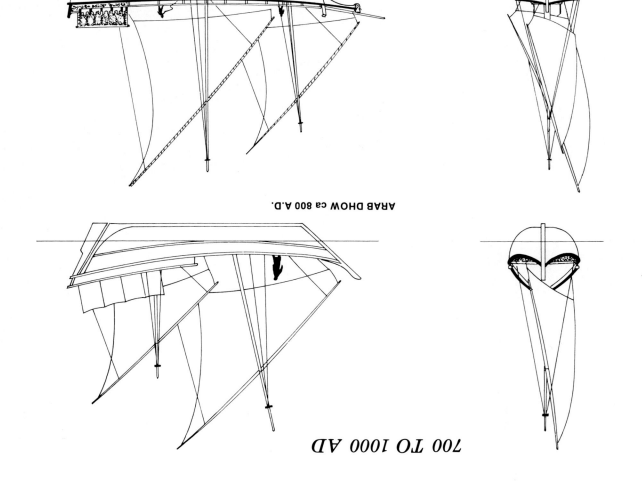

VENETIAN GALEASSE ca 800 A.D.

ARAB DHOW ca 800 A.D.

700 TO 1000 AD

The splendid clinker built ships of the Vikings became the models for shipbuilders in the north. William The Conqueror, the Duke of Normandy, of course, directly descended from the Vikings who invaded and settled France in the tenth century. When, in 1066, he invaded England, he came in the Viking style ships of his ancestors and established with them one of the cornerstones of England's maritime tradition.

During the four centuries following William's invasion of England, the single sail, deckless vessel of the Vikings evolved, with influences from the south, into the ocean-going sailing ships of Drake, Hawkins and Hudson. The first step in the evolution was the development of the stern rudder. Prior to 1000 AD or thereabouts, all ships were steered by an oar or set of oars rigged on the quarters. The Vikings mounted a single oar on the right or "steerboard" quarter. The modern term for the right side of the ship, "starboard," derives from the old practice.

The first evidence of a ship with a stern rudder comes from a relief carving in Winchester Cathedral believed to have been made in 1180 AD. The Kalmar ship of around 1250 AD is the earliest actual vessel yet discovered with a stern rudder.

Sailing ships first began to be built higher in freeboard and deeper in depth of hold. Later platforms were mounted at the bow and stern so that warriors aboard could shoot down on their opponents instead of up at them. By 1300 the fore and aft platforms had grown into huge superstructures known as "castles"—the forecastle, and stern castle.

The idea of building "castles," or raised superstructures on ships originated with the Phoenicians who built full length bridge decks on their galleys above the level of the oarsmen to provide fighting platforms for archers.

The Greeks followed suit with similar full length storming bridges called *katastroma*.

It took the Romans, however, to introduce tower like superstructures clearly reminiscent of a true "castle." They built *dromons* of about 150 feet in length, pulling 100 oars and fitted with catapults in addition to one or two wooden turrets painted to look like stone and manned by marine archers and spearmen.

The naval workhorses of the years between 1100 and 1400 AD were the cogs of the Hanseatic league and England. The largest of these, ranging up to 200 tons and more, featured three castles—a forecastle, stern castle, and a

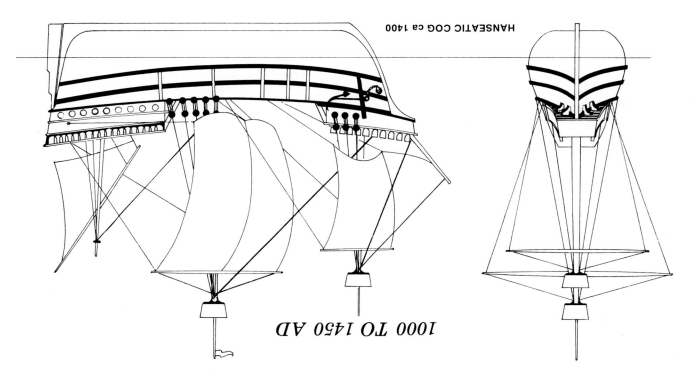

HANSEATIC COG ca 1400

1000 TO 1450 AD

CARRACK ca 1300 3/16" = 1'0"
As merchantmen workhorses of Medieval Europe, Carracks were built as large as 1200 tons. Shown here is a small ship of about 50 tons, 66 feet long, and 22 feet in beam.

masthead castle. With cogs we see the distinctive outline of classical sailing ships for the first time featuring extended stern castles covered by poop and quarterdecks, a lower midship waist and a forecastle covered by a foredeck.

The profiles of many ancient warships as well as merchantmen show raised castle-like cabins in the stern, rather luxuriously appointed, and clearly establishing these areas as "officer country." The tradition of the captain's cabin located in the stern castle was thus born before the time of Christ and continued until our own century.

The castle idea grew slowly through the dark ages until by 1200 AD high fighting platforms were being built fore and aft. At first the platforms were open scaffold structures erected independently of the ship itself. Later the scaffolds were planked in and became integral with the hull.

Throughout history castles were designed to provide advantageous fighting positions. While weapons were limited to bows and arrows, catapults, and boiling pitch, the height of the castles was an essential consideration. As guns came into use, high fore and after castles became more of a hindrance than a boon. The weight of the guns required they be set lower in the hull; the high ship profiles were vulnerable targets and made the ships difficult to maneuver. The coming of guns announced the passing of the great castles.

Model by J. Elem

A SHIP FROM THE REIGN OF PHAROAH SAHURE 2500 B.C.

1/4″ = 1′0″

This vessel, about 50 feet long, had no keel, stepped a bi-pod mast forward, which limited her to downwind sailing. She was lashed together in the same way as Cheop's ship a century earlier, though much more stoutly built. The array of stays and the heavy fore and aft cable were fitted to offset hogging stress, in the same way as on traditional reed boats.

A VOYAGE TO PUNT 1500 B.C.   1/4″ = 1′0″

Queen Hatshepsut organized an expedition of "sea people," probably Cretans, to sail to the land of *Punt* in quest of exotic animals and ivory. They travelled in ships like this one. The vessel exhibits the traditional reed ship lines, but a keel is in evidence. The midship mast provides the potential for sailing wind abeam. The square sail set between upper and lower yards was typical of the early Phoenician *hippos*.

Model by J. Elem

Queen Hatshepsut's ROYAL BOAT 1500 B.C.   1/4" = 1'0"
The great queen impressed her subjects with ceremonial trips on the Nile in a boat like this one. The boat
was about 68 feet long, displaying again the traditional reed ship lines.

GREEK TRADING VESSEL ca 300 B.C.   3/8″ = 1′0″

Model by H. Bridenbecker

The earliest vessel yet recovered through underwater archaeology, this ship was raised near the Greek island of Kyrenia. Though still reflecting reed ship lines, the ship has a full keel, life rails, spray shields, and a raised steering platform aft. The bow exhibits a trace of a ram, characteristic of the warships of the time.

Model by H. Bridenbecker

BYZANTINE TRADING SHIP ca 600 A.D. 1″ = 3′0″
Discovered by underwater archaeologists led by George Bass, the remains of this vessel were brought up
from the sea floor near the Island of Yassi Ada in the Mediterranean. This ship was a true sailing ship
built without oar ports, and the earliest evidence of a vessel constructed with the modern
plank-on-frame technique. Earlier ships were built shell first, with ribs added later. In plank-on-frame
construction, a skeleton was built first, with a lighter skin of planks fastened to it afterward.

ARAB DHOW or SAMBUC ca 700 AD 1/4″ = 1′0″
The Arab dhow is the prototype of the Mediterranean lateen rigged ships still seen in Near Eastern waters today. The term "dhow" is the general term for any Arab cargo ship. A sambuc refers to this particular type of dhow. Sambuc's mast shrouds were set only on the windward side. When the ship came about, the shrouds were shifted to the opposite side as a leeward yard, and sail was hauled up while the windward one was dropped.

Model by H. Bridenbecker

VIKING MERCHANTMAN ca 900 AD 1/4″ = 1′0″
The distinctive feature of northern shipbuilding was clinker or lapstrake construction, where planks were
overlapped like shingles. The shell was built first and ribs added. Since the woolen sails stretched easily,
they were criss-crossed with bands of rawhide or rope.

Model by T. Palen

NORMAN TRADING SHIP
ca 1300   1/60 scale
The Normans, descendents of the
Vikings, learned to build carvel
planked ships during the Crusades
when they ventured into
Mediterranean waters. Platforms fore
and aft were precursors of the later
fore and aft castles.

Model by R. Roos

COCCO VENITA ca 1500   1/72 scale

The "cocco" was the merchantman workhorse of the Mediterranean in the years when Venice and other Italian city states dominated the trade between Western Europe and the East. Regarded then as the best shipwrights and mariners in the western world, the Italians successfully exported their skills. Christopher Columbus sold his talents to Spain in 1492, while Henry the Eighth of England hired Italians to teach in his new school of naval architecture.

Model by C. Chaffin

**LA REALE, a "King's Ship"
of the Seventeenth Century**   1/4" = 1'0"
Louis the Fourteenth of France was the most powerful
sovereign of seventeenth century Europe. His
shipwrights were the leaders of the day. Lateen rigged
galleys like this one were the backbone of Louis'
Mediterranean fleet.

Model by H. Bridenbecker

CARRACK ca 1300   3/16″ = 1′0″

Carracks were the merchantmen workhorses of Medieval Europe which preceded the famous galleons of
the Seventeenth Century. They represented a cross-fertilization of shipbuilding ideas between North and
South. Two, three, or four masted, they flew a southern lateen mizzen sail with northern square sails
forward. Some carracks were built as large as 1200 tons, though the model shown here is of a small ship of
about 50 tons, 66 feet long, and 22 feet in beam.

Model by H. Bridenbecker

A COLONIAL BARK ca 1640   1/4″ = 1′0″

W. A. Baker, a naval architect and leading maritime historian of the twentieth century, drew the plans for this little ship after many years of painstaking research into the shipbuilding practices of the early 1600's. She is thought to be a vessel typical of those built and used by the first American Colonists. Mr. Baker also worked out the reconstruction of the Mayflower of 1620 (Mayflower II), which is on exhibit in Plymouth, Massachusetts.

CHINESE WAR JUNK ca 1850 1/8″ = 1′0″

The Chinese shipwrights built ocean-going junks similar to the one shown here, before the time of Christ, while archaeologists are beginning to think that Chinese navigators visited California as early as 300 A.D. Among other sophistications, junks featured watertight bulkheads dividing the ship into several independently buoyant sections — a safety measure not adopted by the West until Brunel built the *Great Britain* in 1843. This model represents a vessel 100 feet long by 25 feet in beam. She carried a crew of 200 men.

Model by H. Bridenbecker

SPANISH GALLEON ca 1600 1/8″ = 1′0″
The galleons of England and Spain reflected the change in shipbuilding practice initiated by Sir John Hawkins just before the defeat of the Spanish Armada in 1588. The change did away with the towering fore and after castles of the earlier carracks (so-called "high-charged" ships) in favor of a more streamlined profile ("low-charged" ships).

SOVEREIGN OF THE SEAS launched 1637   1:78 scale

H.M.S. *Sovereign of the Seas* served as the flagship of the Royal Navy from the time she was launched until 1696, playing a major role in the great sea battles of the three Dutch wars of the Seventeenth Century. During her career, she was renamed twice. Under Cromwell, from 1649 until 1660, she was called simply the *Sovereign*. Then, when Charles the Second was restored to the throne, she became *The Royal Sovereign*. With 100 guns, 126' in length, 46'6" beam, and 17' deep, the ship weighed in around 1400 tons. Her lavish, gilded decorations matched the tastes of the Baroque Period of which she was a part.

SANTA MARIA
Columbus' flagship

THE AGE
OF
EXPLORATION

The latter half of the fifteenth century ushers in the great age of worldwide exploration. In this century, the sailing ship took on the characteristics and rig that remained essentially unchanged for the next 500 years.

The Portuguese, under Prince Henry the Navigator, perfected the *caravel* as an ideal vessel for the exploration of unknown seas. They were small, stout and seaworthy craft that could sail well to windward under lateen sails (caravella latina) or a combination of lateen and square sails (caravella redonda). They shipped three masts. The caravella redonda added a bowsprit. Vasco da Gama sailed *caravels* around Africa; Columbus to the new world; and Magellan around the world.

The discovery of the *New World* in the fifteenth century touched off an explosion of maritime activity and warfare, spurred the growth of the European national monarchies, flooded the continent with seemingly endless riches, and further inspired the quest for new learning that came with the Renaissance. Portugal, Spain, France, England, Germany, Scandinavia, and Holland joined the mortal combat to control the seas, the trade routes and the wealth of the world.

The small *caravels* so good for exploring were the pathfinders for the great armed ships that followed. Spain and Portugal stuck with

their *carracks* until they matured into the famous *galleons*. The northerners' *"clinker-built"* cogs similarly matured. In the first half of the century, the ships were "high charged" like the earlier *cogs,* sporting towering fore and after castles. When Sir John Hawkins took over Elizabeth's navy, he changed the profile to the "low charged" vessels which beat the invincible Spanish Armada in 1588. From that time forward the height of the fore and after castles gradually diminished. By the time of the American Revolution, the castles had all but disappeared except in name.

The development of marine architecture after 1600 was a steady refinement of the shipbuilding technology that had evolved to that date. Hull designs changed, larger and larger ships were built, multiple decks were added, masts grew masts, and battle tactics relied on more, heavier and better guns. But the structural components of a ship's framing, her planking, her rigging, and basic layout, varied little until the coming of the iron and steel hulls of the nineteenth century. Even then the traditional art of wooden shipbuilding yielded only slowly to the concepts of twentieth century engineering.

Many of the parts of modern steel ships are known by the names assigned to their wooden counterparts five centuries ago, while nostalgic yacht and boat builders still build very much in the manner of our ancestors.

Chapter Four
Details of Wooden
Ship Construction

DETAILS OF WOODEN SHIP CONSTRUCTION

The technique of building a wooden ship evolved from the early reed bundle vessels of the pre-Egyptians through a sequence of events which finally culminated by 1400 in a common Pan-European technology. The methods and terminology in use by 1400 are in essence the same as we use today. The method begins with the laying of a keel to which is fitted a stem and sternpost. Prefabricated frames are then set up along the length of the keel to form a skeleton structure. The skeleton is covered over with a skin of planks or plates. This method is recognized as *plank-on-frame* construction and, while not every ship in the world is built this way, it applies to most large, ocean-going craft. This chapter is devoted to an examination of the structural details of a wooden plank-on-frame vessel.

LOFTING

The construction of a ship begins with the translation of the architect's lines drawings into full scale patterns for the actual structural components. This process is called *lofting*.

The lofting of the keel, stem, and sternpost is a matter of simply expanding to actual size the shapes given in the profile plan, while the patterns for the individual frames must be interpolated from the sections given in the body plan. The latter task is by far the larger and more demanding of the two.

Often the floor of a large room, designated the *loft*, was the scene for this large scale drafting. To one side, a stripe was painted to serve as the keel reference line. The rest of the architect's grid of waterlines and buttocks would be laid out with taut strings. Thin boards would then be sprung under the grid in positions matching the frame being lofted. The shaped boards became the pattern for the final timber.

The plots for the frame came from an extension of the architect's lines plans. Verticals drawn in the profile, and half breadths at each frame, yield intersections with the buttock lines and the waterlines. Thus, for each frame, one has a plot of points up and out from the keel intermediate to those represented in the architect's body plan.

Plots for the rest of the important timbers followed similar procedures.

Modelers, when constructing fully framed vessels, use precisely the same methods, except for the demands imposed by their miniature scales.

PLOTTING THE SHAPE OF FRAMES
FROM THE LINES DRAWINGS

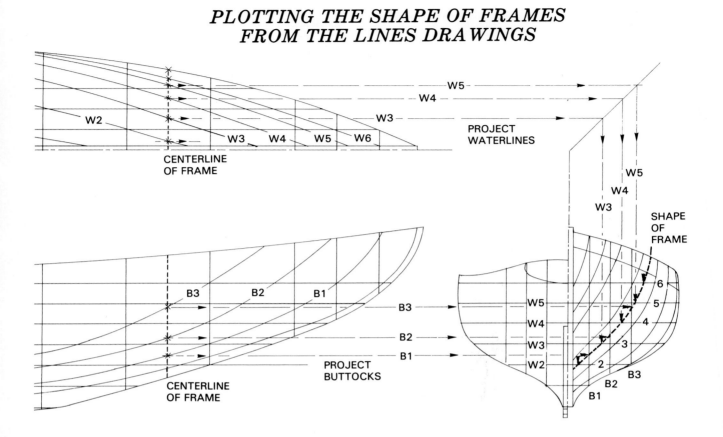

The plots for all of a ship's frames are derived from the lines drawing by drawing perpendiculars across buttocks and waterlines at the frame centerlines. Intersections of the frame centerlines with the buttocks and waterlines provide distances which are plotted on the body plan. The shape of each frame parallels the closest body section.

ROOM AND SPACE

Room and space is the naval architect's term for the center-to-center spacing of a ship's frames. The term derives from the Scandanavian *rum*, which was used as a unit of measurement for a ship's length, and represented the distance between two rowing thwarts.

In the eigthteenth century, rules for ship construction were laid out by the British Admiralty for warships, and by Lloyd's Register for merchant ships. Among these rules were those for room and space. A warship's room and space was to be .0172 times the length of the ship between the posts. The factor for a merchant ship was .027. The width of the frames in both cases was .47 of the total room and space. Thus, from about 1750 onward,

naval ships, regardless of size, always had 58 frames, not counting cant frames, while merchant ships had 37. Though the decimal formulas for room and space did not become official until the eighteenth century, earlier ships probably conformed closely with this specification. The early shipwrights, as we have said, laid out a ship's hull with geometry, e.g., progressively dividing and subdividing lengths with the use of a compass and straight edge. The peculiar decimals of the later years were derived from earlier geometrical methods. These traditional formulas held sway in shipbuilding circles until the results of modern investigative science began to challenge their validity in the early nineteenth century.

SCANTLINGS

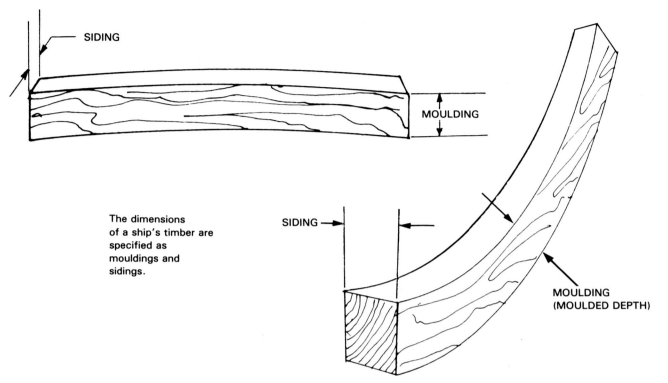

The dimensions of a ship's timber are specified as mouldings and sidings.

It is not enough for the shipbuilder, of course, to simply know the outside shape of a member. He must also know its thickness and general massiveness. Such specifications are known as *scantlings*. It was not uncommon to find ships made from the same lines with completely different performance characteristics because of different *scantlings*. One ship might have especially light scantlings, another very heavy. Merchant ships as a rule were made of lighter scantlings than warships of comparable size.

Naval architects, as well as prospective ship owners, spent considerable effort in specifying ship scantlings because unless they did, they were likely to fall prey to some unscrupulous economics by the shipwrights. Business then, as now, was business.

Today a significant portion of a ship's scantlings are spelled out in a special drawing called the *midship section*. In this single drawing it is possible to show the thickness of frames, planking, keel, and so on at the widest section of the ship, while calling out the variations of these

members at more forward or aft locations. The midship section is supplemented with other structural detail drawings as required.

This comprehensive practice, however, only became common in later years. Blueprints did not come into use until well into the nineteenth century prior to which there was no practical way to reproduce working drawings for use in the shop. In the early years, scantlings were spelled out in words, while hull designs were rendered in models. Beyond this, the old shipwrights designed their ships as they built them using materials as best they could to satisfy rather loose contract specifications.

Among the terms used in specifying a ship's scantlings are *mouldings*, and *sidings*. A moulding is the thickness of a timber in the vertical plane; a siding in the horizontal plane. Thus we read that a ship's keel has a moulded depth of 18 inches, sided 12 inches, and a sternpost is, "British oak - sided 10½ inches, moulded at keel - 19 inches, at top - 10¾ inches, 1 piece."

MATERIALS

Oak from the earliest times to the end of the wooden ship era was the preferred building material for most of a ship's structure. Keel, frames, planking, deck beams, carlings, and many other parts were almost always made of oak. When oak was not available, elm was considered an acceptable substitute. East Indiamen built in the Far East were made of teak.

The fabulous Mackay clipper ships of the 1850's are examples of craft partly built of less expensive, soft wood. The decision to compromise on materials for these ships was justified by the fact that a handsome profit could be made on them within the ten years they were expected to last. But for all their short lives, these ships were nonetheless superbly built and amazingly strong.

In the early days, shipwrights carved frames and other curved structural members from timber shaped naturally somewhat like the component. Later as timber resources diminished and ships grew in size, this practice became impractical giving way to built-up frames and other structures. Smaller elements such as knees, knuckles, breast hooks, and the like, however, continued to be built from naturally grown timber forms. In America, hackmatack, a variety of larch, provided a good source of natural "knee" shapes.

Treenails (trennels or trunnels) fasten a ship's timbers and planks together. Treenails were wooden dowels from one to three inches in diameter driven through holes drilled into the timbers often with expansion wedges slotted in either end.

FASTENINGS

Timbers and planks were fastened together with iron bolts, nails, and wooden pegs called treenails or "trennels." Nails were really more like rivets. Holes were drilled through the timbers to receive them, after which the nails were driven home and cleated back on one side.

Treenails were used everywhere except in places where only the special strength of iron was required. Treenails driven into drilled holes of adjoining members expanded when wet to form solid watertight joints, while sharing the same ratios of expansion and contraction as the surrounding timber.

Treenails fasten down the deck planking on the *Star of India*.

CAULKING

Hulls were made watertight by filling the cracks between the planks with hemp or other fibrous material soaked in tar and pitch. For many years, oakum payed over with hot pitch was the standard caulking material. Oakum was old, tarred rope picked apart into loose, bristly strands. A standard minor punishment for a miscreant crewman was to be sentenced to picking oakum, a boring job that painfully flayed the fingers. Richard Dana tells us in *Two Years Before the Mast* that on wet days when other work couldn't be done, the crew was set to picking oakum just to keep them busy.

To caulk a ship, soaked oakum was pounded into the seams with a light sledge hammer, and a chisel-shaped caulking iron. Since the planks swelled when wet, care was taken not to caulk the seams so tightly that structural damage would take place once the ship was afloat.

SHEATHING

The mighty wooden ships that weathered Cape Horn in winter and resisted assaults by cannon and fire, forever fought a losing battle against a living nemesis - teredo worm. Wooden ships to this day suffer the encroachments of these tropical seaborn termites which have been known to literally eat the bottom out of a ship.

In the early days of worldwide maritime activity, attempts were made to control the ship worms by adding extra layers of sacrificial fir planking to ship bottoms, or applying thick coats of tar mixed with horse hair and other materials. Anthony Deane tried lead sheathing but this approach set up galvanic currents which chewed away underwater iron fittings. Nothing worked really well until copper bottom plating was tried.

After 1780, copperplate sheathing became the accepted method of discouraging worm attack. Copperplate sheathing stayed in use into the twentieth century when it gradually was replaced by modern protective paint coatings.

Nothing so far, however, has managed to completely thwart the scourge of the teredo as owners of modern wooden craft testify.

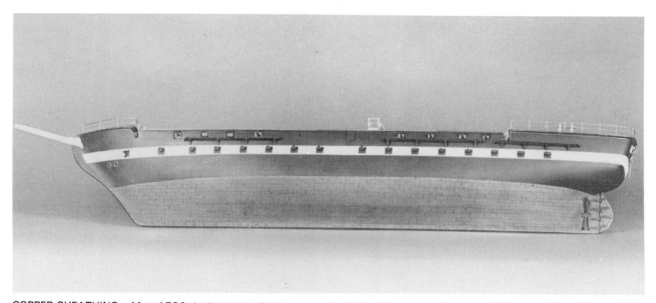

COPPER SHEATHING - After 1780 the bottoms of ships were sheathed with copper plates as a defense against shipworms. Art Robinson's model of the Danish frigate *Jylland* of 1861 shows how the plates were overlapped bow to stern, and from the top down as shingles on a house. Copper nails were used since a different metal would have caused galvanic corrosion.

KEEL, STEM AND STERNPOST

A ship's keel is her backbone providing a major portion of the hull's longitudinal strength.

The keels of smaller vessels were (and are) made of a single, carefully hewn timber. Larger keels necessarily were pieced together, the joints scarphed for maximum strength.

The stem and sternpost are scarphed to the keel at either end and reinforced with knees. The outer edges of the stem and keel are protected by a cutwater piece (gripe), and a false keel or shoe.

Inboard of the stem lies the apron and stemson, which provide the surface to which the planking is nailed. The apron and stemson continue the line of the keel rabbet, the groove cut out to receive the planks on each side. Fore and aft the frames of the ship arise from the keel higher than they do amidships, so the keel is built-up of solid timber in these areas. The sections are called the fore and after deadwood.

The sternpost is comparable in structure to the stem except that it may not have a protective outer shoe. Inboard the inner post provides the shelf for the planking attachment.

Toward the end of the sailing ship era, auxiliary engines came into use, and with them propellers. To accommodate a midship, single screw, as well as a rudder, a second sternpost was contrived aft of the first and called the *prick post*.

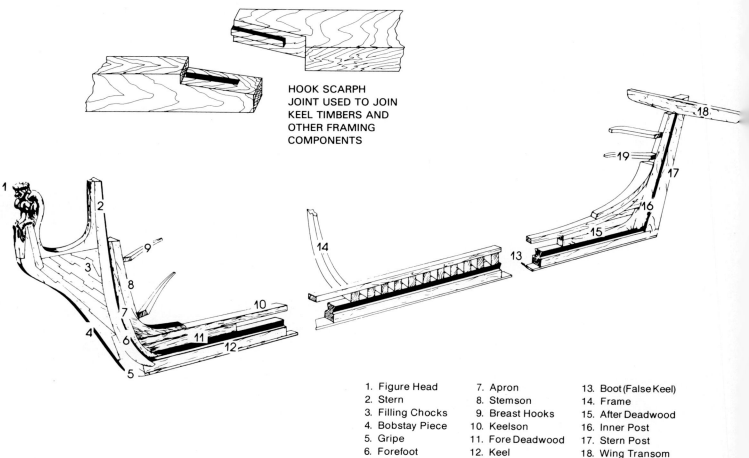

HOOK SCARPH JOINT USED TO JOIN KEEL TIMBERS AND OTHER FRAMING COMPONENTS

1. Figure Head	7. Apron	13. Boot (False Keel)
2. Stern	8. Stemson	14. Frame
3. Filling Chocks	9. Breast Hooks	15. After Deadwood
4. Bobstay Piece	10. Keelson	16. Inner Post
5. Gripe	11. Fore Deadwood	17. Stern Post
6. Forefoot	12. Keel	18. Wing Transom
		19. Lower Transoms

Henry Bridenbecker's plank-on-frame model of the brig *Irene* of 1806 exhibits the structure of frames through the use of vari-colored woods.

The *Jylland* was one of the earliest ships fitted with a *prick post* aft of the sternpost to accommodate a midship propeller.

FRAMES

A ship's frames for most of history were composite structures consisting of the floors and a series of futtocks bolted and treenailed together. The frames straddled the keel and were treenailed to it. On top of them was laid another longitudinal member, the keelson, which followed the "line of floors" up to the stem and sternpost above the deadwood. The heavy stem and stern knees connect the keelson to the two posts.

At the bottom edge of each frame next to the keel, holes were bored so that bilge water would flow to the lowest level of the ship where the pump could remove it. The holes were called *limbers*. The inner ceiling planks just above the limbers, called limber boards, were made removable so that this lowest place in the bilge could be cleaned out from time to time. Sometimes chains were strung through the limbers so that a pull back and forth could keep the holes unclogged.

Frames tapered from keel to rail when viewed either in section or broadside. For most of the ship's length, the frames crossed the keel under the keelson as complete units from side to side, and were known as *full frames*. Toward the stern, as the rise of floors becomes more acute, the frames were built in two halves, and therefore called *half frames*.

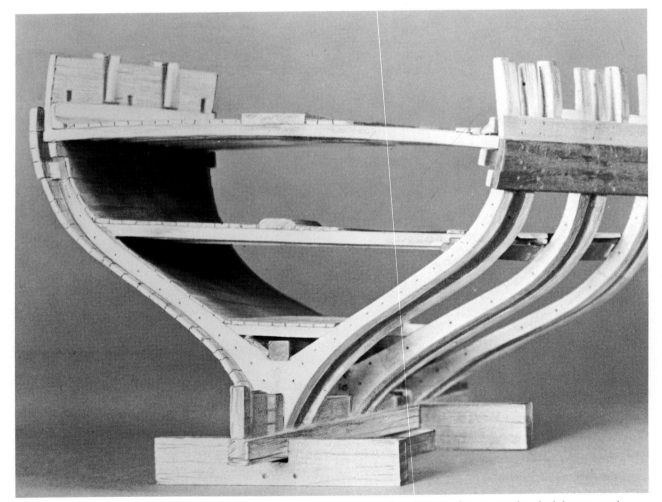

Sections of *Irene* show how half frames are joined to the stern deadwood, the clamp strakes supporting deck beams, and the variations in thickness of ceiling, bottom planking, and wales.

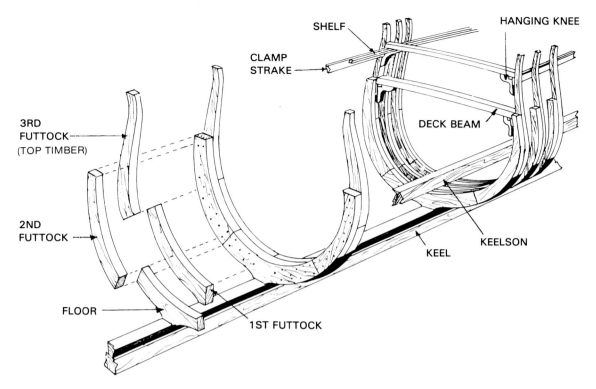

SHELF

CLAMP
STRAKE

HANGING KNEE

3RD
FUTTOCK
(TOP TIMBER)

DECK BEAM

2ND
FUTTOCK

KEELSON

KEEL

FLOOR

1ST FUTTOCK

Model by T. Pugh

The framing of the bow was a near-solid mass of timber, as may be seen here in the *Oliver Cromwell*.

This Spanish galleon of around 1600 exhibits the broad, "square tuck" stern typical of ships built before 1630 when Phineas Pett introduced the "round tuck."

STERN STRUCTURES

The sterns of ships built after 1650 are the most complex structures in wooden ship construction.

Prior to 1650, the taffrail was a simple plane defined by the aftermost frame of the vessel. Longitudinal planks ended on the last frame, and stern planks connected either side of the frame straight across the slightly raked sternpost. This construction was referred to as the "square tuck" and applied to most European vessels. Then Phineas Pett introduced the "round tuck" stern in England about 1650.

The round tuck evolved from the wish to create a hull with a finer run and one which could take a following sea less brutally than the squared-off, flat, backside. Ships with square tuck sterns lived in continuous danger of being pooped, while at best they were cranky sailors.

The stern counter or overhang was developed to direct following water down under the hull.

The basic structure of the round tuck that Pett devised can be found with variations in almost all of the English ships built through 1860,

and constituted Pett's most notable contribution to naval architecture.

There are two key elements — the wing transom and the fashion frame. The wing transom mounts like the cross of a "T" across the inboard face of the sternpost. It is a solid timber shaped like a flattened out frame consistent with the lines of the rest of the ship. Its top edge provides the after shelf for the main deck; the under edge provides the terminus for the bottom planking.

The fashion frame is the aftermost true frame of the ship and is unique in that it is both a cant fame (angled aft from the keel in top view), and raked (slanted aft from bottom to top when viewed from the side). It arises from a point in the after deadwood somewhat forward of the inner post then curves up and aft connecting to the outer corners of the wing transom, then continues up to the poop deck rail.

The stern overhang or *counter* was built out from the wing transom by a system of stern frames running more or less parallel with the keel. These frames were connected athwartship by *knuckle timbers* and tied into the shipsides higher up by *quarter logs*.

CLINKER BUILT SHIPS

Scandinavian shipbuilders planked their vessels "clinker fashion." The planks overlapped one another like shingles. The *Kalmar Ship* of about 1250 A.D., shown here in a 3/8" = 1'0" model by H. Bridenbecker, was built shell first with 13 planks per side. Reinforcing frames, knees, and through beams were added after the planks were riveted together with iron nails. The windlass was used to raise and lower the mast and sails. The ship was 26½ feet long and 15 feet wide. Clinker building is still used in the construction of small boats to this day, though carvel planking became the standard for large ships after 1600. Overlapped planks used more material, and adapted themselves poorly to the more economical plank-on-frame methodologies because of the zigzag cross-section that was created with them.

Model by H. Bridenbecker

THE GOKSTAD SHIP - VIKING 850 AD

The remains of this ship were found in
a burial mound on the Gokstad estate
in Vestfold, Norway about 1880 and
is among the best preserved vessels
of the Viking era.

The ship is 76' overall, 17' wide and
6½' from the gunwale to the keel
amidships. She is built from oak in the
traditional northern lapstrake or clinker
fashion.

The bottom planks were riveted
together then lashed to the ribs with
spruce roots. The garboard strakes
were riveted to the keel. Ribs were
added to the plank structure after the
latter was built out to the 10th, or
waterline strake called the
"meginhufr" in old Norse.

 1 Sternpost
 2 Gunwale
 3 Steering oar (tiller)
 4 Shields lashed to gunwales
 5 Trestle
 6 Rib knees
 7 Top ribs
 8 Oar port
 9 Mast
10 Stern
11 Oar
12 Gunwale
13 Cross beam
14 Rib
15 Mast fish
16 Mast lock
17 Cross beam
18 Keel
19 Strakes (planking)
20 Steering oar

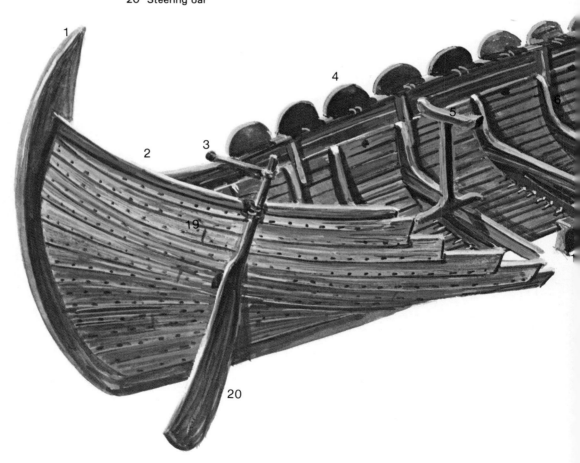

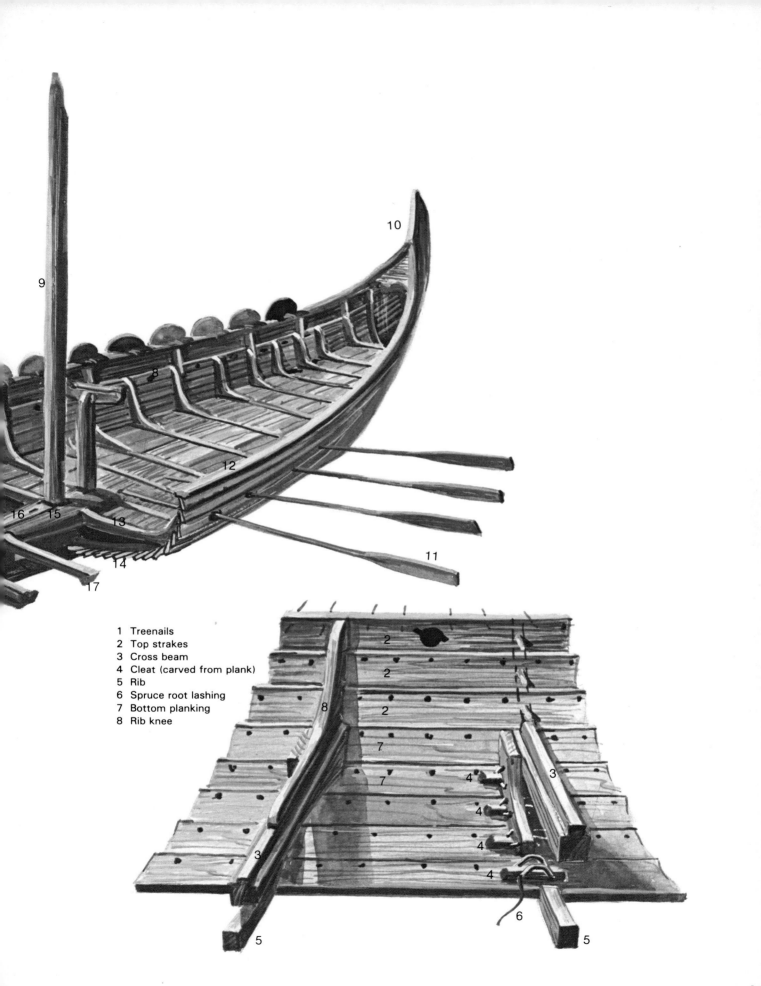

1 Treenails
2 Top strakes
3 Cross beam
4 Cleat (carved from plank)
5 Rib
6 Spruce root lashing
7 Bottom planking
8 Rib knee

THE YASSI ADA SHIP - BYZANTINE SEVENTH CENTURY

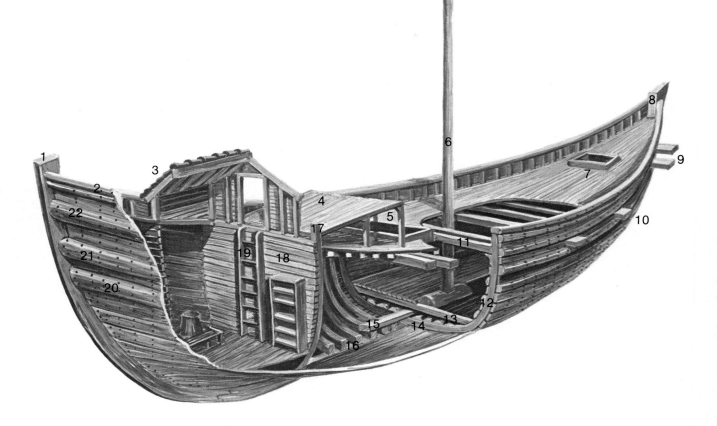

Found by Professor George Bass during an archaeological expedition in the Aegean, the Yassi Ada ship is the earliest evidence we have of true plank-on-frame construction.

The designation "Yassi Ada" derives from the name of the island near which the wreck was discovered.

The ship is thought to be typical of small coastal vessels privately owned by Byzantine traders. She was about 40 tons burdened, 70'0" long, 17'0" in beam, and 6'0" depth of hold amidships.

1 Sternpost
2 Gunwale
3 Tile galley roof
4 Steering platform
5 Hatch
6 Mast
7 Forward hatch
8 Stem
9 Fore through beams
  and catheads
10 Through beams
11 Deck beam
12 Frame
13 Hold deck beam
14 Floor
15 Keelson
16 End of frame
17 Frame
18 Galley bulkhead
19 Ladder
20 Lower wale
21 Middle wale
22 Upper wale

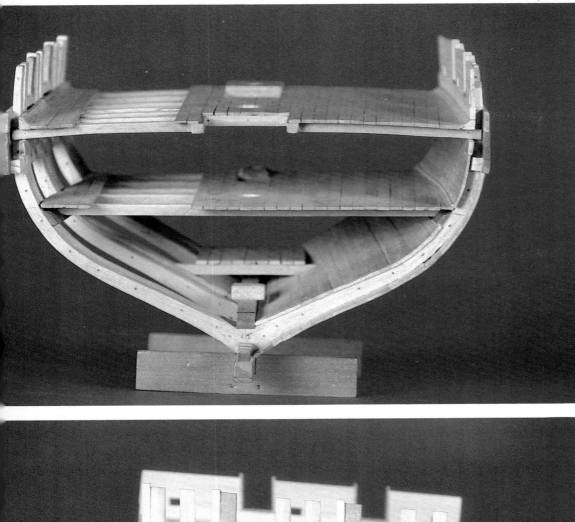

Plank-on-frame built ships were planked carvel fashion or edge-to-edge so each
plank lay firmly against the frames. Heavy inner frames supported a lighter skin of planking.
The open spaces between the outer and inner (ceiling) planks were often filled with rock salt to inhibit rot.
This model illustrates the plank-on-frame construction in perfect detail.

THE CONSTRUCTION OF A WOODEN SHIP *ca 1730*

This generalized view of a wooden ship
depicts major structural elements
common to ships built from 1600 through
about 1825. The particular configuration
shown is approximately that of a small,
English warship of the early
1700's. The vessel would have been
about 100' on deck and about 25' in beam.

26 Poop rail
27 Quarterdeck
28 Mizzen mast
29 Poop deck
30 Taffrail arch
31 Stern lantern
32 Stern timber
33 End of knuckle timber
34 Wing transom
35 Fashion frame
36 Carling
37 Rudder
38 Deck beam
39 Keelson
40 End of frame
41 Deadwood
42 Keel
43 Boot (false keel)
44 Third Futtock
45 Hanging knee
46 Lodging knee
47 Orlop deck beam
48 Second futtock
49 Floor
50 Planking
51 Main wale
52 Frame
53 Mast partner
54 Cant frame
55 Head timbers
56 Hawse timbers
57 Knight timber
58 Forefoot
59 Apron
60 Bobstay piece
61 Filling chocks

8 Cathead
9 Forecastle rail
10 Forecastle deck beam
11 Frame
12 Hanging knee
13 Ends of clamp and shelf
14 Main deck
15 Foremast
16 Woolding
17 Waist rail
18 Bosom knee
19 Hanging knee
20 Main deck beam
21 Gunport
22 Hatch
23 Quarterdeck ladder
24 Quarterdeck catwalk
25 Mainmast

1 Figurehead
2 Hair rail
3 Middle rail
4 Lower rail
5 Head timber
6 Stern
7 Knighthead

THE BRIG IRENE - ENGLISH 1806 1/4" -1'0"

Commissioned by the British in 1806 as a small 18 gun brig of war and originally called the "Grasshopper," the ship was captured by the Dutch in 1811 and renamed "Irene."
At the time, English and Dutch measurements varied. An Amsterdam foot (.283 meters) was shorter than the English foot (.3048 meters) so the ship wound up with two sets of dimensions. The English dimensions were 383 tons, 100'-0" overall length, 30'-6½" in beam and 13'-1" in depth of hold. The ship was armed with 16 32-pounder carronades and two 6-pounder long guns.
The model by Henry Bridenbecker, is rigged in the Dutch manner, after information in E.W. Petrejus' book "Building the Brig of War Irene." Each frame of the vessel was made like the original as a system of floor and futtock timbers. Contrasting color woods point up the construction. Only the most forward or "bridle" gunports had port covers, the rest were left open except in heavy weather when plank covers, carried below, would be fitted.

TYPICAL COMPOSITE SHIP - 1860

In the mid 1800's the advantages of iron for ship building became apparent to some, while many retained old prejudices about the "floatability" of iron for shipbuilding. The compromise was the composite ship built with iron framing and wooden planking. A number of famous clipper ships, the *Cutty Sark* among them, claimed composite hulls. At this time many traditional shipbuilding practices were giving way to science and modern engineering ideas.

1 Bobstay piece
2 Stern
3 Cathead
4 Caprail
5 Bulwarks
6 Foremast
7 Clamp stringer main deck
8 Clamp stringer lower deck
9 Bilge stringer
10 Main deck
11 Mainmast
12 Mast coat
13 Hatch
14 Deckhouse
15 Mizzen mast
16 Poop deck and cuddy
17 Counter
18 Rudder
19 Planksheer
20 Sheer strake
21 Upper deck beam
22 Bracket end of lower deck beam
23 Ceiling
24 Mast step
25 Floor
26 Hold stanchion
27 End of frame
28 Keel
29 Bilge keelson
30 Side intercostal keelson
31 Keel plate
32 Keelson
33 Forefoot
34 Stern
35 Stemson and apron
36 Garboard strake
37 Lower deck tie plate
38 Upper deck waterway

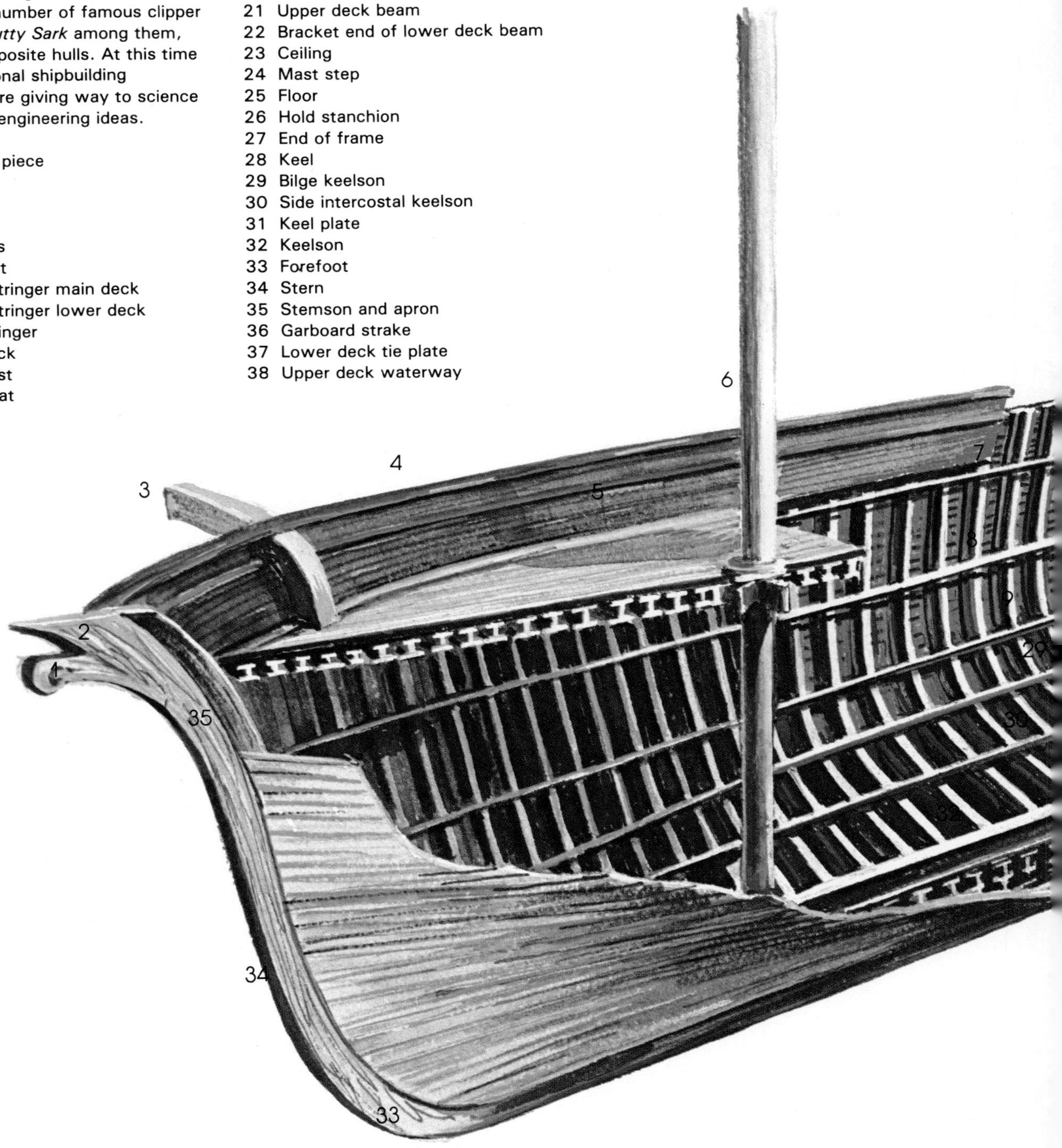

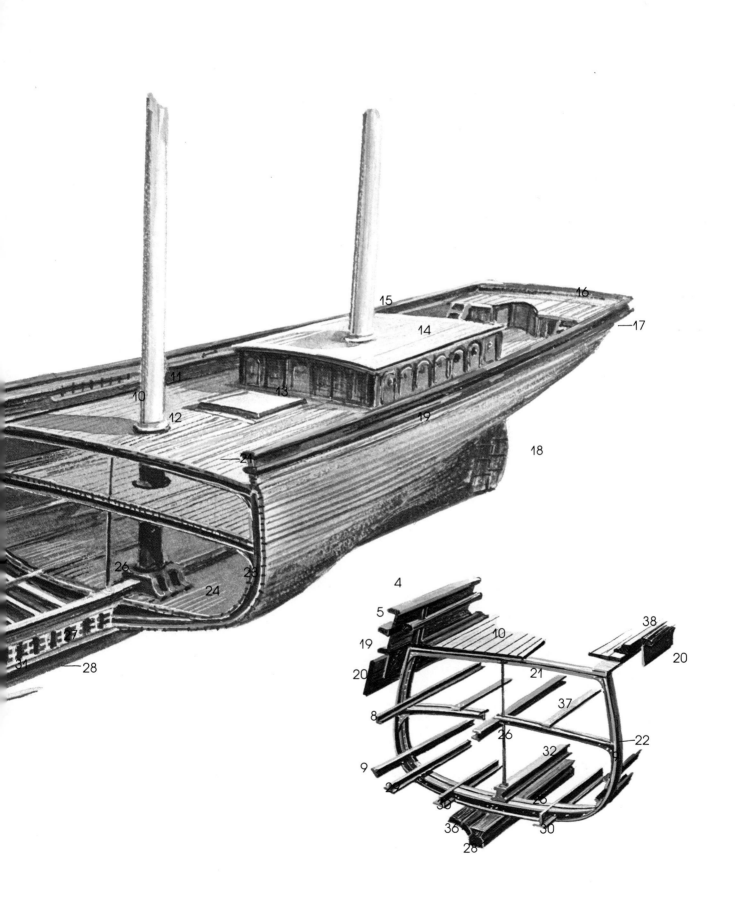

THE STAR OF INDIA
IRON HULLED BARK - 1864

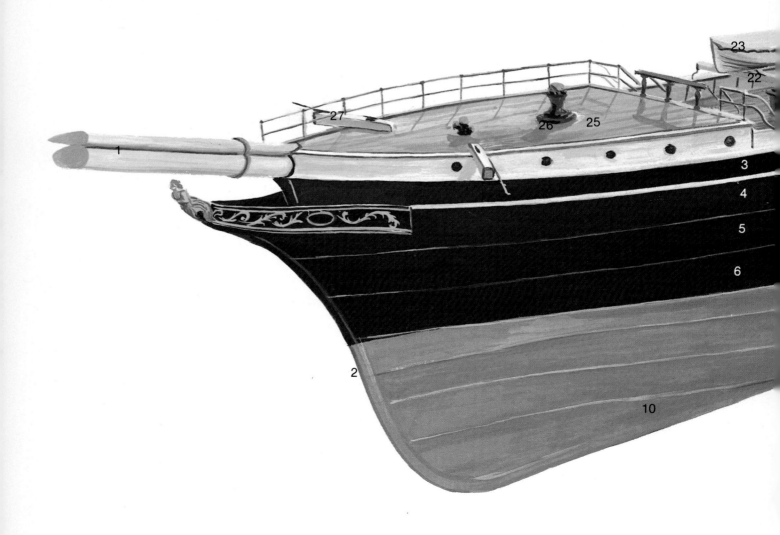

1	Bowsprit	18	Deck beam
2	Stem	19	Steerage deck
3	Bulwark plate	20	Deckhouse (galley forward; carpenter shop aft)
4	Upper sheer strake	21	Main deck
5	Topside strake	22	Skid beam
6	Lower sheer strake	23	Life boat
7	outside plate	24	Foremast
8	inside plate	25	Foredeck
9	outside bilge strake	26	Capstan
10	inside bilge strake	27	Cathead
11	frame	28	Wheel and wheelbox
12	centerline keelson	29	After booby hatch
13	Side intercostal keelson	30	Skylight and passenger benches
14	Bilge keelson	31	Mizzen mast
15	Bilge stringer	32	Stack of main salon heating stove
16	Side stringer	33	Main hatch
17	Lower deck stringer	34	Ship's launch
		35	Mainmast
		36	Pump
		37	Main fife rail

Model by L. McCaffery

"DILIGENTE" SLAVER BRIG   1/16″ = 1′0″

Ships like the *Diligente* played a key role in the grim chapter of American history beginning after the War of 1812, the heyday of the slave trade. Built for speed at minimum expense, the slavers were characterized by sharp "Baltimore clipper" lines and huge spreads of sail suited to passages in light, tropical airs. *Diligente* was 100′ long and 25′ in beam.

Model by J. Seela

"LEON" MERCHANTMAN BRIGANTINE 1880 1/8" = 1'0"
Leon exhibits the characteristics of ships built close to the end of the great days of sail. Speed then was less important than efficiency and carrying capacity. *Leon* is full amidships and less sharp in the run and entry than the clippers of the 1850's. The rigs of *Leon's* period were also simplified. Gone were such as stunsails, moonrakers, and stargazers.

BENT FRAME CONSTRUCTION

Model by H. Judson

PINNACE ca 1825 1/2″ = 1′0″
Small boats were built as lightweight craft with slender frames steamed and bent to fit the plank shell, which was built first over supporting molds. Stringer, rubbing strakes, gunwales, and seat thwarts were added last.

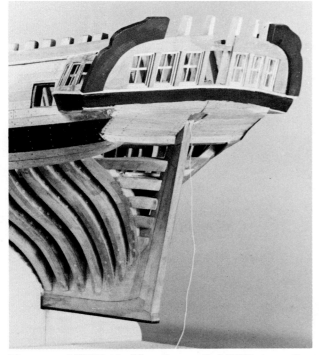

The stern of Bill Wick's *Oliver Cromwell* of 1776 shows the transoms of round tuck construction connecting the fashion frame to the sternpost. The wing transom shows at the bottom edge of the counter planking. Note the 'V'-shaped hole above the sternpost to accommodate the straight stock rudder.

Many smaller vessels from the earliest times were built as "double-enders" where the planking joined the sternpost the same way as at the bow. The small colonial American bark of 1620 illustrates the variation.

The stern of the American schooner *Hannah* of 1776 shows the flow of planking in typical "round tuck" stern construction.

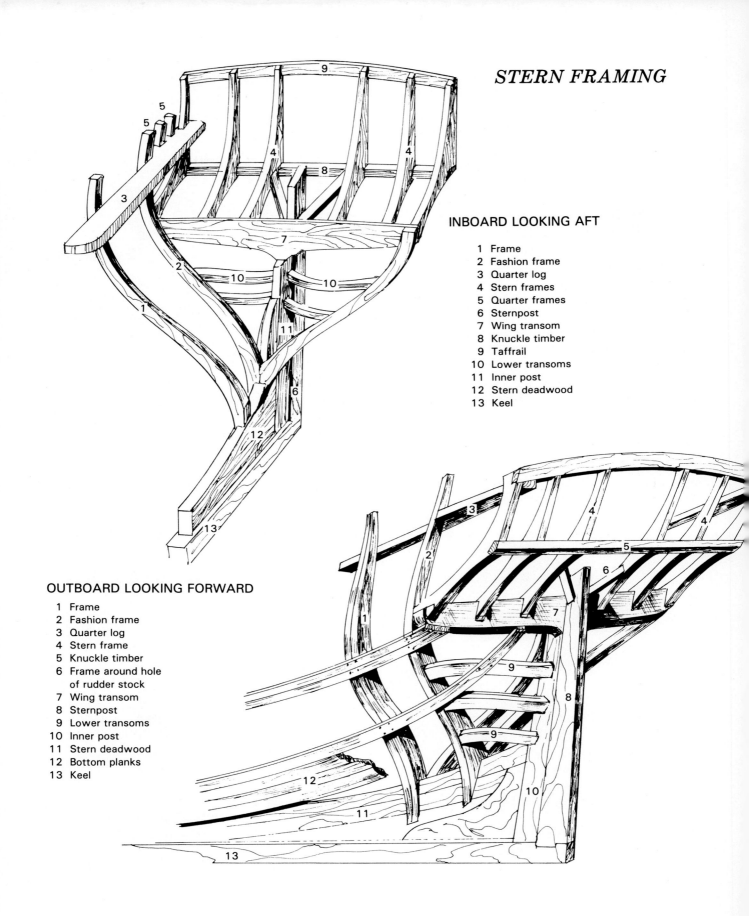

STERN FRAMING

INBOARD LOOKING AFT

1 Frame
2 Fashion frame
3 Quarter log
4 Stern frames
5 Quarter frames
6 Sternpost
7 Wing transom
8 Knuckle timber
9 Taffrail
10 Lower transoms
11 Inner post
12 Stern deadwood
13 Keel

OUTBOARD LOOKING FORWARD

1 Frame
2 Fashion frame
3 Quarter log
4 Stern frame
5 Knuckle timber
6 Frame around hole
   of rudder stock
7 Wing transom
8 Sternpost
9 Lower transoms
10 Inner post
11 Stern deadwood
12 Bottom planks
13 Keel

STERN AND QUARTER GALLERIES

From 1600 through 1825, ships were fitted with stern and quarter galleries. The quarter galleries served as latrines for the officers, while the stern galleries provided a kind of back porch for the pleasure of the ship's VIP's.

In the Seventeenth Century, the galleries were lavishly decorated with gilded baroque carvings of nymphs, cupids, and other assorted figures from classical mythology. These were the years when Northern Europe, including England, France, and Germany, came alive with the Renaissance, which had begun in Italy two centuries before. The time was characterized by a passion for everything from ancient Greece and Rome. The educated spoke and read Latin; students and scholars received the honors of kings and saints, and the humanistic philosophers were beginning to transform the world. Monarchs and citizens, alike, in this atmosphere vied in exhuberant ostentation, and the thirst for it carried over into the ships they built.

We have specific information about the decorations on a few of the most famous ships of this era. For example, the *Wasa*, the Swedish entry in the "grandest ship" sweepstakes, was recovered in an excellent state of preservation from the mud in which she sank over three centuries ago, and most of her carvings are there to see. But little research has been done on the subject as a whole, leaving open an interesting field of speculation and inquiry for modelers and art historians alike.

The tendency to lavish decoration reached its height in the first half of the 1600's. Afterward, Oliver Cromwell's attempts to impose Puritan values on the English contributed to a change of taste in that country, while in Europe, generally, there was a drift toward more subdued and frugal tastes as middle-class businessmen replaced aristocrats in the seats of power.

In the Eighteenth Century, the style of decoration switched from ebullient baroque to more harmonious classical systems of columns, capitals, and entablatures. Throughout the 1700's, this classical architectural style held sway, while the actual amount of decoration applied to ships gradually diminished under the pressure of economics. By 1800, the stern and quarter galleries were but spartan and pragmatic vestiges of their former splendid selves.

Structurally, the galleries consisted of platforms mounted at deck level, which stuck out from the side of the ship proper. The platform areas were walled in and roofed over. The walls were pierced with windows made up of small glass panes, perhaps 8″ x 10″, mullioned together in fine "country home" style. The profile design of the quarter galleries harmonized with the rake of the sternpost. The horizontal lines of the quarter galleries carried around to those of the stern.

The arch of the taffrail carried out to the outer edges of the quarter galleries and formed the after bulkheads for these facilities.

Quarter figures adorned the outer edges of the taffrail through the Eighteenth Century, and were among the last of the ornamental elements to disappear. The quarter figures were almost full round, bigger-than-life-size sculptures of allegorical or mythological personages such as *Neptune*, god of the sea; *Achilles, Venus,* or *Minerva;* or *"Truth"* or *"Commerce,"* or *"Justice"* with her scales.

The aftermost panel of the ship's stern above water was called the taffrail, after the Dutch *"taffreel,"* meaning "panel picture. Through the Seventeenth Century, taffrails were, in fact, billboards announcing the munificence and grandeur of a ship's owner. Coats of arms and, again, classical motifs, characterized these decorations. Later, as we have said, rows of windows and balustrades replaced the solid picture panels.

FRAMING
OF
STERN
GALLERIES

1 Taffrail arch
2 Stern gallery lights (windows)
3 Quarter gallery frames
4 Quarter gallery lights
5 Timberhead
6 Quarter gallery deck
7 Deck
8 Stern gallery frame
9 Stern frame
10 Knuckle timber
11 Sternpost
12 Wing transom
13 Fashion frame
14 Inner post
15 Quarter gallery frame

We are accustomed to see a ship's name spelled out on her taffrail. But this practice did not come into use until well into the 1800's. Owing to the prevailing illiteracy of the times, decorative pictures told the world more about a ship's name and ownership than letters.

PLANKING

A ship's planking, unlike the siding on a house, is made up of individually shaped boards which vary in thickness and width, depending upon their location in the hull.

The planks lie in courses running in smooth curves from one end of the ship to the other.

Each course, or layer, is called a "strake."

The thickest planks (called "thick stuff") were laid near the waterline and at the keel, while higher and lower strakes became thinner, depending on their distance from the waterline.

SPILING

Full-scale shipwrights, as well as modelers, are faced with the problem of plotting the shape and position of each strake on the face of the frames. This process is called *spiling*.

The first step in spiling is to determine the total number of strakes required to cover the hull at midships. This is done by simply dividing the length around the midship frame by the width of the planking material.

The width of the strakes at the other

sections is then determined by dividing their various lengths by the number of strakes required at midships. Thus, it is possible to plot the taper of the strakes from their widest point at midships to their narrowest as they flow toward the bow and stern.

The next step in the spiling process is to vary the shape of the strakes to accord with the way the planks naturally flow over the curves of the hull.

UPPER STRAKES

The upper strakes from the sheer strake down to the turn of the bilge will be found to flow in even, natural curves in accordance with the tapering rule given above. As the strakes taper forward to a width half of their midship width, two strakes may be merged into one with a *joggle plank* to avoid fastening a long, pointed plank at its thin end.

Aft, if the ship is a modern one with a counter, the upper strakes will twist under the stern and join herringbone-fashion along the centerline aft of the sternpost. On an older ship, these planks will end on the wing transom.

BOTTOM STRAKES

The bottom planking from the keel up to the turn of the bilge presents a different pattern.

In general, the bottom planking lies flat amidships, twisting to vertical where it joins the stem and sternpost.

Planking so laid demonstrates a tendency to fan out as it approaches the ends, leaving wedge-shaped holes at bow and stern, which must be filled with "stealer" planks. The stealers are squared off, and the diverging planks notched out to accommodate them. Again,

to avoid the "thin end" problem.

The *garboard strake*, the first strake next to the keel, and the next *broad strakes* often were widest at the stem and stern, and narrowest at midships.

The balance of the bottom planking may best be visualized as a system of meridians laid as much as possible between the two poles of the stem and sternpost. The objective was to minimize the use of stealers, while retaining an even, natural curve for the strakes from end to end.

Profile view of H. Bridenbecker's model of the Hannah shows the shape and flow of strakes over the ship's frames. Note the flare of the garboard and broad strakes where they join the sternpost and stem while higher strakes taper fore and aft.

FASTENINGS

The planks were fastened to every frame with from two to four treenails. At the butts iron nails, as well as treenails, were often used for extra strength. The number of nails in a given fastening depended on the width of the strake at that point. The practice was to have each plank nailed to each of the two futtocks of every frame with at least one nail.

WALES

Up to 1850 nearly all ships and many boats were banded stem to stern with extra heavy strips of planking called *wales*. The wales served several functions. First they provided longitudinal structural support second only to the keel in importance. They also helped to bind the upper ends of the frames together, squeezing them, so to speak, toward the center of the vessel. The wales also served as stout bumpers protecting the ship from damage in case she encountered unfriendly quays, rocks or cannon balls. Finally, the wales bore the strain of the lower shrouds and the abuse of the anchor cables.

After 1850 the wales were built flush with the rest of the side planking making them a less obvious element of the ship architecture.

Depending on size, ships had from one to three wales beginning with the lowest or main wale above which ran the channel wale and finally, the gunwale. The gunwale (pronounced gunnel) refers to the top edge or rail of an open boat as well.

Since the wales were extra heavy planking they were more difficult to steam and bend to the curves of the ship. So often they were elaborately pieced together of a large number of short planks laid "hook and butt" fashion. Hook and butt planking was the equivalent of scarphing as practiced in the joining of keel timbers.

Leon's flow of strakes echos the ship's handsome sheer.

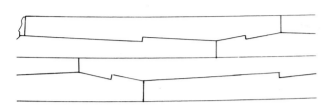

8" or less
single fastening

9" - 11"
alternate
single/double
fastenings

11" or more
double
fastenings

The heavy wales of some ship's defied steam bending and had to be pieced together in a system of scarf joints called 'hook-and-butt' planking. The top and bottom edges of the wales came out as smooth lines while the intermediate joints zigzagged down the hull.

DECKS

1 Caprail
2 Timberhead
3 Waterway
4 Nibbling strake
5 Head timbers
6 Stemson (stem not shown)
7 Eking
8 Midship carling
9 Deck beam (small)
10 Mast beam
11 Bosom knee (after side of deck beam)
12 Lodging knee (forward side of deck beam)
13 Mast partners
14 Deck planking
15 Hatch coaming
16 Head ledges
17 Hatch carling
18 Deck stanchions
19 Hanging knee
20 Dagger knee
21 Frame

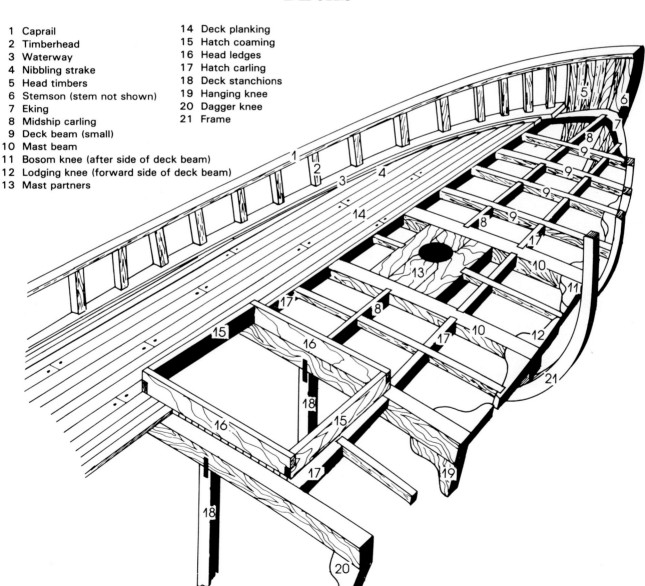

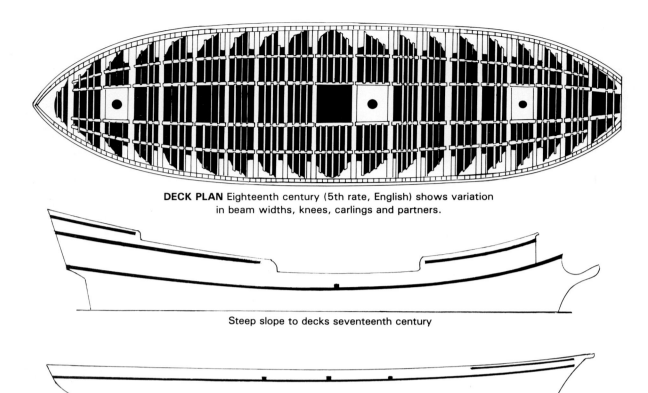

DECK PLAN Eighteenth century (5th rate, English) shows variation in beam widths, knees, carlings and partners.

Steep slope to decks seventeenth century

Shallow slope to decks after 1800

The deck framing of wooden ships consisted of transverse deck beams, longitudinal members called *carlings*, and a variety of reinforcing knees.

Gundecks invariably were more stoutly constructed than those not subject to the weight and recoil of armaments.

Deck beams in a given ship varied in size. Heavier beams spanned the ship where the structure was interrupted by openings such as those for masts, hatches, and scuttles. Lighter beams were used in between.

Carlings running fore and aft also varied in size by the same principle.

The mast partners consisted of timbers as thick as the heaviest deck beams formed into solid masses around the holes where the masts came through.

Lodging knees reinforced the joints on the afterside of the deck beams in the horizontal plane; bosom knees on the foreside; and hanging knees in the vertical plane. Dagger knees descended below the joints diagonally at places where a hanging knee would interfere with a gunport or other important structure.

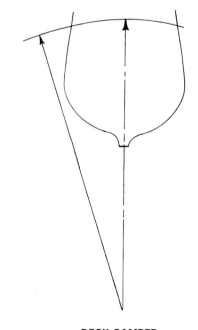

DECK CAMBER
Often an arc of a large circle. Same arc applies to all deck beams in a given deck.

SHAPE OF DECKS

A deck arches across a ship from side to side and slopes downward from either end fore and aft so that water will run down to the sides amidships and overboard through scuppers in the bulwarks. The arch or *camber* of a deck is often simply an arc of a large circle with a center far below the keel.

In certain instances, however, deck camber was designed with more complex geometry because of problems associated with the mounting and firing of guns.

The fore and aft curvature of decks evolved from quite steep around 1600 to almost flat at the end of the sailing ship era. The steep curvatures of earlier decks were there to help offset the tendency of a hull to hog. Later it was found that hogging stress could be managed satisfactorily with flatter and flatter (and therefore more practical deck sheers, so that finally fore and aft deck curvature was reduced to that just sufficient to accommodate water run-off.

SIZE OF DECK BEAMS

The cross section of a heavier deck beam was generally equal in size to that of the frame at the point of their intersection. Since the frames tapered from bottom to top, the beams of lower decks were thicker than those of the higher decks.

Usually in a given deck there would be one deck beam for each frame, though lighter, upper decks sometimes got away with only one beam for each two or three frames.

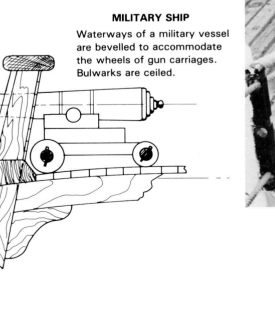

MERCHANT SHIP
Waterways of a merchant ship step up from level of deck. Timberheads exposed.

WATERWAY

MILITARY SHIP
Waterways of a military vessel are bevelled to accommodate the wheels of gun carriages. Bulwarks are ceiled.

View of the forepeak of the *Star of India* shows the deck planking nibbled into the nibbling strake just inboard of the waterways.

DECK PLANKING

Deck planks for the most part were laid side by side parallel with the keel throughout the length of the ship except for certain portions along the outermost edges and around hatches, companionways, and the like.

The outer edges of a deck consisted of the waterway and the nibbling strake. The waterways were thicker than the deck proper forming a raised shelf in the areas between the timberheads and inboard of them a few inches. In warships, the waterways were bevelled so that the wheels of the gun carriages could be bowsed up close to the bulwarks. The waterways curved with the shape of the shipsides.

Immediately inboard of the waterways and parallel with it, the nibbling strake was laid. The nibbling strake was the same thickness as the rest of the deck planks, but its inner edge was notched to accommodate the ends of the planks laid square with the keel.

The ends of parallel deck planks were never allowed to taper to fine points but rather were squared off and fitted to the notches in the nibbling strake. As with all planking it was not possible to adequately fasten a sharply pointed board.

Facing planks fitted all around the edges of openings in the deck in order to simplify the caulking job.

Some ships had fancy decks where the planks were laid parallel with the shipsides rather than the keel.

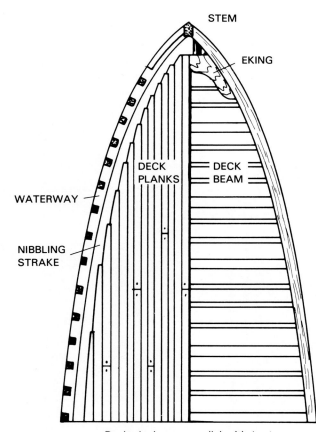

Deck planks run parallel with keel

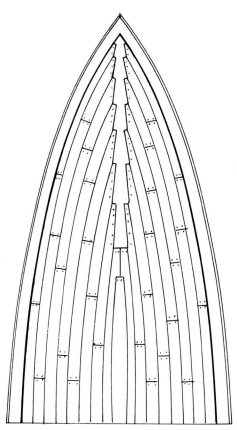

Some decks laid fair with ship sides.

BULWARKS AND RAILS

A ship's sides above her upper deck are called bulwarks. The bulwarks consist of the upper ends of the frame timbers planked over the outside and, in warships, on the inside as well. (Inside planking is referred to as "ceiling" whether it occurs above or below decks.) The top edge of the bulwarks is finished with the caprail.

As a rule, the bulwarks of a ship are the site of many important and interesting details of her architecture. Here, for example, may be found pinrails, kevels, knights, and cleats essential to the rigging of the vessel. Midships one finds scuppers to funnel water overboard. And on warships the bulwarks are pierced with gunports while to either side of the ports will be the ring bolts and other gear used to rig the cannon.

Cape Horners rigged netting extensions to their bulwarks as a safety precaution in the raging southern waters.

In the 1700's it was a practice to build-up bulwarks with "hammock nettings" as a defense against flying splinters in combat. These nettings were so called because they were made up of the crews' sleeping hammocks.

Earlier when naval tactics centered on grappling and boarding, nets were stretched tent-like from bulwark to bulwark across the entire ship and held aloft in the middle by tackles.

Outboard the bulwarks of seventeenth century ships would often be decorated with carvings only slightly less lavish than those of the stern and quarter galleries. A common practice in English naval ships was to surround the upper gunports with elaborate carved wreaths.,

The bulwarks of older ships varied in height above the various decks. The lines of their rails usually echoed that of the wales and were carried through the whole length of the ship.

Later the line of the rails echoed that of the sheer strake and hence the line of the decks.

The boarding port was a typical feature of large ships of the early centuries. They were counted the "front doors" of the ships through which only V.I.P.'s passed. Ordinary sailors went aboard over the rails.

Inboard side of the *Star of India's* bulwarks shows the belaying points on the port rail at the main shrouds.

Chapter Five
Deck Furniture

The quarterdeck of the *USS Franklin* typifies the clear uncluttered deck layouts of the first American 74's. This photo shows the *Franklin's* double wheel, the skylight over the captain's cabin, a mizzen fife rail tucked as close to the mast as possible, and hammock nettings which in battle would be stuffed with the crew's sleeping rolls as a defense against flying splinters.

Model by J. McDermott

The term *deck furniture* is a general term used to describe the gear permanently fastened down or built into a ship's deck. It includes such items as capstans, windlasses, deckhouses, hatches, and companionways. Of the many things ships had in common, deck furniture, and deck layout were not among them. More than anything, a ship's deck furnishings declared her individuality.

Yet, to function, all ships required one version or another of certain basic bits of equipment, in the sense that all houses need roofs and windows.

Broadly, a given piece of deck furniture will fall into one of three categories. It may be installed for the purpose of accommodating crew, passengers, or cargo; for the purpose of operating the ship, either at sea or in port; or it will have to do with the ship's seagoing business. In the first category fall *ladders, cabins, hatches, galleys, skylights,* and *barrels* (otherwise known as *scuttlebutts).* In the second, fall *steering wheels, binnacles, running lights, capstans, fiferails, bitts, knights,* and *mooring bollards.* In the last category, we find such things as a warship's *guns,* a fisher-

man's *bait box,* or a whaler's *trypots.*

Whether building or evaluating a ship model, one should be sensitive to the fact that a ship is and was an integral "life support system." Men spent long periods confined in small wooden hulls upon which their very lives depended. The ship was everything. A good model reflects this vital human element, and nowhere is it more apparent than in the details of her deck furnishings.

For example, a galley stack, or *Charley Noble,* as it was called, tells us where the crew filled their *kids* (mess kits), and grabbed a moment of warmth after a cold, wet trick aloft. An open companionway hatch may invite the speculation that the skipper has just gone below to get his sextant. A drinking cup beside the scuttlebutt suggests a welcome break in a sailor's tedious day.

This sort of detail explains a vessel's uniqueness, as well as her place in history. How different are the deck furnishings of an 1820 slaver as opposed to those of an Atlantic packet ship of the same period. Both carried immigrants to America, but under grossly different circumstances.

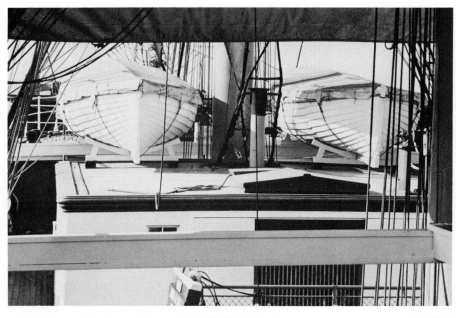

The *Star of India's* boats were shipped in cradles, one pair of which mounted on the forward deckhouse and the other on a forward skid beam. The ship's galley and carpenter shop shared the deckhouse. The galley stack (Charley Noble) can be seen rising into the iron bridle of the mainstay - an ingenious arrangement for keeping unwary hands off the hot stack.

Star's quarterdeck features finely varnished benches for the enjoyment of passengers and officers in good weather. The benches are built into the skylight which illuminates the ship's main salon below.

GROUND TACKLE

The ground tackle of a ship consisted of her anchors, anchor cable, and the riding bitts to which the cables were rigged while the ship was at anchor.

The anchors of large ships were and are massive affairs weighing well into the tons. More modern ships use heavy chain for the cables while oldtimers used cable-laid, hemp hawsers, 10 or more inches in diameter depending on the size of the ship.

Ships carried a number of anchors made to precise specifications. The most important were the "bowers" and the "sheet" anchors. Others might be smaller, special purpose hooks stowed in the hold.

The bowers were carried toward the bows attached to their cables ready for instant use. The starboard bower was called the "best bower" though there was no difference between it and the "small bower" to port.

Sheet anchors were carried aft on either side near the main channels or below in the hold. The sheet anchors were considered spares and only occasionally were rigged ready to use.

Below are given specifications for anchors from two periods in English history:

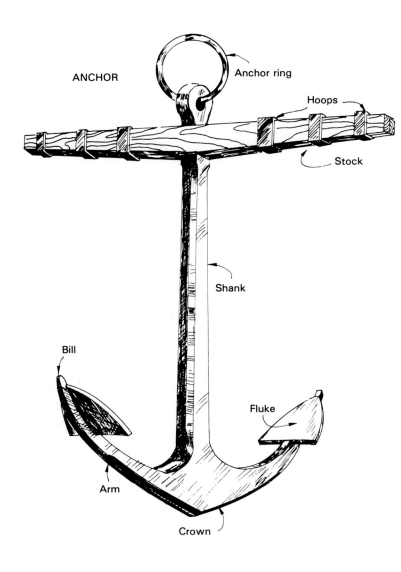

ANCHOR — Anchor ring — Hoops — Stock — Shank — Fluke — Bill — Arm — Crown

DIMENSIONS OF ANCHORS
Sutherland "Shipbuilding Unveiled" (1717)

	Size for 1677 ton ship	Size for 364 ton ship
Shank	18'6''	12'2''
Shank's thickness (max)	0'11½''	0'7½''
Shank's thickness (min)	0'8¾''	0'5½''
The square	2'11''	1'11''
From end of shank to nut	1'11''	1'3''
Square of nut	0'2¼''	0'1½''
Inner diameter of ring	2'1½''	1'3''
Thickness of ring	0'4''	0'3''
Hole in shank for ring	0'4½''	0'3''
Length of crown	1'2''	0'8¼''
Length of arm	7'0''	4'0''
Breadth of fluke	2'8''	1'9''
Length of fluke	3'9''	2'5½''
Thickness of fluke	0'3''	0'2''
Square of arm at fluke	0'7''	0'4½''
Length of bill	0'10½''	0'7''
Rounding of fluke	0'1''	0'¾''
Clutching of arm	3'6''	2'4''
Inside meeting	6'6''	not given
Outside meeting	6'6''	not given
Middle meeting	6'6''	not given

ENGLISH ANCHOR SIZES ca 1840
Fincham "Naval Architecture"

Ship	Shank Ft	In	Arms Ft	In
100-120 guns	17'	0''	5'	7''
80-92 guns	16'	6''	5'	5''
72 guns	15'	4''	5'	1½''
Frigates				
50 guns	15'	2''	5'	0''
40 guns	13'	10''	4'	7½''
38 guns	13'	0''	4'	4'
Razee	12'	8''	4'	3''
Corvettes	11'	7½''	3'	10½''
Sloops				
16 guns	10'	10''	3'	7½''
8 guns	9'	2''	3'	0''

ANCHOR TYPES

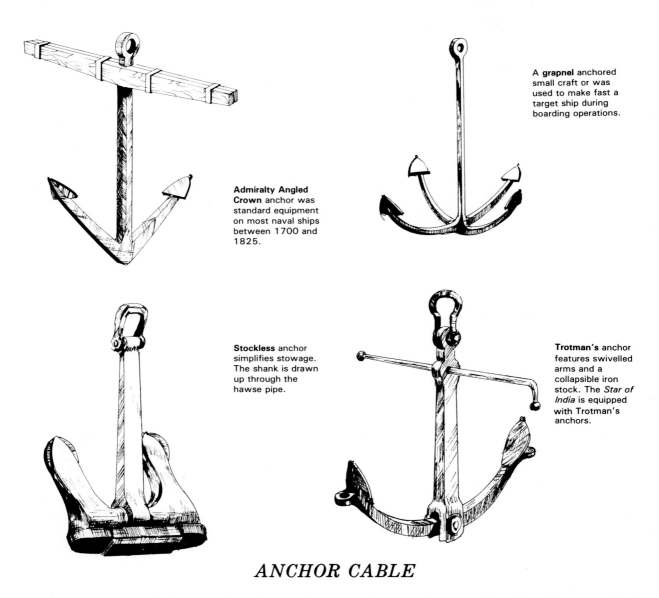

Admiralty Angled Crown anchor was standard equipment on most naval ships between 1700 and 1825.

A **grapnel** anchored small craft or was used to make fast a target ship during boarding operations.

Stockless anchor simplifies stowage. The shank is drawn up through the hawse pipe.

Trotman's anchor features swivelled arms and a collapsible iron stock. The *Star of India* is equipped with Trotman's anchors.

ANCHOR CABLE

Anchor cable varied in size according to the size of the ship. Up to about 1800, hemp was the universal material for cables, after which, iron chain link came into use.

In 1780, the standard size of cable was specified as "½ inch of circumference for each foot of the ship's beam."

Chain link was measured by the circumference of the material in a link. The size may be computed fairly accurately by computing the size of a hemp cable circumference and dividing by 10. The chain link equivalent of a 10" cir-

cumference hemp cable, therefore, would be about 1".

Hemp and chain anchor cable were also measured by conventional lengths of manufacture. A rope cable length was between 100 and 115 fathoms (about 200 yards); a hawser laid cable length was about 130 fathoms.

Chain cable was measured in "shackles", about 12½ fathoms. The name "shackle" grew from the fact that the several lengths of chain would have to be shackled together to make-up the full length of the cable.

CATHEADS AND BILLBOARDS

Old-timers carried their anchors outboard, "fished" up against the bows. The ring end of the anchor was hoisted clear of the water through tackle rove into the catheads. The bill end was hoisted up with tackles rigged high on the mast or topsail yard. Once fished, the anchor was lashed up tight to the fore chains or to the fore rail. The shipside where the bill of the anchor rode was protected by billboards.

Later, ships carried their anchors inboard lashed down to the foredeck. The catheads and billboards still functioned while the anchor was in process of being dropped or weighed.

The *Leon's* small bower hangs acockbill from her catheads. Billboards protected her topsides when her later Nineteenth Century iron stock anchor was fished up.

Hannah's best bower was the typical wooden stock **fisherman's** anchor of her 1776 era.

The *Star of India's* **Trotman's** anchor, shown here catted and fished to the fore rail.

129

ANCHORING A SHIP

Anchoring a ship is a tricky bit of business requiring expert seamanship. The skipper, having selected a spot in the harbor at which to let go the hook, maneuvers his vessel so that she can be steered into the wind (brought to) at that place.

Meanwhile, the anchor is prepared. Hawse bags are removed from the hawse holes, the cable is flaked out on the deck aft of them, the end rove out through the holes and bent to the anchor ring. Casts of the lead line determine how much cable is called for and *keckling*, chafing gear, is bent to that portion of it expected to ride in the hawse holes. A slip hook or slippery hitch fastens the anchor, acockbill, at the cathead, and the cat purchase is eased away. At the exact moment, the captain commands, "veer away", and a yank or a pound instantly lets the hook fall into the sea.

As the anchor hits bottom, it falls on its side, one of its fluke ends is forced to bite the bottom ground by the stock. The ship having heaved to into the wind, now drifts stern first to leeward and cable is veered out to a good swinging length. The cable needs a long horizontal drape (catenary) for the anchor to hold well, so a good anchorage is one where the ship has a wide swinging radius.

Enough cable is now veered out and turns are taken around the riding bitts. *Nippers* bind the cable to the deck which otherwise would work loose or *render*.

The ship is now securely anchored and one would suppose that all hands could now go ashore and relax. Not so. At anchor a ship swings with the wind and tide. If left unattended, the combined effect of these forces can cause her to drift willy-nilly on the end of her cable, twisting one way only to be dangerously jerked the other by a cable alternately made slack then taut. Such aimless drift can cause a slack cable to foul the upstanding fluke of the anchor itself and cause a disastrous breaking of ground.

The task of the anchor watch is to keep a steady tension on the anchor cable by steering the ship and setting different sails as the conditions of wind and current change. So managed, the ship is said to be *holding her sheer*.

Crowded ports often lacked sufficient room for ships to either come to anchor or swing in a wide enough scope once secured. Here the practice of *mooring* solved part of the problem. A moored ship is secured by two anchors, the bower as described above, and a sheet anchor whose cable leads astern. The ship is held more or less on a line between the two separate anchoring points.

Normally a ship would be able to manage the placement of her two mooring anchors unassisted, but many ports employed anchor hoys to assist incoming or outgoing traffic. As a ship approached her mooring, a hoy came alongside and carried her anchors out a sufficient distance fore and aft and let them go.

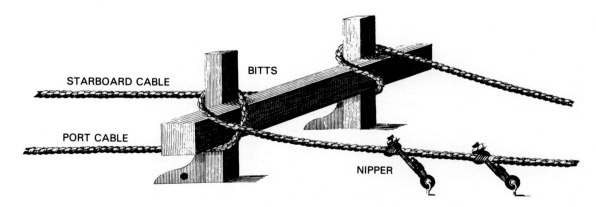

STARBOARD CABLE

BITTS

PORT CABLE

NIPPER

Anchor cables were turned around the riding bitts and nippered to the deck while the ship rode to anchor. Some larger ships had two sets of riding bitts, one a few feet behind the other. The unused part of the cable aft of the bitts was called the cable's "bitter end."

ANCHOR HOY

Anchor hoys, like modern tugboats, helped larger ships into anchorages and moorings in crowded harbors. The hoy came alongside an incoming ship, hooked into the larger vessel's anchor, and carried it out with cable attached to a proper anchoring distance. Henry Bridenbecker's model shows the hoy's broad, buoyant bow, its special cathead-like spar, and running bowsprit. Note the short, heavy mast shrouds rigged to bear the weight of the anchor the hoy carries.

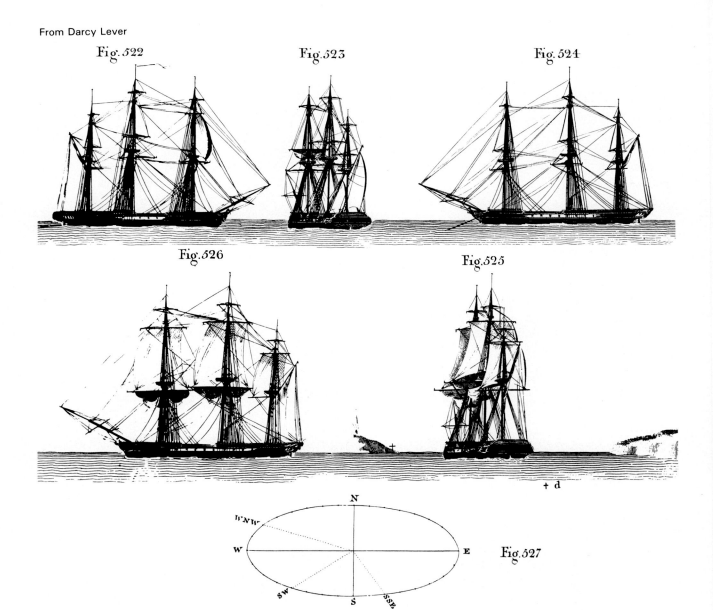

Fig. 522   Fig. 523   Fig. 524

Fig. 526   Fig. 525

Fig. 527

MANAGING A SHIP AT ANCHOR

If the wind be large, or right aft, like Fig. 522, and the Stream from windward, or what is called a leeward Tide, then all the Sails are handed, except the Fore Topsail, and the Cable is bitted: the Ship is hauled up sooner, the Helm put a-lee, the Fore Topsail clewed up, the Mizen hauled out, the Mizen Staysail Sheet aft, to bring her to the wind, like Fig. 523; and when she comes head to wind, like Fig. 524, she loses her Headway, at which time the Anchor is let go, and according to the strength of the Wind and Tide, a long Scope of Cable is veered out. The Mizen, and Mizen Staysails are taken in.

The Ship, Fig. 525, is driving with the Tide setting to the Southward, against the wind, which is on the Quarter: this is called a Weather Tide. Proportioning her Sail according to the strength of it, she sometimes sets her Top Gallant Sails, by which she remains stationary, and sometimes as occasion may require lets fall the Foresail, by which she shoots a little a-head; so that she is under every Command that can be wished.

WEIGHING ANCHOR

Heaving up the anchor was a bone and muscle job where all hands laid onto the capstan handle bars. The anchor cable itself was too large and stiff to go around the capstan barrel so a smaller rope called a *messenger line* provided the purchase. The messenger line was a large loop rather like a conveyer belt, which was alternately stopped and unstopped along lengths of the cable as it was hauled inboard and consigned to the hawse locker.

As the cable shortened the ship was drawn closer to the anchor's place on the sea floor. The angle between it and the water became gradually steeper until the mate could report "straight up and down, sir." And then, as the cable began to sway a little, he would know the anchor was clear of the bottom. "Anchor's aweigh, sir." The ship was underway and would be steered to catch the wind.

When the anchor cleared the water, the cat purchase was paid out and hooked into the ring, then the anchor was heaved up acockbill. Down from the foremast top came a big triple sheaved *"fishing tackle"* or *burton* which fastened to the fluke of the anchor.

With all hands laying on, the bill of the anchor was finally heaved to the rail or fore channel and made fast.

Below, the hawse holes were once again filled with hawse bags before breaking waves could slosh through them and soak the forepeak.

MESSENGER LINE

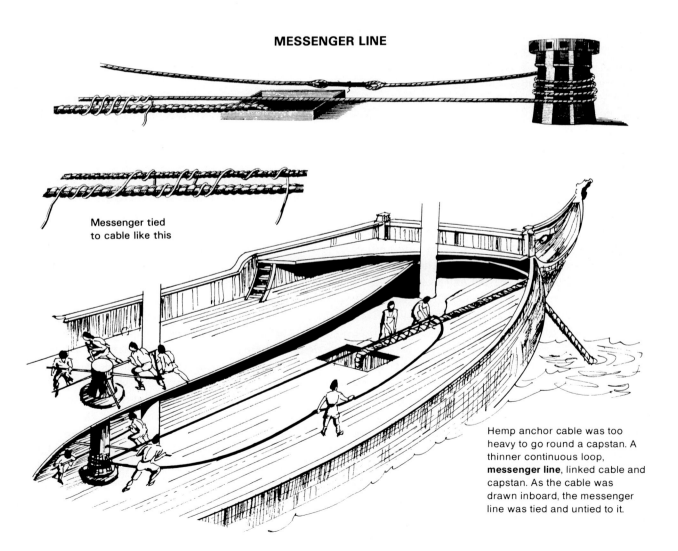

Messenger tied to cable like this

Hemp anchor cable was too heavy to go round a capstan. A thinner continuous loop, **messenger line**, linked cable and capstan. As the cable was drawn inboard, the messenger line was tied and untied to it.

BELLS AND HOUR GLASSES

Timekeeping for sailors was vital because of its importance in navigation. Many of the inventions of our modern world owe their inspiration to the attempt by early engineers and scientists to make precise clocks that would work dependably at sea. Such clocks, today called *chronometers*, did not come into existence until well into the nineteenth century. Before the introduction of the chronometer, navigators lacked a truly practical method for determining longitude. The best they had was a complicated procedure based on observations of the moon which, in turn, depended on the possession of accurate lunar timetables. The latter were often neither available nor accurate. Thus early navigators could never be completely sure of their position in the East-West direction. They could only estimate it by *dead reckoning* which is a matter of multiplying time by speed to arrive at a distance travelled in a given direction. As speed, direction, winds, and currents continually varied with ships under sail the possibility for error in dead reckoning one's longitude was substantial. But whether one dead reckons or shoots the stars, the navigator is obliged to measure the passage of time as accurately as he can.

Until chronometers, the half-hour glass was the most dependable of timepieces available to the mariner, because shore-side clocks failed when subjected to the roll and heave of a ship at sea. Yet to work with any accuracy they had to be watched and instantly turned as the last grain of sand tumbled through the neck. Often this duty fell to the boys shipped as apprentices who lived in fear of hell and torment if they failed in it. A number of glasses mounted on gimbels were kept around the ship to provide a mean average.

As the glasses were turned, the fact was simultaneously announced by the ringing of the bell. The day was divided into six four-hour periods called watches. Each watch was divided into eight half-hour periods. Thus a watch progressed from one to eight bells and seamen came to perceive time accordingly.

Sailor's ended the day with the dogwatch which was divided into two two-hour work

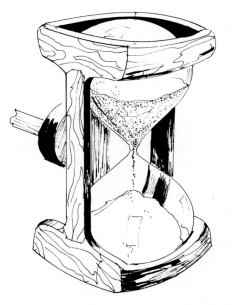

The half-hour glass was the seaman's clock until the invention of the chronometer in the Nineteenth Century. Accurate timekeeping is essential to navigation, particularly in the computation of a ship's longitude. Half-hour glasses, however strenuously attended to, were hardly accurate enough to give a navigator much more than the crudest approximation of his east-west position.

periods called the first and last dogwatches. Crews were divided into halves so that one half rested while the other worked. Each group worked four on and four off around the clock until the split dogwatch interrupted the routine. By this means, the work hours of each crewman varied from day to day. The watch from 8 p.m. to midnight was known as the First Watch; midnight to 4 a.m., the Middle Watch; followed by the Morning, the Forenoon, the Afternoon, and the final Dogwatch. Thus we hear a sailor declare the time as "three bells in the forenoon." He means 10 a.m.

The main bell of old ships, most often, was mounted forward near the break of the forecastle deck probably because it was easier for all to hear it from there. Later in the nineteenth century, they are found aft near the wheel where the helmsman had the duty to ring it. Smaller crews on the latter vessels likely prompted the move.

In the seventeenth century, the belfry was an elaborate gilded cage in style with the rest of the ship, while later the structure was simplified to a crossbar on top of two heightened deck stanchions. The bell itself was brightly polished brass.

All aboard knew the time of day from the ringing of the ship's bells. In the seventeenth century, a ship's belfry provided another opportunity for elaborate decorations as this one on John Dupray's model of the *Sovereign of the Seas* shows.

Of the two bells aboard the *Star of India*, this one mounts under the foredeck rail. The other, smaller one mounts aft on the wheel box.

PUMPS

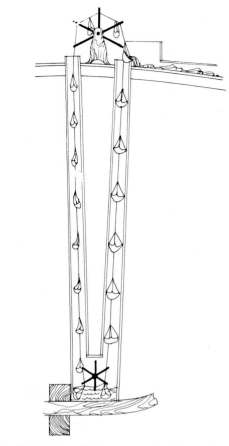

Keeping the old wooden ships dry was a perpetual problem from the day the ship was launched. As a ship aged, the problem became more acute as plank fastenings weakened, caulking worked free, and ship worms took their toll. Even the dryest ships required daily pump operation, and seamen were forced to pump day in and day out for weeks on end just to keep their ship afloat. Pumps, therefore, were vital to the life of all vessels in all eras.

Among the simplest of pumps was the sort used on small Baltic Sea craft in the Seventeenth and Eighteenth Centuries. It consisted of a hollow wooden pipe that extended down into the bilge, through which a leather bucket was lowered and raised by a long wooden handle. The bailed-up water might dump into a pump dale and be piped overboard, or simply spilled onto the deck to run overboard at the scuppers.

Sir Walter Raleigh is said to have invented the chain pump. The chain pump carried leather buckets attached to a conveyor belt sort of arrangement that moved up and down through a pair of wooden pipes. Turned at deck level by long-handled cranks, and manned by a half dozen or more men, the chain pumps could discharge up to a ton of water per hour. In spite of this efficiency, only the British Navy seems to have adopted their use.

Wooden suction pumps presumably became the standard between 1650 and 1850, after which iron ones superceded them. The wooden pumps had one or two cylindrical barrels made of hollowed out tree trunks. The plunger consisted of an iron rod fitted with a set of leather flap valves which opened on the down stroke, and closed on the up stroke. At deck level, the water fell from spigots that were notched or formed into the heads of the barrels, and then ran across the deck into the scuppers. Some of the larger vessels had pipe dales to the shipsides.

The handles for these pumps varied from small, single levers and cranks to large cranking systems that were manned by teams of crewmen. The latter normally involved two-barrelled pumps, the rods of which connected to

Sir Walter Raleigh, it is believed, introduced the chain pump to the British navy around 1600. No one knows exactly what it looked like but in principle it was a bucket carrying conveyor belt somehat like the one shown here.

a common crankshaft. Two large wheels on either end of the crankshaft were equipped with handles on the rim sufficient for three or four men to share in the turning.

Rocking-arm handles were also common. With this system, the pump rods pivoted at points halfway out from a center fulcrum on a rocking beam. The beam had long handles perpendicular and horizontal to it and fixed to its outboard ends. This enabled teams of crewmen to participate in the heaving.

The most usual location for the pumps was immediately abaft the mainmast where, just as often, the main fiferail was adapted to hold some of the pump mechanism.

After 1850, some ships enjoyed the presence of a steam-driven donkey engine on deck to help with the heaving chores. Chain drives from these engines turned the pump cranks.

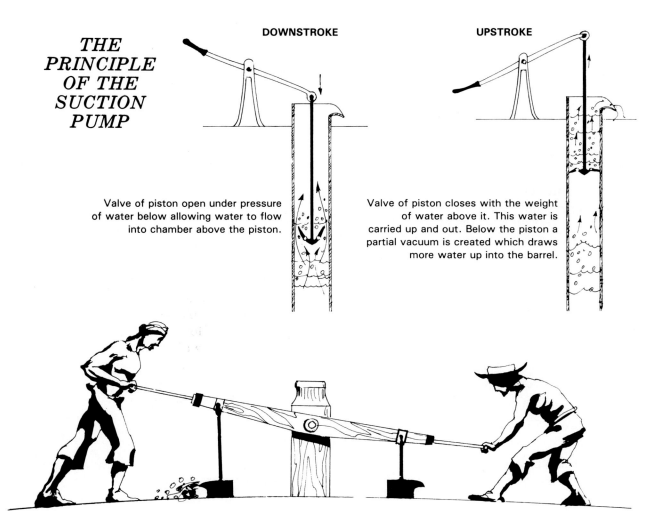

THE PRINCIPLE OF THE SUCTION PUMP

DOWNSTROKE

UPSTROKE

Valve of piston open under pressure of water below allowing water to flow into chamber above the piston.

Valve of piston closes with the weight of water above it. This water is carried up and out. Below the piston a partial vacuum is created which draws more water up into the barrel.

Double-barrelled pumps used rocker arm handle.

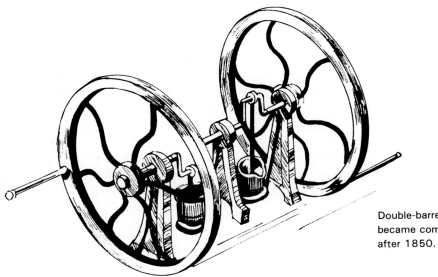

Double-barrelled **Downton** pump became common on larger ships after 1850.

SHIP'S LIGHTS

"My Lady Sandwich, my Lady Jemimah, Mrs. Browne, Mrs. Grace, and Mary and the page, my Lady's servants and myself all went into the lanthorne together."

Until the Nineteenth Century, light in all ships was a rare and potentially dangerous luxury. The only source of artificial light was fire, and fire to the inhabitants of wooden ships was more feared than the sea itself. Such light as there was consisted of candles mounted in horn-lensed lanterns. The captain's cabin, and a few areas in "officer country" might be lit by these on a regular basis. Otherwise, lanterns appeared in no other part of the ship except on an "as needed" basis, and then only under the strictest control of an officer.

A particularly fire-sensitive area was a ship's powder room, which was deliberately located deep in the hold, below the waterline. No lantern was ever lit there. However, so men could see to work in the room, windowed bulkheads were built, and lighted lanterns were placed behind them.

Lanterns played a larger role on shipboard as signals. Maritime traffic, then as now, faced the possibility of collision while underway at night. Ships in convoy particularly needed to know the whereabouts of other vessels in the fleet. To satisfy these requirements, ships were fitted with one or more large stern lanterns set on, or somewhat outboard, of the taffrail arch. The stern lanterns of the largest vessels were truly enormous. Samuel Pepys reported upon his visit to the *Royal Sovereign* in 1661 that, *"My Lady Sandwich, my Lady Jemimah, Mrs. Browne, Mrs. Grace, and Mary and the page, my lady's servants and myself all went into the lanthorne together."*

Stern lanterns remained in use until the latter half of the Nineteenth Century, though they gradually diminished in size and became more functionally austere as the years wore on. Toward the end of the Eighteenth Century, oil lamps replaced candles on some ships.

In the first half of the Nineteenth Century, candles were allowed in the forecastles of merchant ships, while whalemen enjoyed the light of whale oil lamps whenever they wished. The whalers, whose lives otherwise were the least desirable of sailormen, at least manned the best illuminated ships afloat at the time.

The breakthrough in lighting aboard ship came after 1854, when Abraham Gesner introduced kerosene, or coal oil, to the world. Kerosene lamps soon lit all of a ship's living and working spaces, and new navigation lights appeared. After the American Civil War, the now-standard red and green, port and starboard, sidelights were adopted and fishing schooners always anchored under a masthead lantern to light their dorymen home.

The other source of light aboard ship, of course, was the sun. All effort was made to make maximum use of it. Early seventeenth and eighteenth century ships admitted light to the stern quarters through the gallery windows. Open gunports and companionways reasonably illuminated the higher decks, and some light penetrated into the lower decks through grating hatch covers. Thus, most of the ship was modestly lighted until weather or heavy seas required that all of these openings be closed.

In the Nineteenth Century, glazed portholes, and skylights made their appearance, as confidence was gained in the technology of making these fittings watertight.

Ships of all periods face special hazards while navigating at night. Stern lanterns, among the few lights allowed on an old wooden ship, played the important role of announcing her position to other ships in her vicinity.

The *Star of India's* starboard (green) sidelight consisted of a kerosene lamp behind a tinted Fresnel lens, which optically enhanced the light. The three-sided mounting board shown here was typical of the day, though many were lashed into the fore shrouds instead of being fastened to the rail.

Kerosene lamps, like this one in the *Star of India's* salon, lit below deck areas on ships in the last couple of decades of the Nineteenth Century.

STEERING GEAR

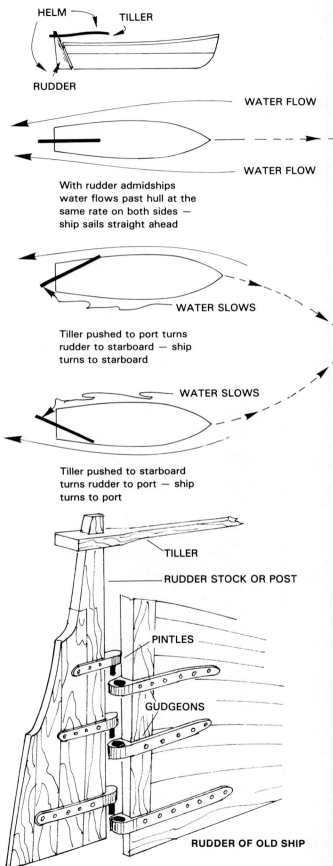

HELM — TILLER

RUDDER

WATER FLOW

WATER FLOW

With rudder admidships
water flows past hull at the
same rate on both sides —
ship sails straight ahead

WATER SLOWS

Tiller pushed to port turns
rudder to starboard — ship
turns to starboard

WATER SLOWS

Tiller pushed to starboard
turns rudder to port — ship
turns to port

TILLER

RUDDER STOCK OR POST

PINTLES

GUDGEONS

RUDDER OF OLD SHIP

The key element of a ship's steering gear is her rudder. A rudder works by slowing down the flow of water on one side of the ship. The effect is to turn the bow of the ship toward the side where the water has been slowed.

The rudder in most ships is turned to either side with a tiller, an arm attached to its upper end or stock. The steerage of smaller ships and boats often consists of no more than the rudder and its tiller.

In larger ships, additional gear was used to turn the proportionately heavier and more remote tiller/rudder apparatus. The sum of all this gear is called a ship's *helm* and the man who steers the ship is the *helmsman*.

Up to about 1700, a ship's tiller worked by a "whipstaff." The lower end of the whipstaff was loosely attached to the inboard end of a long tiller. The staff then went up through the deck where it was pivoted to a beam or block. The helmsman swung the whipstaff from side to side to operate the tiller.

The whipstaff would not permit the rudder to be turned very far so the helms of these old ships were not too efficient. In fact, the sailors of the time depended more on their headsails for maneuvering than they did on their rudder. The rudder did more in holding a course than it did in changing course.

After 1700 steering wheels began to replace the whipstaff so that by the middle of the century the latter were obsolete.

The wheel operated the tiller through the agency of tackles, the hauling ends of which were wrapped around a wheel drum. The arrangement permitted a somewhat wider swing for the tiller than the whipstaff, but a disproportion between the length of haul on the tackles and the arc of the tiller's swing still limited the system's efficiency.

The solution to this problem came along with the invention of the sweep, later the quadrant, which had the effect of matching the length of haul to the length of arc swept out by the tiller.

These tiller rope steering systems were more or less standard from about 1725 to 1825 when chain drives came into use.

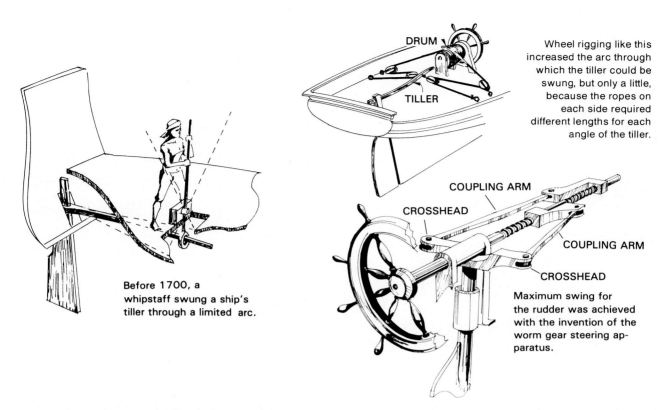

DRUM

TILLER

Wheel rigging like this increased the arc through which the tiller could be swung, but only a little, because the ropes on each side required different lengths for each angle of the tiller.

COUPLING ARM

CROSSHEAD

COUPLING ARM

CROSSHEAD

Before 1700, a whipstaff swung a ship's tiller through a limited arc.

Maximum swing for the rudder was achieved with the invention of the worm gear steering apparatus.

After 1850, a worm gear arrangement turned the rudder stock through a pair of coupling rods connected to a kind of thwartship, double-ended "tiller" called a *crosshead*.

The terminology surrounding a ship's helm often refers to the wind direction. For example, a captain wishing to bring his ship about orders, "Make ready to come about." When the lines are properly manned the mate reports, "Ready to come about, sir." The captain at the crucial moment then says, "Ready about!" This alerts the crew. Then follows, "Helm alee!" On this command the helmsman pushes the tiller as far to the lee side of the ship as possible, so that the rudder turns to windward and the ship heads up into the wind. "Lee helm" on a ship is considered a safe helm because it means that the ship has a natural tendency to head up into the wind (a safe situation), and the helmsman must keep pressure on the tiller to keep the ship "off". The opposite is a "weather helm" where the ship tends always to steer downwind and it becomes hard work to get her to head up.

Rudders were mounted on the sternposts of ships with a system of *pintles* and *gudgeons* analagous to pin hinges. The gudgeons of the rud-

der rested over those of the sternpost, and the "pins" or pintles went down through the matched holes like carriage bolts.

Rudders were known to become unshipped given certain sea conditions, so it was a practice to prevent their total loss by connecting them to the hull with a pair of *rudder chains*. The chains ran from either face of the rudder near the top to convenient points on the stern above water.

Up to about 1790, the inboard edge of a rudder was a straight line from the foot to the top of the stock. This put the stock aft of the turning centers of the pintles, so that a large, pie-shaped hole in the counter was required for it to turn. In spite of all efforts to seal the hole with canvas, sea water inevitably penetrated through it. The answer to the problem was found with the development of a round sectioned stock offset forward of the rudder edge so as to line up with the turning centers of the pintles. The stock then could turn in a cylindrical pipe. This arrangement became known as a *plug stock* rudder.

In larger vessels where the position of the tiller was hidden from the men on deck, *spurling lines* were rigged from the rudder head up to a telltail which reported the position of the rudder.

Sir Joshua Slocum developed a unique "self-steering" rig for his *Spray*, the boat he single handed around the world in 1895-98. The rig, a forerunner of modern self-steering vanes, had the wheel connected to the sheet of the small mizzen sail. If the vessel veered off course, downwind, the extra force applied to the rudder steered her back to her correct point of sail.

Steering wheels varied in size and number of spokes. The number of spokes was determined by a man's reach.

6 spokes

8 spokes

12 spokes

THE GALLEY

The galley is a ship's kitchen whose primary feature in the old ships was a cooking stove or hearth. It was the one place aboard where fire and heat was allowed in sufficiency.

The galley was commonly located under the forecastle deck just aft of the foremast. A chimney stack, or Charley Noble as it was called, rising from the stove below was a characteristic element of foredeck furniture.

Before 1750, the galley stove was made of brick, and the stack a brick or mortar lined wooden box. After 1750, iron stoves and stacks replaced the brick fireplaces. At first the iron stacks were square in cross section, later to become round, sheet metal pipes with elbowed tops which could be turned away from the wind. Through the years the stacks diminished in diameter as the stoves became more efficient and coal replaced wood as the standard fuel.

In the nineteenth century, heating stoves were added to the ones for cooking. Stacks were made removable so that the deck apertures could be made watertight in heavy weather.

As the nineteenth century wore on, it became a practice to locate galleys and forecastles in separate deckhouses above the main deck in order to maximize below deck cargo space. The deckhouse galley became known as the *caboose*.

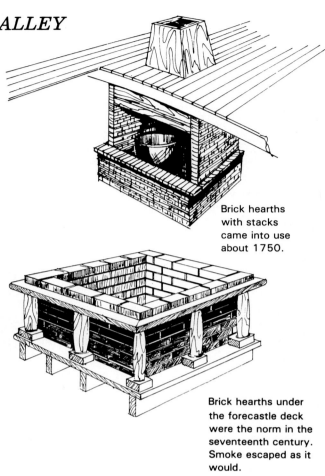

Brick hearths with stacks came into use about 1750.

Brick hearths under the forecastle deck were the norm in the seventeenth century. Smoke escaped as it would.

A *scuttlebutt* held a crew's daily ration of drinking water.

The galley stack of the *Star of India* emerges from the caboose located just aft of the foremast. The cook shared this forward deckhouse with the carpenter.

GUNS

Between 1500 and 1835, more or less, the great oceans were battlegrounds. The seafaring nations of Europe were at war for the trade of the world, not least of which was that of the "New World" — the Americas. Therefore, all ships whether merchantmen or naval vessels went to sea prepared to fight. Guns were the major weapons.

The gun deck of a ship in those days in combat was a horror. The deck would be crowded with perhaps a hundred men or more. The only light and ventilation was that which crept through the deck gratings and gunports. Lanterns or candles were lethal in the atmosphere of wood and gunpowder. It was dark, wet and stinking.

With the order to fire, the guns would go off one after another in a series of mind numbing explosions made worse by the restricted space. If they were all fired at once the combined recoils would tear out the side of the ship. They had no recoil mechanisms, so the guns would buck off the deck at each firing and slam back into their breechings. The smoke of burnt powder and steam from cooling water would choke the atmosphere.

Let a man touch a gun chase in the pandemonium and his hand would fry. Let him misjudge his place in the thundering gloom and he would be crushed by a rearing gun carriage.

Add to this, enemy fire, splinters flying like buckshot, the moans of wounded, disoriented crew mates, and blood, fear and pain. Such was the glory of naval warfare that one can feel fortunate to have missed.

Between 1600 and 1850 naval warfare depended on muzzle loading guns, the technology of which varied little through the entire time. The guns were essentially heavy iron or brass tubes mounted on four wheeled carriages. The load, consisting of gunpowder, wadding and the shot, was rammed in through the front end of the cannon. The powder charge was ignited through a "touch hole" near the rear of the gun.

The carriages were wooden, engineered to allow a minimum of aiming, and crudely rigged to manage recoil.

THE PARTS OF A GUN

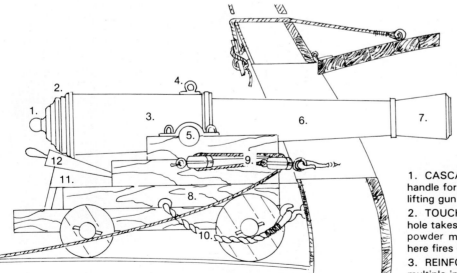

Front wheels larger than rear makes gun level on cambered deck

1. CASCABEL
handle for aiming or lifting gun
2. TOUCH HOLE
hole takes priming powder match touched here fires gun
3. REINFORCE
multiple in some guns, e.g. first reinforce, second reinforce, etc.

4. DOLPHIN
lifting ring
5. TRUNNION
bar that supports gun in carriage
6. CHASE
main barrel of the gun
7. MUZZLE SWELL
8. GUN CARRIAGE
9. TRAIN TACKLE
hauls gun out and helps in aiming
10. BREECHING
controls recoil
11. BED
adjusts gun elevation - works with quoin
12. QUOIN
adjusts gun elevation - works with bed

SEVENTEENTH CENTURY DECK DETAILS

A typical ship of the seventeenth century
would include most of the details
shown in this illustration. This ship is
a warship though in all but a few
particulars it would represent a
merchantman as well.

1 Main shroud	15 Waist rail	29 Cathead
2 Mainmast	16 Gun	30 Cat purchase
3 Fore shroud	17 Main fife rail	31 Anchor
4 Foremast	18 Quarterdeck catwalk ladder	32 Billboard
5 Bowsprit	19 Quarterdeck catwalk	33 Channel
6 Bowsprit gammoning	20 Quarterdeck	34 Gunport wreath
7 Gammoning stop cleat	21 Companionway	35 Gunport
8 Forecastle rail	22 Mainmast	36 Framing of gunport
9 Woolding	23 Hatchway facing board	37 Channel wale
10 Fore fife rail	24 Hatch coaming	38 Main wale
11 Belfry	25 Hatch grating	39 Rider (fender)
12 After Forecastle rail	26 Capstan	40 Boarding ladder
13 Forecastle catwalk	27 Forecastle door	41 Deadeye laniard
14 Fore catwalk ladder	28 Beakhead	42 Chain plate

STERN
AND QUARTER
GALLERIES

Model by J. Dupray

Rich carvings embellished quarter and stern galleries, particularly in the Seventeenth Century. The taffrail normally carried the owner's coat-of-arms, which in the case of a military ship, was the King's emblem. Decoration grew less lavish through the Eighteenth Century. The last carvings to disappear from the stern were the quarter figures, such as those on the *Oliver Cromwell*.

Model by T. Pugh

Model by J. McDermott

Large ships, then as now, carried a flotilla of boats of various classes and sizes. While at sea on long passages where boats had little use, they would be stowed on deck or in the hold. As need became imminent, the boats were rigged to the davits and made ready for use on quick notice. Six of the *Franklin's* boats are shown here in stern and mizzen davits.

The *Sovereign of the Seas* carried a sheet anchor at the bow, abaft of her best bower in its own hawse pipe, ready to be let go at any time.

The *Franklin* is shown below with her sheet anchor lashed up to the fore channels, while her small bower hangs acockbill.

Model by J. McDermott

Model by J. Dupray

Model by R. Pranka

Leon's best bower anchor is shown here, fished to the rail, with the cat purchase unrove.

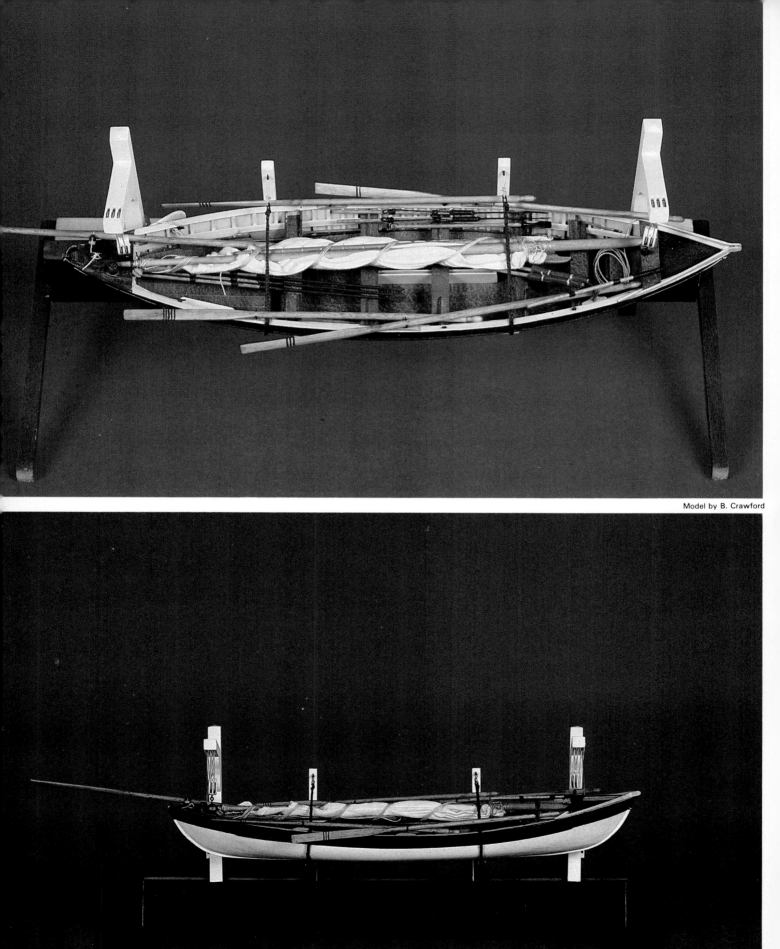

Model by B. Crawford

WHALEBOAT (opposite)
Fast, lightweight but strong, double-ended boats like this one were standard equipment on Nineteenth Century whaling ships. Each whaler would carry several of these boats on stern and quarter davits, ready for instant response to the lookout's cry, "There she blows!" A mate manned the stern steering oar, and the boat crew laid on the oars during the chase. Standing in the bow, the harpooner flung his weapon. If he hits his mark, the angered whale churned off at a frantic speed. The tub line whizzed out and was finally snubbed off on the loggerhead, after which the whale would tow the boat for miles. Often enough, the whale escaped, and the disappointed hunters faced a long row or sail back to their mother ship.

Model by H. Bridenbecker

LONGBOAT
The *Irene's* longboat was a smaller version of the type. Note the wide beam and bluff bow of the longboat in contrast to the sharp bow of the pinnace.

JOLLYBOAT
Clinker-built jollyboats were among the smaller of a ship's boats pulling one or two pairs of oars. Often, the jollyboat was carried in stern davits, as shown here on the brig *Irene*.

PINNACE ca 1800 1/2″ = 1′0″

Model by H. Judson

Ships carried a complement of boats, the largest and most important of which was the long boat or launch. A pinnace was the second largest, and was built with a view to speed and sailing qualities.

RUDDERS

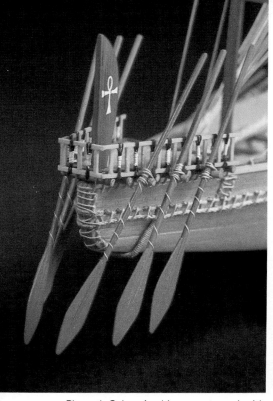

Pharoah Sahure's ship was steered with six steering oars.

Early straight stock rudder joined the tiller outboard requiring a large hole in the stern so the tiller could swing.

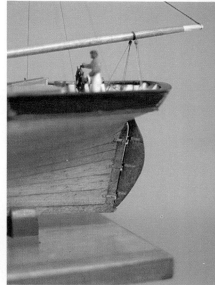

The stock of the plug stock rudder offsets forward so its axis lines up with those of the pintles.

Rudder of a power driven ship with midship propeller mounted on a prick post.

The rudder of a Chinese junk is perforated to ease the water pressure on it. It also may be hoisted up out of of the water when circumstances require.

STEERING
WHEELS

The *Star of India's* helm was of the latter worm gear variety, the mechanism protected by the handsome wheel box shown here. (opposite)

Early steering wheels were rigged to the ship's tiller like this one on the *Oliver Cromwell*. Since the length of haul on the wheel ropes was disproportionate to the distances struck out by the arc of the swinging tiller, elaborate block and tackle systems were required to maintain tension on the ropes. The problem was not fully solved until the development of the quadrant, around 1800.

Model by T. Pugh

CAPSTANS
AND PUMPS

A.

B.

A. The *Star's* iron capstan.
B. The turning wheel of the *Star's* Downton-type bilge pump.
C. The *Oliver Cromwell's* wooden capstan with turning bars in place.
   The barrel of this capstan would go down to a socket on the deck below.

C.

Model by T. Pugh

GUNPORTS AND
OTHER DETAILS

Oliver Cromwell's gunport lids were hauled open by single ropes through the gunwales attached to rings in the centers of the lids.

The *Franklin's* port lid openers featured bridles to a pair of rings. Note the manner in which the chainplates are staggered to clear the ports below.

Canton
1st Quarter
2nd Quarter
3rd Quarter
4th Quarter
Hoist
Fly

FLAGS

Flags were important signals on ships of all eras. The designs have their roots in the traditions of Heraldry from which flag nomenclature derives.

HOIST - The width of the flag as well as the edge toward the flagstaff.

FLY - The length of the flag as well as the edge farthest from the flagstaff. Thus the dimensions of a flag are given as 4 feet in the hoist, 6 in the fly.

CANTON or first quarter - The upper corner of hoist.
2nd Quarter - Upper corner of the fly
3rd Quarter - Lower corner of the hoist
4th Quarter - Lower corner of the fly

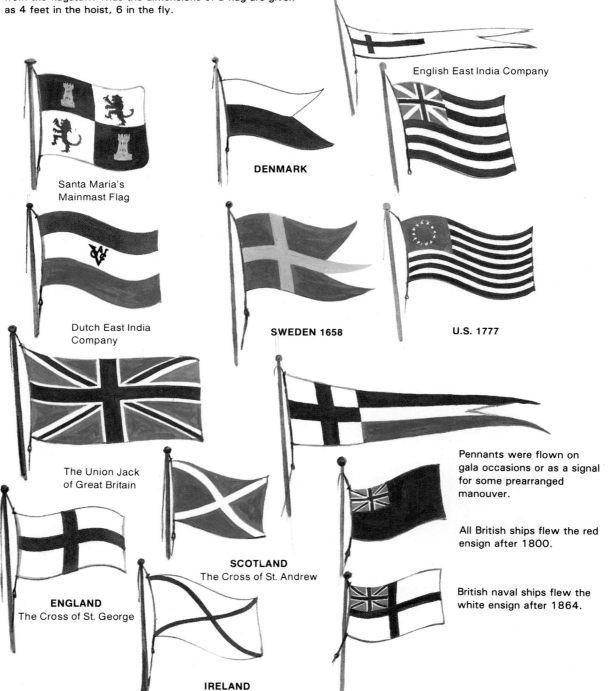

English East India Company

Santa Maria's
Mainmast Flag

DENMARK

Dutch East India
Company

SWEDEN 1658

U.S. 1777

The Union Jack
of Great Britain

SCOTLAND
The Cross of St. Andrew

ENGLAND
The Cross of St. George

IRELAND
The Cross of St. Patrick

Pennants were flown on gala occasions or as a signal for some prearranged manouver.

All British ships flew the red ensign after 1800.

British naval ships flew the white ensign after 1864.

Private merchant fleets adopted house flags as modern corporations use specially designed emblems. A few of the notable ones are illustrated here.

BLACKBALL LINE

The Blackball Line was the first regularly scheduled shipping service between Europe and America begun in the 1830's. Blackballers were identified by the great black balls on their foresails.

GRINNELL AND MINTORN

A clipper ship operator of the 1850's. Their fleet included the famous *Flying Cloud*.

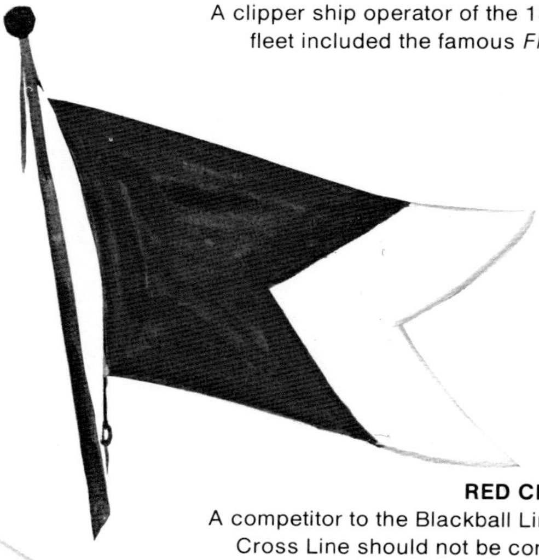

RED CROSS LINE

A competitor to the Blackball Line, the Red Cross Line should not be confused with the modern "Red Cross." The line was one of the two that declared her colors on the foresail.

THE WHITE DIAMOND LINE

Established in the 1840's to run between Boston and Liverpool, the White Diamond Line was among the first to commission Donald Mackay. Mackay later became the most famous of all clipper ship builders. Many of his ships flew the White Diamond ensign.

ALASKA PACKERS ASSOCIATION

The house flag of the *Star of India* during the final years.

Model by L. McCaffery

The *Star's* figurehead recalls her original name, *Euterpe*. One of the nine Muses of Greek mythology, Euterpe was the goddess of "lyric poetry."

Captain Bligh's famous ship *HMS Bounty* bore this figurehead.

Art Robinson's scratch built, 1/8'' = 1'0'' scale model of a 32-pounder long gun is accurate to the smallest bit of hardware. Carriage wheels turn, and the quoin adjusts elevation as it does on the real gun.

Some development did take place, however. Originally, each size of gun carried a distinctive name such as "demi culverin" or "saker." By 1700, these designations were replaced by reference to the weight of the shot the gun fired, such as "42 pounder," or "12 pounder," and so forth.

While some feeble attempts were made to standardize the size of shot and guns through the period, a large number of gun sizes stayed in use. By 1820, the Royal Navy had reduced the number to 10 shot sizes and 29 gun lengths.

In 1779, the carronade came into use. The carronade was a short-barrelled, short-ranged, low velocity weapon which used less powder than a comparatively sized canon. The slower moving shot of the carronade inflicted more damage and rained more splinters on a target than that of the long gun.

British experience with carronades during the War of 1812 proved frustrating in en-counters with the large U.S. frigates. The latter kept out of carronade range while pounding the British ships with long guns.

SEVENTEENTH CENTURY GUN TYPES			
Type of Gun	Length	Caliber	Shot Weight
			Lbs
Cannon	11'0''	7''	42 Plus
Cannon drake*	8'10''	7''	42 Plus
Demi-cannon	11'	6''	32
Demi-cannon drake	8'6''	6''	32
Culverin	8'13''	5''	18
Culverin drake	6'-7'6''	5''	18
Demi-culverin	8'11''	4''	9
Demi-culverin drake	6'	4''	9
Saker	6'9''	3''	5
Saker drake	5'-6'6''	3''	5
Minion	9'	3''	4
Falcon	--	--	2 or 3
Falconet	--	--	1 or 2

*A drake is a shorter and lighter version of a standard gun. Drakes also were characterized by a tapered bore.

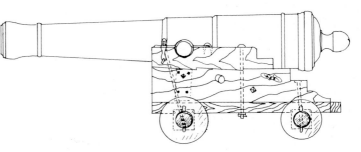

DIAMETERS OF SHOT

SHOTWEIGHT pounds	DIAMETER inches
68	7.809
42	6.684
32	6.106
24	5.546
18	5.040
12	4.403
9	4.0
6	3.494
4	3.053
3	2.793

The gun and gun carriage
shown here is fairly typical of
naval guns in use between 1700 and 1800.

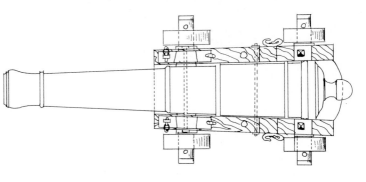

TYPES OF SHOT

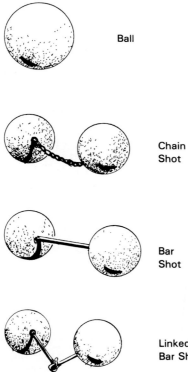

Ball

Chain
Shot

Bar
Shot

Linked
Bar Shot

ROYAL NAVY GUN DIMENSIONS FROM 1732 thru 1839

Shot Weight (name of gun)	1732 length	1790 length	1839 length largest	smallest
68	--	--	10'10''	10'10''
68 carronade	--	--	5'4''	5'4''
42	10'0''	9'6''	--	--
42 carronade	--	4'3''	--	--
32	9'6''	10'0''	9'6''	8'6''
32 carronade	--	4'0''	--	--
24	9'5''	10'0''	9'6''	6'0''
24 carronade	--	3'7''	--	--
18	9'0''	9'6''	9'0''	6'0''
18 carronade	--	3'3''	--	--
12	9'0''	9'6''	9'0''	7'6''
12 carronade	--	2'2''	--	--
9	8'5''	9'6''	9'0''	7'0''
6	7'0''	9'0''	8'6''	6'0''
4	6'0''	6'0''	6'0''	5'6''
3	4'6''	4'6''	4'6''	4'6''
½ (swivel)	--	3'6''	3'0''	3'0''

Around 1800 the conventional wheeled carriage gave way, in part, to the swivel platform mounting shown here. The carriage provided better control of recoil and was somewhat easier to aim. This type of carriage was universally used with carronades. Art Robinson's model is to a scale of 1/8" = 1'0".

Model by A. Robinson

GUNPORTS

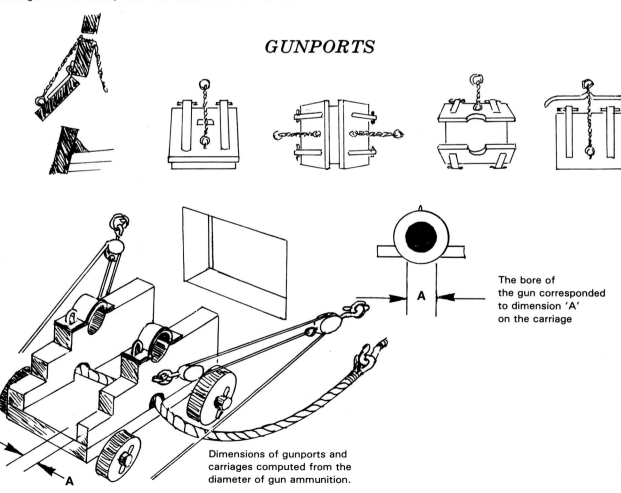

The bore of the gun corresponded to dimension 'A' on the carriage

Dimensions of gunports and carriages computed from the diameter of gun ammunition.

BOATS

The most famous confusion of the landsman in nautical lore is the difference between a boat and a ship.

One goes to sea aboard a ship, not a boat. Boats are small service vessels for a ship. Classed among boats are the captain's *gig*, the fisherman's *dory*, a ship's *longboat*, the whaler's *whaleboat*, and *lifeboats*.

Before the day of motors, most boats were rowboats, sometimes fitted up for a mast and sail. As a rule, boats were open, that is deckless. Oarsmen sat on plank thwarts, one or two men to a thwart with their backs to the bow. The gunwales (the upper rails of a boat) had thole pins fitted into them as the lever points for the oars. Aft a bos'un manned a tiller.

Small ships sometimes towed their boats astern with a painter line, though this was frequently a problem in heavy seas. Most often, as soon as a ship was off-soundings, her boats were shipped and lashed to the deck upside down. In other cases, boats were stowed right side up in chocks on deck or on skid beams mounted athwartship on top of a deckhouse.

Ships carried a variety of boats depending on their size, period, nationality and mission. Boats came in a great many styles, classes and sizes. There were 57 sizes of boats in use in England in 1817 for example, so the question about a particular ships' complement of boats cannot be answered in general terms.

The information given below is approximate, the intention being to convey a general sense of proportion along with some suggestion of the types and classes of boat a ship might have aboard.

LONGBOAT   (before 1780)

Primary and largest service boat for a ship; 20 to 50 feet long; length to beam ratio 3.5 to 3.8 to 1; 8 to 16 oars; sloop rigged; one per ship. Length of longboat equal to 50% of keel of the mother ship before 1700; 25% to 40% thereafter. Rigged with a windlass to handle anchors.

LAUNCH   (after 1780)

Successor to the longboat — from 34 to 42 feet long; 12 to 18 oars. Many 1800 naval launches carried guns.

PINNACE

20 to 50 feet long; length to beam ratio 3.8 to 4 to 1; 16 oars; sloop rigged. Generally one per ship. Faster than longboats, pinnaces were used for dispatch, reconnaissance, and inshore exploration. Pinnaces were smaller than longboats in proportion to the mother ship. Pinnaces also referred to a type of small seventeenth century ship over 50 feet and carrying 6 guns.

BARGE

Secondary service boat frequently reserved for officers, V.I.P.'s and their effects. They were 25 to 35 feet long; length to beam ratio 3.5 to 3.8 to 1; 8 to 16 oars, sloop rigged; one per large ship.

SKIFF

Light service boat 16 to 20 feet long; 2 to 4 oars; sloop rigged. Several per large ship. Often used for inspection tours of the ship while she was underway.

JOLLYWAT   (Jollyboat)

Similar to a skiff but more often clinker built and mounting up to 6 oars. The jollyboat frequently was carried in the stern davits.

CUTTER   (after 1750)

Similar to a pinnace, but 24 to 32 feet long; 8 to 14 oars and cutter rigged (two masts; dipping lug foresail, and standing lug mainsail); several per large ship.

YAWL   (after 1750)

Same as cutter except the aftermast is smaller and stepped abaft the rudderhead. Alternate to cutter.

GIG   (after 1800)

Fast, narrow service boats usually reserved for transport of personnel (i.e., the captain's gig); from 20 to 28 feet long; 4 to 6 oars; cutter rigged. Two per large ship. Often clinker built.

DINGHY   (after 1800)

Small, one or two man boats; 12 to 16 feet long; 2 oars, occasionally sloop rigged; 1 to 3 per large ship.

DAVITS

Davits are the special cranes rigged to lower or ship boats. Old ships used straight wooden davits, while after 1850, curved iron davits became the rule. Many davits were semi-permanent fixtures. That is, they could be taken down when not in use and stowed in the hold. Often, however, it was convenient to simply leave the davits rigged up and tied off at the shipside or stern.

Some ships, whalers for example, carried boats outboard in permanent, rigidly fixed davits. Stern davits in the case of whalers were stout beams bolted to the after rails or the deck.

Later, ships carried lifeboats pre-rigged to davits along the shipsides.

Boats carried in the davits were lashed up with gripes to keep them from banging around.

The more modern curved iron davits were designed to pivot around so that the suspended boat could be swung in and out over the rail with some ease.

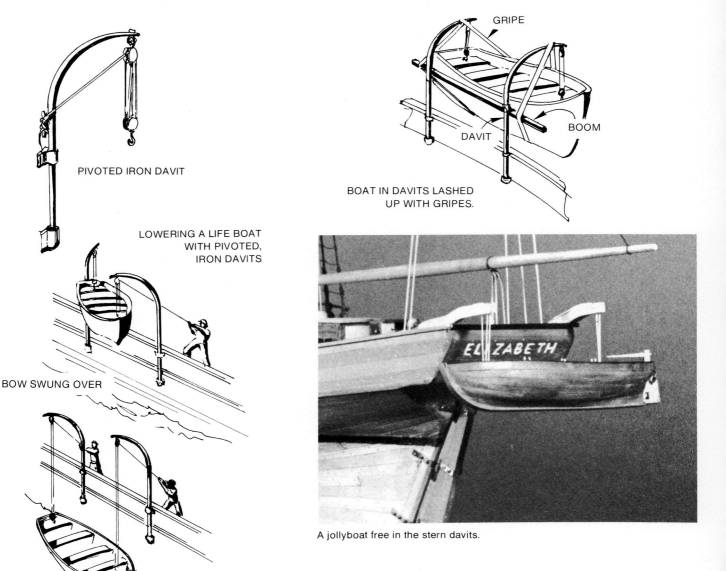

PIVOTED IRON DAVIT

LOWERING A LIFE BOAT WITH PIVOTED, IRON DAVITS

BOW SWUNG OVER

BOAT LOWERED

GRIPE

DAVIT

BOOM

BOAT IN DAVITS LASHED UP WITH GRIPES.

A jollyboat free in the stern davits.

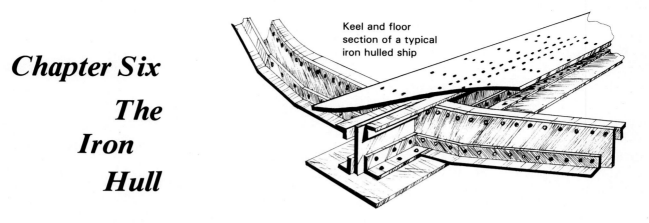

Keel and floor
section of a typical
iron hulled ship

Chapter Six
The
Iron
Hull

W hoever heard of iron floating?" was the rallying cry of those in the early 1800's who would not accept a metallic threat to their beloved and ancient wooden ship tradition. At first, the traditionalists had good reason, as well as prejudice, to resist iron as a shipbuilding material, and only conceded the issue after nearly a century of debate and refinement of the new technology.

The first small experimental iron-hulled vessel to astonish the world by not sinking appeared on the Thames River in the 1790's, but a generation passed before the *Aaron Manby*, in 1820, became the first true iron ship in commercial service. She was a small steamer of about 116 tons which made regular runs between London and Paris up until 1855, when rust finally forced her into retirement. After the *Manby* was launched, a few more vessels were tried out, but the first large iron ship did not appear until 1843, when Isambard Kingdom Brunel's ship *Great Britain* came off the ways. The *Great Britain* was a screw-propelled steamer, 322 feet long, displacing 3,270 tons.

It was Brunel's engineering of the *Great Britain* that set the precedents for true iron ship architecture. Previous efforts with iron were essentially cases of replacing wooden ship components with iron ones, without consideration of the structural properties of the latter.

Brunel, before turning his attention to the design of ships, had been a railway engineer well acquainted with iron as a building material. He came to shipbuilding free of wooden ship preconceptions, and so introduced innovations which lie at the heart of marine architecture to this day.

Before Brunel entered the picture, however, iron, for all its apparent advantages, displayed discouraging disadvantages. First of all, it was difficult to shape by the then available casting and hot forging techniques. The structural members produced by these methods often cracked and became undependably weak. Second, it rusted at a formidable rate in salt water environments. Third, barnacles and other underwater growth, for some reason, grew more rapidly on iron bottoms than on wood. Fourth, iron disrupted the operation of the magnetic compass. And, fifth, iron was comparatively expensive. Until Brunel's time, little could be gained by replacing wood with metal.

Several developments in the iron industry, between 1784 and 1840, paved the way for Brunel. In 1784, Henry Cort devised a technique for changing brittle pig iron into a more flexible sort of wrought iron, which in turn led to the first rolling mills. Thereafter, it was possible to produce structural iron in the forms familiar

The Stern of the iron hulled *Star of India.*

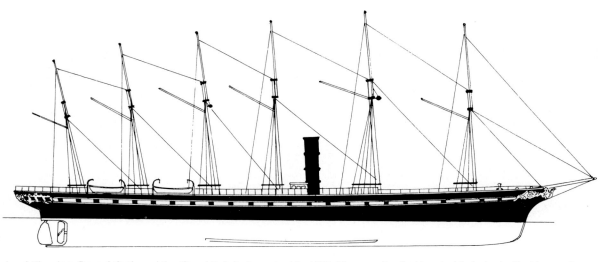

Isambard Kingdom Brunel designed the *Great Britain*, launched in 1843. She was the first large ship to be built of iron using modern structural engineering principles.

to us today as angle iron, "T" bar, and "I" beam. His "puddled" iron, as it was known, was precisely the material familiar to Brunel, the railway engineer.

Then, in 1828, James B. Neilson, true to his Scottish heritage, found a way to reduce the price of puddled iron by inventing the blast furnace.

The combination of these events gave rise to extended experiments with iron truss girders.

The frames of the *Great Britain"* were made of angle iron, while "T" bar and "I" beams connected them in the fore and aft direction into a large truss structurally consistent with a bridge girder. Since iron took up far less space than wood of comparable strength, Brunel divided up the hull into six watertight compartments, with transverse and longitudinal bulkheads. These added both strength and a safety factor to his ship.

Brunel's work introduced several new terms to the shipbuilder's vocabulary. His new fore and aft framing members became known as *bilge keelsons, side intercostal keelsons,* and *bilge stringers.*

After Brunel, iron shipbuilding gained momentum. Certain die-hards, however, continued to believe that the only proper material for a ship was wood, yet conceded to the structural advantages of iron framing. Their thinking inspired the composite hull. The only essential difference between the iron ship and the composite was that the latter was planked with wood. The famous *Cutty Sark* of 1860 had a composite hull.

The navy was the last to concede to iron, because iron, as well as the steel of the Nineteenth Century, could not withstand shell fire. The wooden ship, although armor plated, remained the staple of the sailing navy until the latter disappeared between 1880 and 1890.

The *Star of India*, now moored as the main attraction of the Maritime Museum of San Diego, is the last iron hulled sailing merchantman still afloat. She was launched November 14, 1863, at the yard of Gibson, McDonald and Arnold, at Ramsey, Isle of Man. Originally christened *Euterpe*, she began her career as a full-rigged ship, and after a romantic world roving career of nearly 40 years, she was finally sold to the Alaska Packers Association of San Francisco. The Packers rechristened her *Star of India*, reduced her rig to that of a bark, and committed her in 1902 to annual up and down runs between San Francisco and Alaska. She lasted in this service until 1923 when, at last, Twentieth Century economics caught up with her. Nonetheless, she remains seaworthy to this day.

The *Star of India* is 205 feet long, 30 feet in beam, 23 feet 6 inches deep in the hold, and has a deadweight tonnage of 1197.01. She is a living testament to the ingenuity of Isambard Brunel, as well as to the skill of the Manx shipwrights who built her.

PAINTS AND FINISHES

Before 1850 there was no such thing as commercially prepared paint. Wherever paint was used it was mixed on the spot by the painter-craftsmen, and it was relatively far more expensive than it is today. So it is understandable that paint as such was used conservatively in shipbuilding.

Wooden hulls were sealed from the elements with pitch "tar." The term *tar*, so frequently mentioned in maritime history, should not be confused with the usual, modern idea of "tar." The tar used today for roofing or road building is in fact coal tar. The old seaman's tar was a variety of gum turpentine derived from certain kinds of tree sap. Pitch pine as well as other pine species were the most important sources of it. The sticky ooze from a wounded pine tree once melted down became varnish. It dried to a hard durable finish when applied paint-like to the wood of a ship.

The initial applications of "tar" left the wood a more or less natural color. With time the varnish oxidized darker and darker, and as more and more coats were added the color of the ship turned to a warm black.

The bottoms of ships were further coated with tallow, a yellow white wax-like material obtained from animal fat. Since tallow will not dissolve in water it makes an excellent waterproofing agent. Tallow was and is well known as a material for the making of candles. Dissolved in alcohol or turpentine, tallow was brushed onto the ship and left to dry to a hard surface.

Turpentine, or refined tar, and tallow were both used in paint, except that paint included at least two or three more ingredients. To make paint (then as now) a finely ground pigment was thoroughly mixed with a vegetable oil, most often linseed oil. The paste mixture was then thinned with varnish and turpentine, and small amounts of "drier" were added.

The pigments used were those found naturally in the earth. Reds were made from iron oxides; yellows from sulphur; blue and green from copper and chromium oxides, though, of course, the modern chemical names of these materials were unknown to the old painters.

The colors produced with the pigments were, by modern standards, rather dull. The brightest yellow obtainable was a mustard color or "yellow ochre." The brightest red, a brick red, and so on. The brilliant modern paint hues for the most part obtain from dyes, most of which have been developed in our own century.

So such paint as appeared on old ships was rather drab to begin with, while time darkened it in the same way it darkened unpigmented varnish.

In our own day, we are accustomed to ships painted to a clearly defined waterline. This practice only became common during the latter 1800's.

Chapter Seven
Masts and Other Spars

MASTS AND SPARS

S par is the general term for the various poles that support a ship's sails. Masts are the vertical spars that rise off the deck. Most of the other spars are attached to the masts.

Masts (except in the case of small vessels and most modern yachts) were built-up one on top of the other in a structural system that remained essentially unchanged from Columbus' Day to the end of the classic days of sailing.

The lower mast rose to the *trestletrees* and *cross trees*, which supported the top on which the crew worked. The trestletrees also supported the heel of the *topmast*, which rose up through the *cap* of the lower mast. This overlapped section was called the *doublings*.

Above the topmast was rigged the *topgallant mast*, in much the same way.

The lower masts of a vessel went down through the decks, most often to the top of the keel or keelson, but sometimes to a lower deck beam. The foot of the mast was mounted in a base structure called the *mast step*, while the hole in the deck was stoutly reinforced all around with *partners*. A *mast coat* was fitted around the mast at the uppermost deck to make the juncture watertight.

Some masts were built of a single tree trunk. Others were pieced together from cut lumber. The latter were nailed and bolted together along their length, then reinforced with iron hoops or heavy lashings called *wooldings*.

Sometimes single-trunk masts were also reinforced with wooldings to keep them from splitting.

PROPORTIONS OF MASTS

The dimensions, proportions, and placement of the masts of a sailing vessel are perhaps the most important considerations in her rig. Raging controversy over the "correct" way to mast a ship has occupied shipmen for centuries.

The proportions of the various masts on a ship were most often expressed as fractions of the dimensions of the main lower mast. The length of the main lower mast was expressed as a multiple of the ship's beam.

The fractions varied through history, as well as with size, type and nationality of the vessel. There were also rules for the thickness of masts, though these rules were less rigid than those for length because materials varied.

A mast made from a single trunk of fine spruce would be considered stout, even though it fell short of the prescribed thickness. On the other hand, if a mast was built-up from less desirable material and lashed together with wooldings, the shipwright might insist on greater than normal thickness.

In this respect, it is interesting to note that one of the major reasons for England's interest in North America was the latter's great store of tall, straight pines needed for masts. By the Colonial Period, England had all but used up her timber resources in shipbuilding, so that to this day, England is but sparsely wooded.

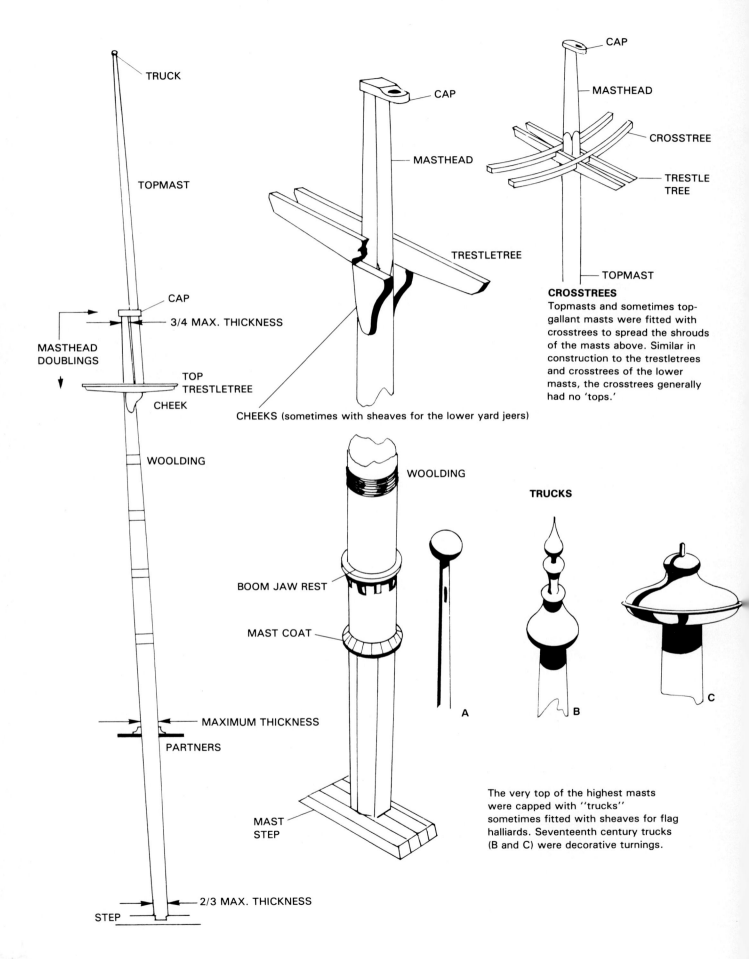

TRUCK

TOPMAST

CAP

3/4 MAX. THICKNESS

MASTHEAD
DOUBLINGS

TOP
TRESTLETREE

CHEEK

WOOLDING

MAXIMUM THICKNESS

PARTNERS

2/3 MAX. THICKNESS

STEP

CAP

MASTHEAD

TRESTLETREE

CHEEKS (sometimes with sheaves for the lower yard jeers)

CAP

MASTHEAD

CROSSTREE

TRESTLE
TREE

TOPMAST

CROSSTREES
Topmasts and sometimes top-gallant masts were fitted with crosstrees to spread the shrouds of the masts above. Similar in construction to the trestletrees and crosstrees of the lower masts, the crosstrees generally had no 'tops.'

WOOLDING

TRUCKS

BOOM JAW REST

MAST COAT

A

B

C

MAST
STEP

The very top of the highest masts were capped with ''trucks'' sometimes fitted with sheaves for flag halliards. Seventeenth century trucks (B and C) were decorative turnings.

172

The lower masts tapered from thickest at the partners to thinner at the top and bottom. They were about 3/4 as thick at the top and 2/3 as thick at the bottom as they were at the partners. The taper followed the line of a large arc tangent at the partners.

The upper masts tapered similarly except that there was no taper to the lower portions.

In cross section, the lower masts were square at the step, octagonal up to the partners, round up to the cheeks, square at the trestletrees and round again from there to the cap.

The upper masts were square from the fid up to above the top, then round up through the cap to the next doubling.

The mast doubling varied in length. In the early years of 1600, the upper masts were lighter and carried less sail so that the masts required little overlap. As time went by both topsails and topgallants grew bigger and mast couplings grew longer commensurately.

MAST PLACEMENT

In principle, the placement of masts in a hull depends on where one decides the sails should be to obtain optimum sailing performance. Generally, this means that somewhat more than half of the total sail area will be set forward of the hull's center of gravity. Such an arrangement has the sails always pulling the ship forward. The alternative would have the sails always pushing the stern around.

But if the sails are too far forward the ship becomes unmaneuverable. The answer lies in finding the exact spot where the ship will maintain a steady forward course under various sail settings, yet still respond favorably to the helm.

Every ship is unique and many a skipper has ordered his masts re-stepped because the builder had failed to find the "right spot" initially.

Captain Woodes Rogers, for example, tells us in his log dated August 11, 1708. *"We lengthened our Mizen-Mast four foot and a half, by placing it on a step on the gun-deck; got our fore-mast forward, and did what we could in order to be in a better trim than before..."*

SEVENTEENTH CENTURY

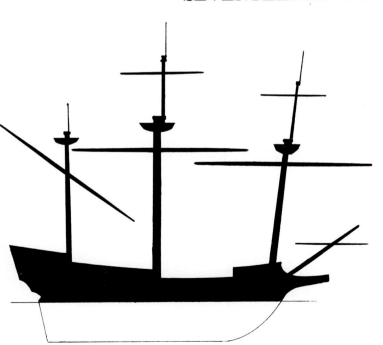

The *Mayflower,* the ship of the Pilgrim Fathers, illustrates the typical rig of small ships of the era. The mainmast steps at the center of the keel; the foremast is well forward and raked forward. The top masts are small while no sails were set on the flagstaffs above them.

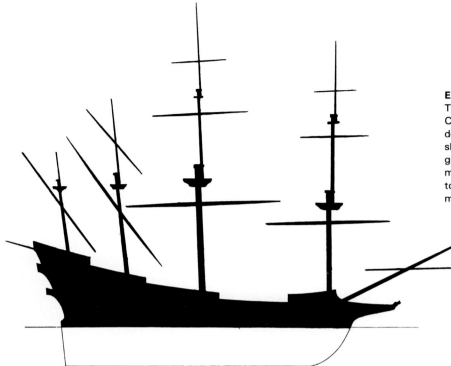

EAST INDIAMAN - 1650
The formation of the East India Company in 1600 inspired the rapid development of ever larger merchant ships. The profile below illustrates the growth. The topmasts grew topgallant masts; the mizzen sported a lateen topsail and a fourth bonaventure mizzen mast was added.

The ships of the seventeenth century were built rounder forward, more slender aft, with the result that their centers of gravity were considerably forward of amidships. Their rigs therefore were concentrated forward.

The mainmast was stepped at or a few feet forward of the center for the keel. The foremast was stepped on the stem at a point just below the waterline. The mizzen, when it was single, was stepped a little forward of halfway between the taffrail and the main. The bonaventure mizzen, as a fourth mast of the period was known, was stepped so that the sheet of the lateen sail was just inboard of the taffrail while the main mizzen (when the ship had a bonaventure) was moved forward. The bowsprit ran out forward beside the stem and a spritsail topmast was stepped on its most forward end.

Given this it is easy to see that the sum of the sail area forward is quite a bit more than that aft where almost all of the latter is taken up with the lateen mizzen "steering sails."

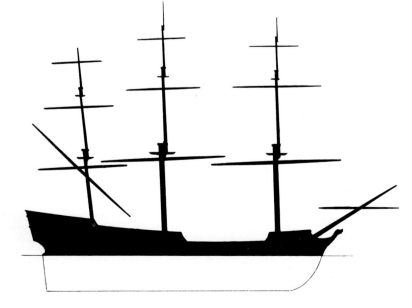

BRITISH 3RD RATE - 1725
Main and foremasts moved aft through the century and the bowsprits longer. The mizzen was rigged with a topsail and topgallant sail.

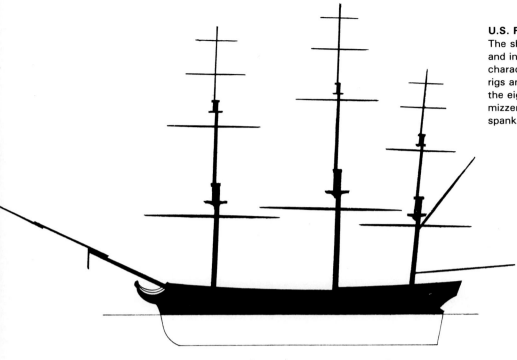

U.S. FRIGATE - 1812
The ships of the American Revolution and into the early 1800's were characterized by their extremely high rigs and very long head spars. During the eighteenth century the lateen mizzen gave way to the gaff headed spankers.

EIGHTEENTH CENTURY

Eighteenth century hulls, underwater, varied little from those of the Seventeenth. The center of gravity still tended to be forward, though not as far. But the high stern castles of the earlier century were cut down, and so reduced the sail-like windage of these structures. The masts moved aft.

The mainmast moved aft of the center of the keel, and the foremast moved aft to the point about where the stem and keel met. The mizzen mast (the *bonaventure mizzen* was not in use at this point) stayed where it had been earlier.

The space between the fore and mainmasts was filled with staysails, and the bowsprit was extended almost half the keel length or more before the bow, and loaded with jibs and fore staysails. In spite of the more aft placement of the fore and mainmasts, the balance of sail was still forward of the center of gravity, as it had to be.

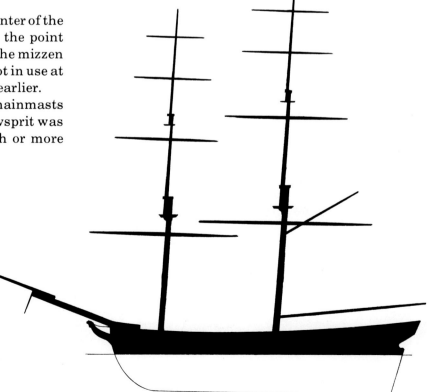

BRIG - 1825
The early nineteenth century witnessed the development of the packet ships, forerunners of the great clippers of the 1850's. The ships like this brig carried enormous areas of sail while hull design favored a sharp entry and run, soft chines and steeply rising floors (pronounced "V" bottoms) all in the interest of speed. These early "clipper" designs while fast were also dangerous.

NINETEENTH CENTURY

Hull lines changed dramatically about the middle of the century with the coming of the clipper ships. With them we find the center of gravity moved aft to a point just forward of midships, and the masts moved even further aft to accommodate the new hull plan. The mainmast is now considerably aft of the mid point of the keel and the foremast is a third of the way between the forefoot and the mainmast step. The mizzen is halfway between the main and the taffrail. Though headsails abound, the bowsprit is considerably diminished to less than a quarter of the keel length.

Earlier ships carried only a single lateen sail on the mizzen. By 1800 ships replaced the lateen

steering sail with a gaff headed spanker and crowded square sails above it.

The American fishing schooner reached a magnificent level of efficiency in this century also, and illustrates further the correlation between hull and rig. The center of gravity of the fishing schooner compares with the clippers. In fact, many schooners were designated as "clippers." The mainmast is stepped forward of the center of gravity, and the foremast about halfway between the main and stem. The mainsail is huge, bent to a boom that overhangs the stern a quarter of its length. The foresail and headsails are diminutive by comparison.

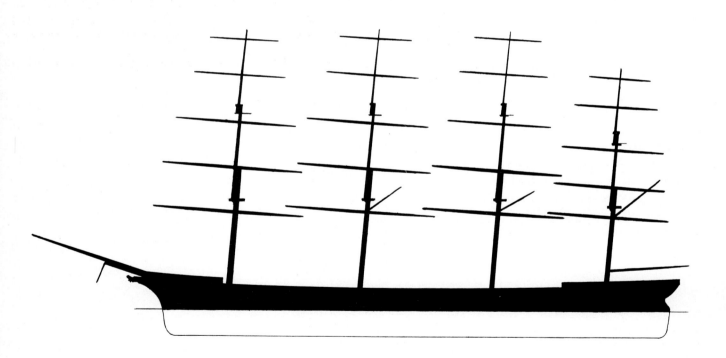

FOUR MASTED FULL RIGGED SHIP - 1860
The great clippers of the 1850's finally evolved into the giant windjammers which, like supernovas, announced the end of commercial sail.

A.

B.

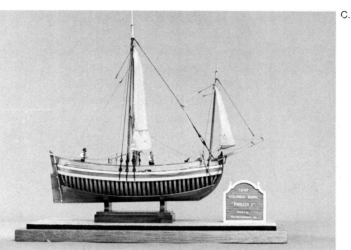

C.

D.

A. The masts of medieval ships were massive timbers built to stand without benefit of shrouds and stays. Note square, battlemented fighting top on this Thirteenth Century Norman ship.

B. This early Seventeenth Century Spanish galleon shipped a bonaventure mizzen. Note the rake of the masts.

C. The foremasts of early Seventeenth Century ships raked forward, the mainmast was nearly vertical, as this model of a small Colonial bark shows.

D. The strong aft rake of the masts on the brig *Malek Adhel* of 1840 was typical of the sharp Baltimore clippers of this era. Most masts of the Nineteenth Century raked aft, though not as radically as those shown here.

TOPS

The design of mast tops, as did other ship elements, changed through the centuries. Few features, however, are as apparent as the tops for clues to a ship's period.

Up to the end of the fifteenth century, tops were thought of as fighting platforms. Naval warfare in the medieval centuries was a case of a limited number of mariners taking a large contingent of land soldiers to sea and bringing them into hand-to-hand contact with the enemy. Ships were viewed as water-borne siege engines.

The top at that time was a battlemented "castle tower" from which archers could fire down on their foes, and from which rocks, hot oil and other missiles could be poured down. The platform was round with heavy sides built-up so that it resembled a wooden tub.

During the sixteenth and seventeenth centuries we see a steady development in the use of guns. The warship was now designed as a gun carrier and the tops changed to accommodate the new role.

The first feature of the medieval tops to disappear was their high sides. In the 1600's they dropped to about knee height; in the 1700's they were at almost six or eight inches. By the 1800's, the sides had diminished to the thickness of a plank.

In size the tops varied with the height of the topmast. When topmasts were small in the early 1600's the diameter of tops was about 25% of the ship's beam. By 1700 they had expanded to about 1/3 of the beam in diameter.

Sixteenth century tops, as we have said, were round and this configuration held up to about 1750, after which they became 'D'-shaped.

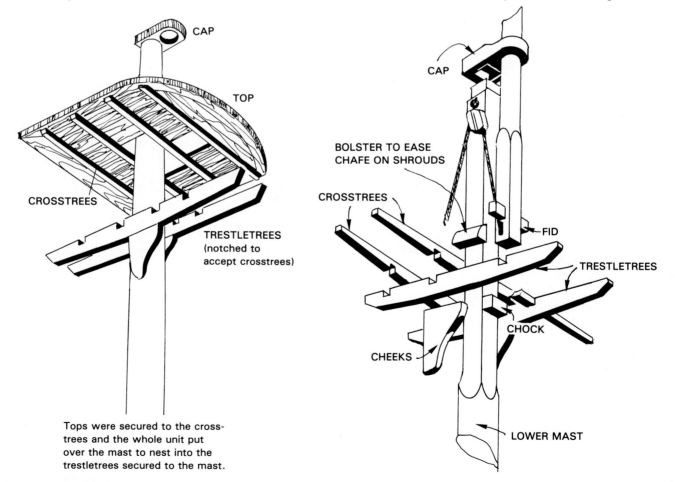

CAP

TOP

CROSSTREES

TRESTLETREES
(notched to accept crosstrees)

Tops were secured to the crosstrees and the whole unit put over the mast to nest into the trestletrees secured to the mast.

CAP

BOLSTER TO EASE CHAFE ON SHROUDS

CROSSTREES

FID

TRESTLETREES

CHOCK

CHEEKS

LOWER MAST

Up to 1800 the top still had value as a fighting platform aloft. After that date the latter function declined in importance, leaving as the purpose for the top the spreading of the topmast shrouds, the support of other upper rigging, and the provision of a work platform.

The basic construction of tops, regardless of shape, followed similar principles throughout the sailing ship era. Just under the top, the mast was fitted with cheeks or "hounds" as they were sometimes called, over which were mounted trestletrees. The trestletrees consisted of two beams, one on either side of the mast in the fore and aft plane.

The basic frame of the top consisted of the crosstrees, two or three beams in the thwartship plane. The trestletrees were notched on the upper side to take the crosstrees.

The crosstrees and trestletrees together formed a criss-cross underpinning that led out to the inner edges of the top's rim. The balance of the structure was variously planked over depending on the shape of the top and the type of vessel it belonged to.

The tops of naval vessels were solidly planked like decks except for a single "lubber's hole" at the center. Merchant ship tops were lighter with grating-like planking.

The lubber holes sometimes provided access to the tops inboard of the futtock shrouds. Most of the time, however, crewmen climbed into the top outboard on futtock shroud ratlines.

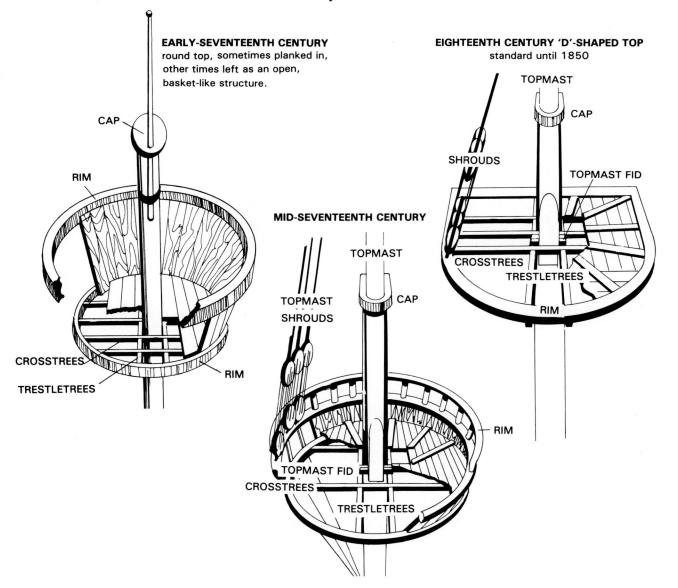

EARLY-SEVENTEENTH CENTURY
round top, sometimes planked in, other times left as an open, basket-like structure.

CAP

RIM

CROSSTREES

TRESTLETREES

RIM

MID-SEVENTEENTH CENTURY

TOPMAST

TOPMAST SHROUDS

CAP

TOPMAST FID

CROSSTREES

TRESTLETREES

EIGHTEENTH CENTURY 'D'-SHAPED TOP
standard until 1850

TOPMAST

CAP

SHROUDS

TOPMAST FID

CROSSTREES

TRESTLETREES

RIM

RIM

A rope ladder aft of the mast provided access to the tops of medieval ships.

Sprit topmast top.

Main top of the *Sovereign of the Seas.*

NINETEENTH CENTURY DETAILS

During the final half-century of the age of commercial sail, iron and steel played a larger role in ship's rigging. In many cases, the masts themselves were metal, while blocks, eyebolts, trestletrees, tops and the like were welded or bolted to them.

Lower topsail and lower topgallant yards were often permanently fixed to the caps with iron cranes. Chain ties and iron trusses similar to universal joints fixed lower yards, while upper sails were raised and lowered on tracks. Turnbuckles and wire rope replaced deadeyes and hemp for shrouds. Chain sheets led through sheaves in the yardarms then inboard to bullock blocks (replacements for the old quarter blocks).

The heavy upper topsails were hauled aloft with tie and halliard systems including a chain span rove through a "gin block."

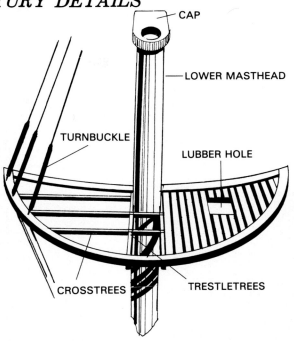

After 1850 crescent shaped tops characterized clipper ships and iron sparred windjammers. Note the outboard lubber holes.

A. Foreyard crane of the *Star of India* as seen looking down from the top.

B. Chain sling supports the *Star's* main yard.

C. The chain tie of the *Star's* upper topsail yard.

D. Main lower topsail crane.

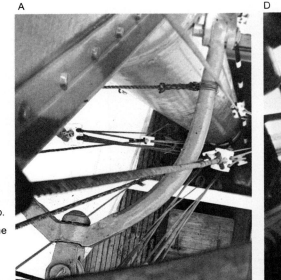

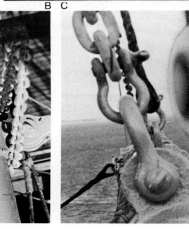

After side of the *Star's* crosstrees. The view reveals backstay spreaders, turnbuckles for the tensioning of the topgallant shrouds, and the sheave of the upper topsail's chain span.

The *Star's* fore top as seen from aft. Note that the topmast shrouds are "set up on their own ends" without deadeyes or turnbuckles. This is an uncommon feature of the *Star's* rigging.

The *Leon's* top as seen from forward.

YARDS

The yards of a ship were rigged like so many crosses of a "T" up the masts of a square-rigger. The sails were bent (fastened) onto the yards. The yards and sails were fitted out with lines, tackles, sheaves, cleats, and other gear for maneuvering the system about.

Early yards were rigged exclusively with hemp, while later, as we have said, chain and steel cable replaced rope where the strains were heaviest.

Yards, like masts, are a major determinent of the number, shape, and placement of sails on a vessel. The largest sails were the lower courses (the main and foresails). The higher sails tapered upward, the yards becoming proportionately shorter the higher they were set. Through the centuries, the taper of the sails changed from quite radical in the 1600's, to very gradual by 1850. The lengths of the upper yards, therefore, came more and more to approximate the lengths of the yards just below.

About 1730, square spritsails gave way to fore and aft jibs. This innovation, however, unbalanced the rigs, and the first solution to the problem was to lengthen the yards. Thus, for a period in the Eighteenth Century, we find main yards up to 1.15 times the beam of the ship. Later, about 1800, the main yard length was cut back to about twice the beam, and the rig was balanced by enormous jibbooms extending nearly half the ship's length before the bow.

The diameters of the yards, like masts, had prescribed values, but varied from ship to ship for the same reasons — inconsistency of material and method of manufacture.

In general, the maximum diameter of a yard was about 2% of its length. This held true of all spars in the Seventeenth Century. As the length of the upper yards increased in the Eighteenth and Nineteenth Centuries, however, their diameters diminished to about 1½% of their lengths.

Yards tapered like masts along the line of large arcs, tangent at the center, to a diameter at the outer end of about 40% of their diameter at the center.

Throughout the Eighteenth Century, the center third of a yard was octagonal in section. Sail robands (rope bands) went around the entire spar, while the head cringles were lashed to the yardarms around stop cleats.

Shortly into the Nineteenth Century, yards were made round throughout their entire length, and were fitted with jackstays to which the sails were bent. A jackstay consisted of a piece of line (later a steel rod), rove through eyebolts, which were set into the upper forward edge of the yard. The jackstay held the sail up on the spar and thus make it easier to furl.

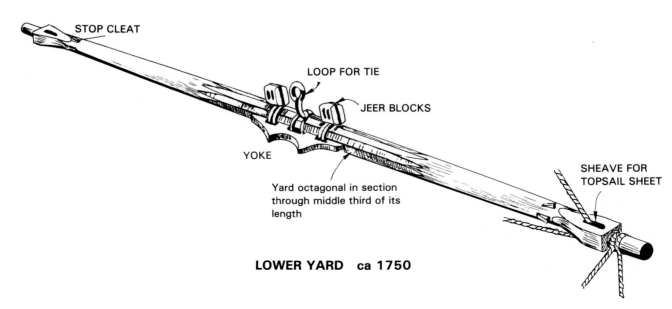

STOP CLEAT

LOOP FOR TIE

JEER BLOCKS

YOKE

Yard octagonal in section through middle third of its length

SHEAVE FOR TOPSAIL SHEET

LOWER YARD   ca 1750

LOWER YARD AFTER 1850

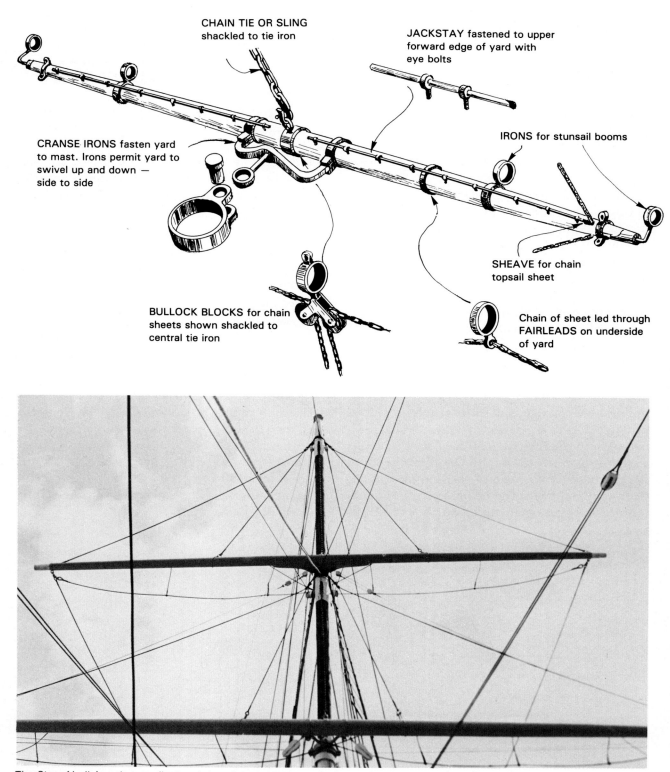

CHAIN TIE OR SLING shackled to tie iron

JACKSTAY fastened to upper forward edge of yard with eye bolts

CRANSE IRONS fasten yard to mast. Irons permit yard to swivel up and down — side to side

IRONS for stunsail booms

BULLOCK BLOCKS for chain sheets shown shackled to central tie iron

SHEAVE for chain topsail sheet

Chain of sheet led through FAIRLEADS on underside of yard

The *Star of India's* main topgallant and skysail yards. The topgallant yard is fixed at the cap, while the royal yard raises and lowers. These yards are wooden, while the lower yards are iron.

SEVENTEENTH CENTURY
Yards diminished rapidly in length from lower to higher. Lower main yard length: 2 times beam.

EIGHTEENTH CENTURY
Yard lengths increased. Lower main yard length: 2.25 times beam.

NINETEENTH CENTURY
Yard lengths tending to be more equal in length. Lower main yard length: 1.9 times beam.

Parrels fastened higher yards to masts. They were designed to permit the raising and lowering, rotation and tilt of the yards. Early seventeenth and eighteenth century parrels consisted of wooden balls strung together with spacers. Iron tub parrels (right) came into use in the nineteenth century. Masts on which parrels were mounted were greased but never painted.

EARLY PARREL

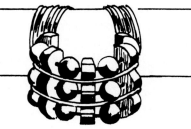

The *Star of India's* bowsprit. Note the lead of the fore topmast stay through the bees at the cap and straight aft to its fastening on the bow.

BOWSPRIT

The bowsprit through the centuries changed in function, shape and manner of rigging more than any other spar.

Originally in the twelfth century, the bowsprit was used exclusively as a means of holding the windward tack of the mainsail forward. Then around 1450 it occurred to someone to set a square sail on it and the spritsail was born. A second sail, the spritsail topsail, appeared in the seventeenth century and these two sails stayed in use until about 1710 when the spritsail topsail was replaced by fore and aft jibs. Finally the square spritsail itself was retired about 1800.

The steeve (the angle between the sprit and the deck) progressed from about 22 degrees in 1650, to 35 degrees in 1750 and back again to about 20 degrees in 1825.

The spritsail topmast was a curious development of the seventeenth century that came with the sail of the same name. It grew out of the need to get more sail area forward as mentioned above, but securing a little, short mast on the end of another spar led to difficulties. The spritsail top-

mast was a frequent casualty in heavy weather.

Jibbooms, fixed parallel with the bowsprit itself, proved more practical. Originally, the jibboom was rigged off to the side of the sprit so as not to interfere with the stays. Later it followed the center line of the sprit, and the stays were led to the side through bee blocks.

Around 1800, jibbooms sprouted flying jibbooms, and jib-of-jib-booms. The flying jibboom mounted on the upper portside of the jibboom; the jib-of-jib-boom on the upper starboard side of the flying jibboom.

The first bowsprits up to about 1550 sailed "on the wood." They had no rigging but the bow timbers, knightheads and steps inboard to hold them in place. A little later in the century a "gammoning" appeared. The gammoning lashed the sprit down to the beakhead and helped offset the powerful up and after haul of the forestays.

Around 1700, the bobstay came into use to assist the gammoning and finally toward the end of the eighteenth century, martingales played bobstay to the way outboard jibbooms.

SEVENTEENTH CENTURY BOWSPRITS

STEEVE - 22 degrees
LENGTH - 88% of mainmast
LENGTH, SPRIT TOPMAST - 27% of mainmast
About 25% of the bowsprit was inboard.

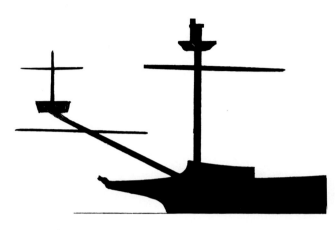

The original purpose of the
bowsprit was to carry tacks
and bowlines.

The *Sovereign's* bowsprit was held in place with heavy gammoning.

187

EIGHTEENTH CENTURY BOWSPRITS

STEEVE - 35 degrees
LENGTH - 45% of main mast
LENGTH, JIBBOOM - 41% of main mast
30% of the bowsprit was inboard, while
the jibboom overlapped the bowsprit
about 25% of its length. Additional jibbooms might add to the overall length.

Bowsprit and jibboom of the *Racehorse* represents typical Eighteenth Century rigging practice.

Hannah's bowsprit had no dolphin striker. Her jibboom only partly overlapped the sprit, in contrast with later Nineteenth Century practice, where the jibboom doubled the entire length of the sprit.

DIMENSIONS OF SPARS

To Use This Chart:

1. Measure the beam of the ship at the widest point. For example: Beam equals 25'

2. Determine era of vessel and use only the columns so marked. ex. 1650

3. Determine height of mainmast - multiply the number under the era opposite entry "A. LOWER" in the MAINMAST column by the beam. ex. 2.4 x 25' equals 60'

4. To find the height of any other mast or yard multiply 60' times the decimal fraction in the appropriate box. ex. the fore topmast entry under 1650 is .42; .42 times 60' equals 25.2'. Hence the fore topmast of the ship will be 25.2' long. ex. the length of the lower mizzen (cross jack) yard would be .50 x 60' equals 30'.

Remember that the dimensions given are but mean averages for the general run of ships in these periods. The mast dimensions of a particular vessel could vary from those shown depending on type, nationality, or dozens of other factors.

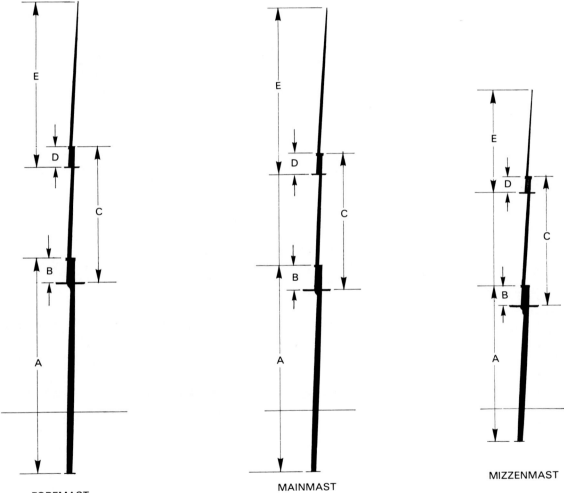

FOREMAST   MAINMAST   MIZZENMAST

MASTS as fractions of lower main mast	MAINMAST			FOREMAST			MIZZENMAST		
	1650	1750	1850	1650	1750	1850	1650	1750	1850
A LOWER	2.4 x Beam	2.28 x Beam	2.1 x Beam	.80	.90	.96	.75	.84	.86
B LOWER DOUBLINGS	.06	.13	.23	.05	.13	.18	.08	.095	.17
C TOPMAST	.52	.58	.77	.42	.57	.77	.34	.43	.60
D TOPMAST DOUBLINGS	.05	.06	.27	.05	.06	.15	.08	.095	.19
E TOPGALLANT MAST	.26	.31	*.91*	.21	.29	.86*	—	.22	.66

*Topgallant, Royal and Skysail on a single pole

189

PROPORTIONS OF TRESTLETREES

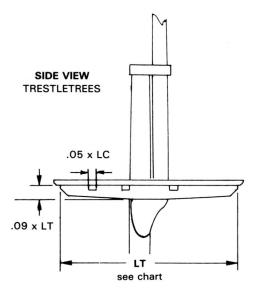

SIDE VIEW
TRESTLETREES

.05 x LC

.09 x LT

LT
see chart

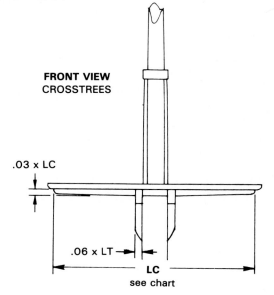

FRONT VIEW
CROSSTREES

.03 x LC

.06 x LT

LC
see chart

as fractions of main lowermast length	MAIN			FORE			MIZZEN		
	1650	1750	1850	1650	1750	1850	1650	1750	1850
LT TRESTLETREES (length)	.13	.145	.08	.10	.14	.075	.085	.108	.06
LC CROSSTREES (length)	.17	.19	.10	.11	.19	.095	.10	.14	.086

PROPORTIONS OF YARDS

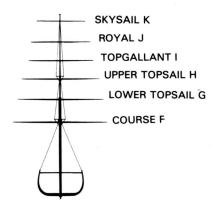

SKYSAIL K
ROYAL J
TOPGALLANT I
UPPER TOPSAIL H
LOWER TOPSAIL G
COURSE F

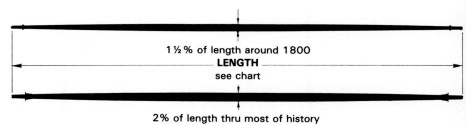

1½ % of length around 1800
LENGTH
see chart

2% of length thru most of history

YARDS	MAIN YARDS			FORE YARDS			MIZZEN YARDS		
as fractions of lower main yard	1650	1750	1850	1650	1750	1850	1650	1750	1850
F COURSE	2 x Beam	2.25 x Beam	1.9 x Beam	.85	.88	.88	.50	.60	.61
G TOPSAIL	.50	.70	.91	.43	.62	.80	.25	.30	.56
H UPPER TOPSAIL	—	—	.83	—	—	.73	—	—	.51
I TOPGALLANT	.25	.47	.66	.22	.41	.58	—	.24	.40
J ROYAL	—	—	.63	—	—	.55	—	—	.38
K SKYSAIL	—	—	.50	—	—	.44	—	—	—

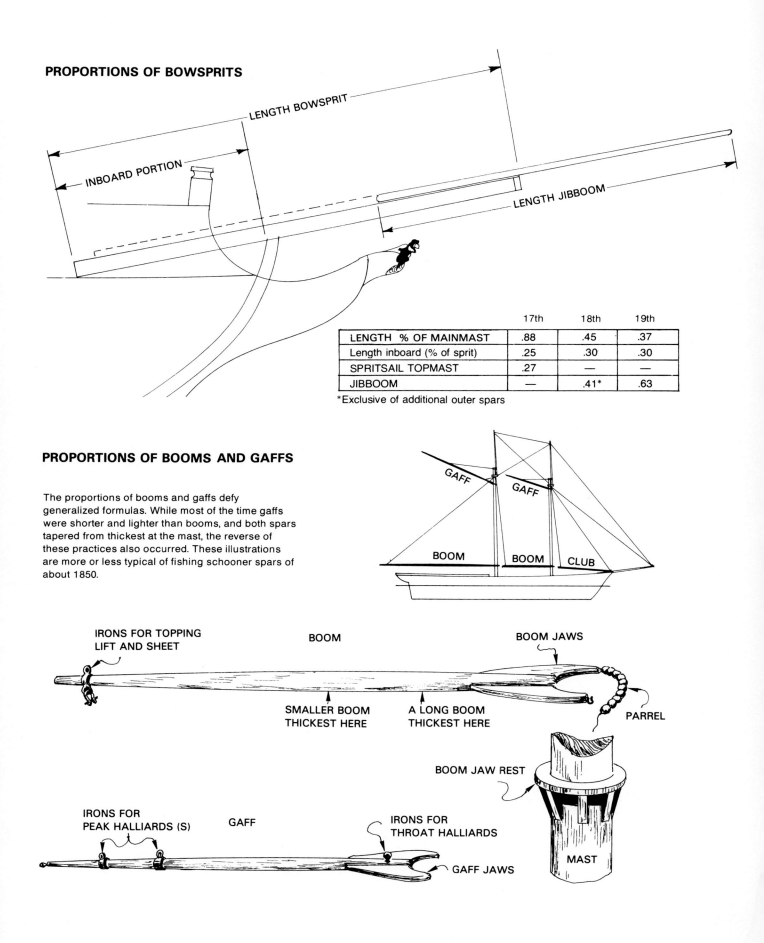

PROPORTIONS OF BOWSPRITS

LENGTH BOWSPRIT

INBOARD PORTION

LENGTH JIBBOOM

	17th	18th	19th
LENGTH % OF MAINMAST	.88	.45	.37
Length inboard (% of sprit)	.25	.30	.30
SPRITSAIL TOPMAST	.27	—	—
JIBBOOM	—	.41*	.63

*Exclusive of additional outer spars

PROPORTIONS OF BOOMS AND GAFFS

The proportions of booms and gaffs defy
generalized formulas. While most of the time gaffs
were shorter and lighter than booms, and both spars
tapered from thickest at the mast, the reverse of
these practices also occurred. These illustrations
are more or less typical of fishing schooner spars of
about 1850.

GAFF   GAFF

BOOM   BOOM   CLUB

IRONS FOR TOPPING
LIFT AND SHEET

BOOM

BOOM JAWS

SMALLER BOOM
THICKEST HERE

A LONG BOOM
THICKEST HERE

PARREL

BOOM JAW REST

IRONS FOR
PEAK HALLIARDS (S)

GAFF

IRONS FOR
THROAT HALLIARDS

GAFF JAWS

MAST

Chapter Eight
Rope

ROPE

Rope was the sailor's constant companion. Awake or asleep, he depended on rope for survival, for comfort, and for amusement. Rope not only controlled masts, sails and spars, but made up the hammock nettings of the sailor's bed, and served as the raw material for artistic expression during long passages. Such intimacy often made up the sum of a sailor's intellectual life. He knew by looking how strong a rope was, what it was made of, how old it was, how it would behave when wet, dry, hot or cold; where it was weak, how to fix it, tie it, bend it, whip it, worm it, weave it, and above all, how to make it handsome.

Rope is among the earliest of man's inventions. He probably learned to make it about the same time that he learned to weave, about 6000 years ago, during the Neolithic or last Stone Age. The neolithic lake dwellers of Switzerland made linen cloth from flax, which might well have been the first rope making material. Certainly flax is among the oldest vegetable fibers man has put to use.

Hemp, however, eventually became the primary material for rope making. Precisely when this occurred is difficult to say, because the different cultures of the ancient world developed at different rates with different access to raw materials.

Hemp was originally an Asian plant indigenous to the territory of ancient Sumeria, which flourished about 3000 B.C. The Sumerians, therefore, may be responsible for the introduction of the material for rope making. In any event, hemp rope became the standard from a very early date.

Hemp, *cannabis sativa,* was transplanted to Europe, and later to North America, where today it is grown as a cash crop specifically for making rope.

The Portuguese and Spanish, during their explorations of the Fifteenth and Sixteenth Centuries, introduced Europe to a new variety of "hemp," which grew only in the Phillippines. The material, taken from a banana-like plant called *abaca,* proved tougher, smoother, and more weather resistant than true hemp, and it rapidly took over as the preferred material for ship rigging. The material became known as *Manila hemp.*

As Europeans investigated other parts of the world, they discovered more fibers adaptable to rope making, though none of them matched Manila for seagoing purposes. *Sisal hemp,* about 75% the strength of Manila, derived from the *agave* plant found in South America, Mexico, and Africa, turned out to be the next best choice.

An eighteenth century ropewalk after an illustration in J.H. Roding's "Allgemeines Worterbuch der Marine," 1798.

Three-stranded **HAWSER LAID** rope ("z" laid) twists from right to left, counterclockwise.

Four-stranded **SHROUD LAID** rope also twists from right to left, counterclockwise.

Nine-stranded CABLE LAID rope, twists three hawser laid ropes together in a clockwise direction.

Jute from India, derived from a variety of linden plant, was inexpensive but far weaker than Manila, true hemp or sisal. Jute was used for chafing gear, padding of one kind or another, and later as a core for steel wire ropes.

Coir rope is made from the outer husk of the coconut. It has only a quarter of the strength of Manila, but it floats and stands up well in water.

Coir was valuable on shipboard when used as a sea anchor. The rope could be payed out astern in a blow without sinking and so helped to keep the ship's bow into the wind.

New Zealand hemp or flax was a latecomer in the quest for natural rope fibers, and turned out to be on a par with Manila for strength and durability.

ROPE MAKING

The useful fibers of these rope raw materials lay, for the most part, in the inner bark of the various plants described above. Separating them involved a process of allowing the rest of the plant to rot away. This was accomplished either by soaking the stalks in water (water retting) or hanging them out in the weather for a period (dew retting). When rotten enough, the stalks were beaten with a club and the fibers picked out.

Next the fibers were combed into ribbons which in turn were twisted into yarns. Depending on whether one was making 'Z'-laid rope or cable-laid rope, the yarns were twisted either right-handed (clockwise) or left-handed (counter clockwise). A half dozen or more twisted yarns

then were twisted together in the opposite direction to make up strands. Three (sometimes four) strands were finally twisted together in the same direction as the yarns to make up the finished rope.

Until the arrival of steel wire rigging in the middle of the nineteenth century, seamen concerned themselves with three kinds of line and cable - *hawser-laid* (right-handed) rope, *shroud-laid* (four stranded, right-handed) rope, and *cable-laid* (left-handed) rope.

The left-handed cable-laid rope was usually a heavy line made-up of three hawser-laid ropes, hence "9 stranded."

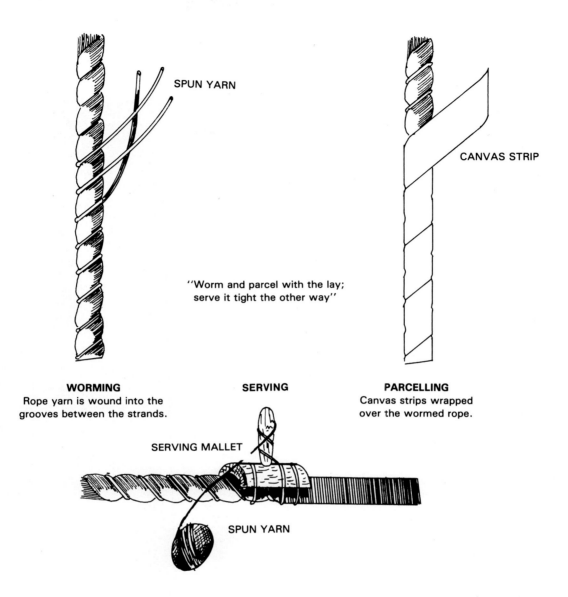

SPUN YARN

CANVAS STRIP

"Worm and parcel with the lay;
serve it tight the other way"

WORMING
Rope yarn is wound into the
grooves between the strands.

SERVING

PARCELLING
Canvas strips wrapped
over the wormed rope.

SERVING MALLET

SPUN YARN

The strength of any of these ropes, of course, depended on the number of yarns per strand (hence the size) and the fiber material. But a rule-of-thumb for rope strength (presumably fairly new Manila hemp) came into use in the eighteenth century. The rule was to divide the square of the circumference of the rope by 3 to get the number of tons required to break it. As a margin of safety, a rope was never used to handle a load greater than 1/6th of its breaking load.

Ropes were protected against fraying, chafing, rotting, and unravelling in a variety of ways. Many lines, particularly in the standing rigging, were soaked with tar to protect them from the corrosive effects of the salty sea.

Large portions of the standing rigging were also *wormed, parcelled,* and *served.* To worm a rope was to lay thin line in the *cunting* (the spiral cracks) between the strands. Parcelling was to wrap old strips of canvas over the wormed line after which the whole was served, or wrapped around and around with marline or spun yarn.

Spun yarn was simply two or three yarns (frequently derived by picking apart old rope) loosely twisted into string. Marline was essentially the same thing but twisted tighter.

The ends of rope were whipped, pointed or knotted depending on the need.

The size of rope used for each of the many rigging lines varied extensively from ship to ship and era to era. More will be said of this later.

SEIZINGS, SPLICES, KNOTS

Ropes were fastened to one another and to various elements of ship's gear in a large number of ways. The ends of all ropes were variously treated depending on the type of attachment it was to have.

A main or forestay, for example, had an eye at the upper end. The lower end passed through the eye as with a cowboy's lariat to form the loop for the attachment at the masthead. To prevent the eye from snugging up tight around the mast, a "mouse" or fat bump was woven into the stay as a stopper.

The lower end of the stay went around a heart and was "seized up on its own end" with a "round seizing."

Shrouds for the most part went double around the masthead, the two ends hanging down to the shipsides where deadeyes were turned in. When shrouds were cable-laid ropes (left-handed), they also went left-handed (counter clockwise) around the deadeye and vice versa with hawser-laid shrouds. They were seized to their own ends with throat seizings. Shrouds were also turned into deadeyes "cutter stay" fashion.

The stropping of blocks was another important element of ropemanship. The standard strop (strap) consisted of a short length of rope with its two ends short spliced together so that it made a ring. The ring went around the block and was made fast with a round seizing with riding turns.

A block set into an eye splice on one end of a line became a "tail block."

A clew line block was stropped in the bight of a short line with an eye splice in both ends.

Some strops consisted of a bight where one end was short with an eye splice in it and the other was long. Such a block might do for a quarter block.

In all cases, the strops were wormed, parcelled, and served.

A fairlead is shown here seized to the *Star of India's* main shroud.

SPLICES AND SEIZINGS

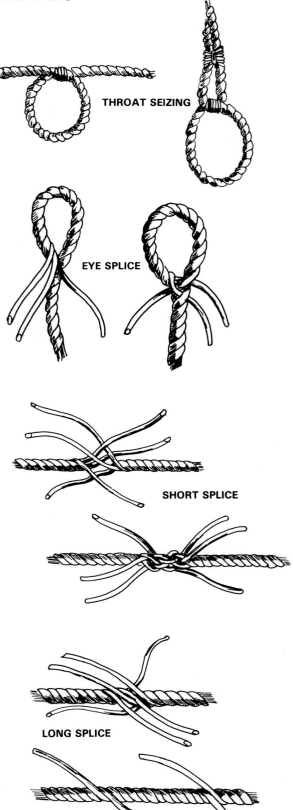

BIGHT

RIDING TURN

ROUND SEIZING

THROAT SEIZING

EYE SPLICE

SHORT SPLICE

LONG SPLICE

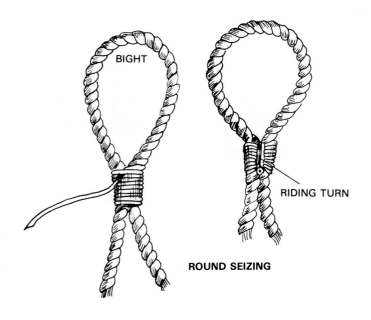

An eye splice with a thimble forms an attachment of a line to a pair of sister hooks which in turn are hooked to a padeye fastened to the deck.

BLOCKS, TACKLE AND RIGGING HARDWARE

Central elements of the rigging of a ship were blocks. A block consisted of one or more sheaves, or grooved wheels mounted on an axle in a wood or metal shell. The block formed a roller bearing and guide for leading a rope around corners or back and forth through other blocks.

Blocks through the centuries took on a wide variety of shapes and sizes, some of which are illustrated here. Older blocks had wooden shells and external hemp strops. More modern blocks had metal or wood shells and internal metal strops.

Blocks with an attachment loop on the bottom, as well as the top, are called becket blocks, the lower loop being referred to as the becket.

The size of a block was determined by its sheave size. The sheave size was a function of the size of rope it was to accommodate. Thus we find the diameter of seventeenth century sheaves specified as "2¾ times the circumference of the rope" which converts to about 9 times the diameter. Later in the eighteenth century, the English specified blocks of 6 times the rope diameter, while American ships fitted blocks of about 8 or 9 times. Other countries adopted slightly different ratios. Nonetheless, seventeenth century blocks were about 1½ times as large as their later counterparts because the ropes themselves were that much larger.

The early blocks were made entirely of wood, usually hard, oily *lignum vitae*, which fact dictated larger size. About 1750, Walter Taylor, an English block maker, introduced iron axles and sheaves making smaller blocks feasible and this inspired the new "six times diameter" formula, which was found to be about the smallest sheave of practical use. Diminished sheave size yielded heavier work and sailors came to view ships with small blocks as "work houses." Hence Americans never lost their preference for larger blocks.

After 1850, iron blocks with internal iron strops came into use. Since these strops, unlike hemp strops, were rigid, the blocks had to be made with hooks facing in various planes. Beckets, shackles and other attachments were attached the same way or fitted with ball joints.

EXPLODED VIEW OF BLOCK

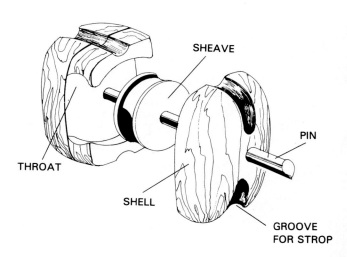

SHEAVE
PIN
THROAT
SHELL
GROOVE FOR STROP

Lighter, specially designed sheet blocks for the jibs were easier to handle than the heavier blocks needed elsewhere.

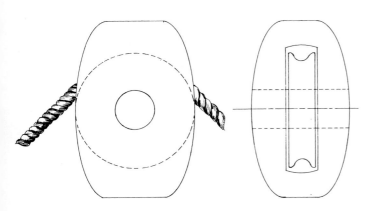

ENGLISH 1700
Sheave 9X rope dia.

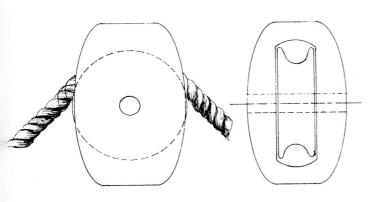

ENGLISH 1800
Sheave 6X rope dia.

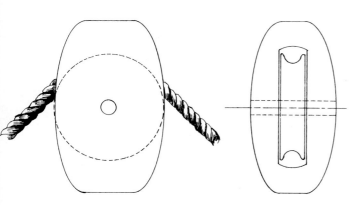

AMERICAN 1800
Sheave 8X rope dia.

Heavy double block makes up the running end of the *Star's* burton tackle. The burton tackle, with its standing end at the foremast top, was used to fish the anchor. Here its big hook is shown tied off at the foot of the forestay.

Bumkins on the *Star's* quarters hold the leading blocks for the main braces. Similar bumkins farther forward hold the forebrace blocks.

BLOCK TYPES

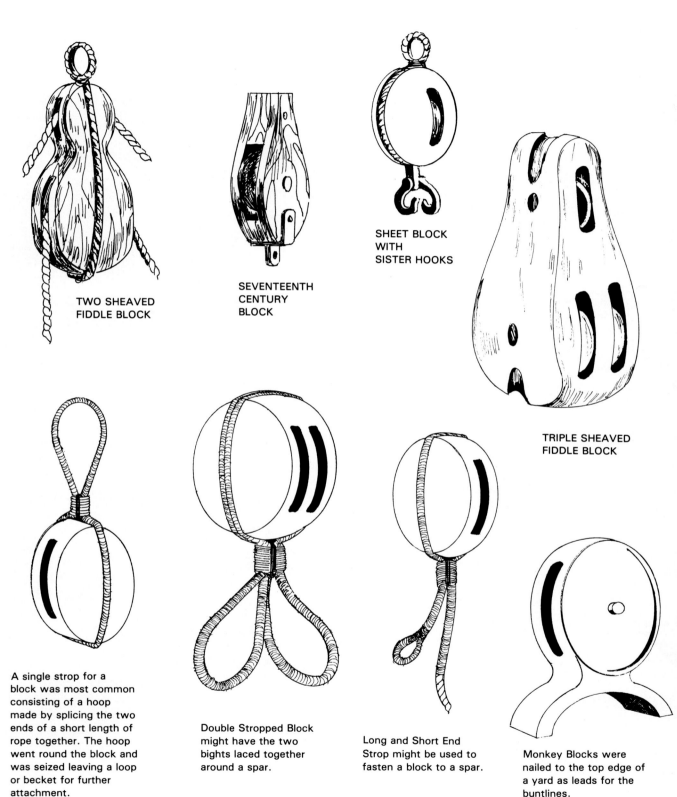

TWO SHEAVED FIDDLE BLOCK

SEVENTEENTH CENTURY BLOCK

SHEET BLOCK WITH SISTER HOOKS

TRIPLE SHEAVED FIDDLE BLOCK

A single strop for a block was most common consisting of a hoop made by splicing the two ends of a short length of rope together. The hoop went round the block and was seized leaving a loop or becket for further attachment.

Double Stropped Block might have the two bights laced together around a spar.

Long and Short End Strop might be used to fasten a block to a spar.

Monkey Blocks were nailed to the top edge of a yard as leads for the buntlines.

TACKLE

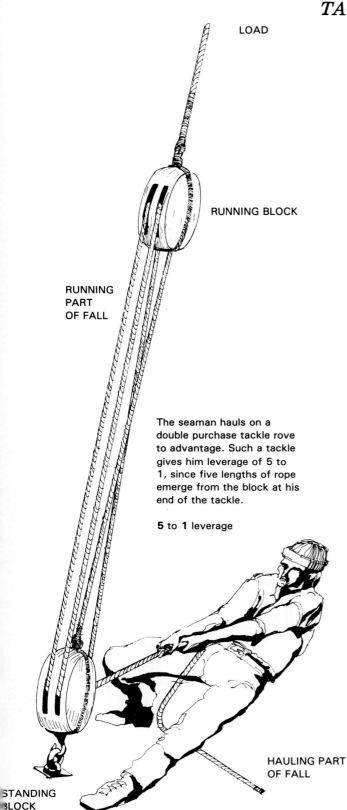

LOAD

RUNNING BLOCK

RUNNING PART OF FALL

The seaman hauls on a double purchase tackle rove to advantage. Such a tackle gives him leverage of 5 to 1, since five lengths of rope emerge from the block at his end of the tackle.

5 to 1 leverage

HAULING PART OF FALL

STANDING BLOCK

Sailors pronounced the word "taykle"; landlubbers "tackle." A tackle consists of a rope rove back and forth through a pair of blocks each of which may have one or more sheaves. The purpose is to gain mechanical advantage or purchase with a line. To increase purchase is to decrease the amount of effort required to move a load.

A tackle is similar, in principle, to a lever. A lever works by having a long "effort arm" moved by a small force balanced against a heavy load on the end of a short "load arm." Thus, a small child on the long end of a teeter-totter can lift a heavy adult on the short end.

The fall of a tackle is equivalent to the length of the effort arm of a lever. The amount of mechanical advantage gained with a tackle depends on the number of rope ends that begin and emerge from the standing block. A gun tackle, for instance, consists of two single blocks where two rope ends emerge from either side of the block. So one can lift twice as much weight with the same effort with a gun tackle as he can without it.

A luff tackle has three rope ends emerging from the standing block. The mechanical advantage is increased by a factor of three. The mechanical advantage of a "three" by "four" tackle is eight times that of a straight haul since eight rope ends (four each side) emerge from the four sheaved standing block.

The *fall* of a tackle is all the rope that is rove through the sheaves. It has two parts. The part that runs back and forth between the sheaves is called the *running part*. The part emerging from the last sheave and on its way to the hands of the hauler is called the *hauling part*.

The hauling part of a tackle may emerge from either the standing block or the running block, and the fall may originate on either of the two. If the fall originates on the running block and the hauling end also comes from it, both ends count in computing the mechanical advantage of the system.

Therefore, a tackle made up a given pair of blocks, may be either *rove to advantage* or *rove to disadvantage* depending on how many rope ends are made to come from the standing block.

A ship may have a large variety of tackles in her rigging; some rove to advantage, some not, depending on whether the hauling end is convenient. Warships, because they had plenty of money and a need for speed, had a special standing tackle for almost every hauling job aboard. The frugal merchantmen, however, traded urgency for money. Often their practice was to equip their ships with a minimum number of portable tackles which could be shifted about as need required. Variously, these tackles were called *handy billies* or *watch tackles*.

Most of the hauling jobs on a sailing ship were handled with tackles made up of one or two sheaved blocks. Treble or four-fold blocks normally were reserved for only a few very heavy hoists such as the main or fore jeers, or the main or fore topsail halliards. Catheads and boat davits might have three sheaves.

The treble or quadruple block tackles, while powerful, were also slow, and except where the load was immense and time of little object, these tackles were impractical.

After 1850, though, when several thousand ton sailing ships were being manned with smaller crews more of the big tackles were used.

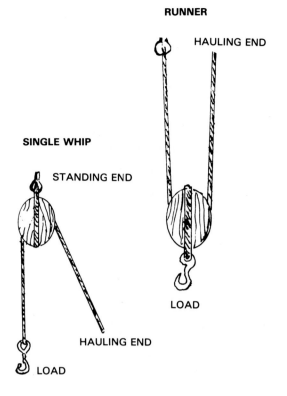

RUNNER

HAULING END

SINGLE WHIP

STANDING END

HAULING END

LOAD

LOAD

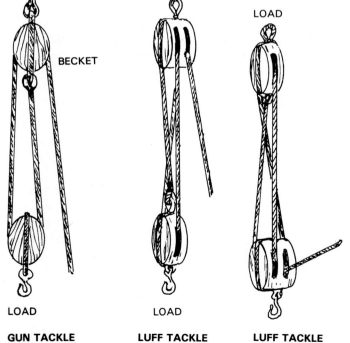

BECKET

LOAD

LOAD

LOAD

LOAD

LOAD

GUN TACKLE

LUFF TACKLE

LUFF TACKLE ROVE TO ADVANTAGE

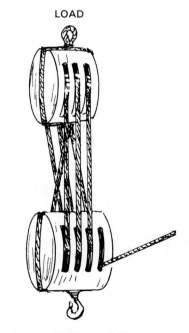

WINDING TACKLE

THREE BY FOUR TACKLE ROVE TO ADVANTAGE

RIGGING HARDWARE

Rigging attached to the hull, spars and sails of a ship with a variety of hardware.

On deck, *ring bolts, pad eyes, bitts, bollards,* and *cleats* would be found in great abundance. *Kevels, cleats, fairleads, built-in sheaves, knights* and *pinrails* lined the inboard side of the bulwarks, while *ring bolts, chesstrees, bumkins, channels* and *chain plates* protruded from the shipsides outboard. Masts and spars had their share of *rings, cleats, stops, sheaves* and *bee holes.* In addition to blocks and deadeyes, rigging was also rove through *bullseyes, deadblocks, euphroes* and *hearts.* Later in the nineteenth cen-

tury, *turnbuckles, shackles* and an assortment of new bits of iron showed up to accommodate wire rope and chain rigging.

The general term "iron" gradually came to be used to designate many parts of hardware such as *cap irons, cranse iron, yard iron* and *stunsail boom iron.* The *parrels* and *trusses* which attached the yards to the masts were often called simply the yard's "irons" instead of the more accurate term. The iron bands equipped with rings which went around yards and masts had this designation also.

The fore fiferail of the *Star of India* presents an array of rigging hardware in use. Many lines draped from the pinrail, while angling down from the left can be seen the mainstay and the main preventer stay. A spider ring goes round the mast where the paint changes color.

A fairlead for a jib sheet.

Sister hooks in a pad eye.

Sheaves in the main fife rail take the leads of upper sail halliards.

Iron stropped bullseye is used to set up each part of the lower end of the Star's divided forestay.

Bee holes in the Star's main top guide upper sail rigging down to the deck.

Shackles link the sheet and clew garnet blocks to the mainsail's clews.

RIGGING HARDWARE

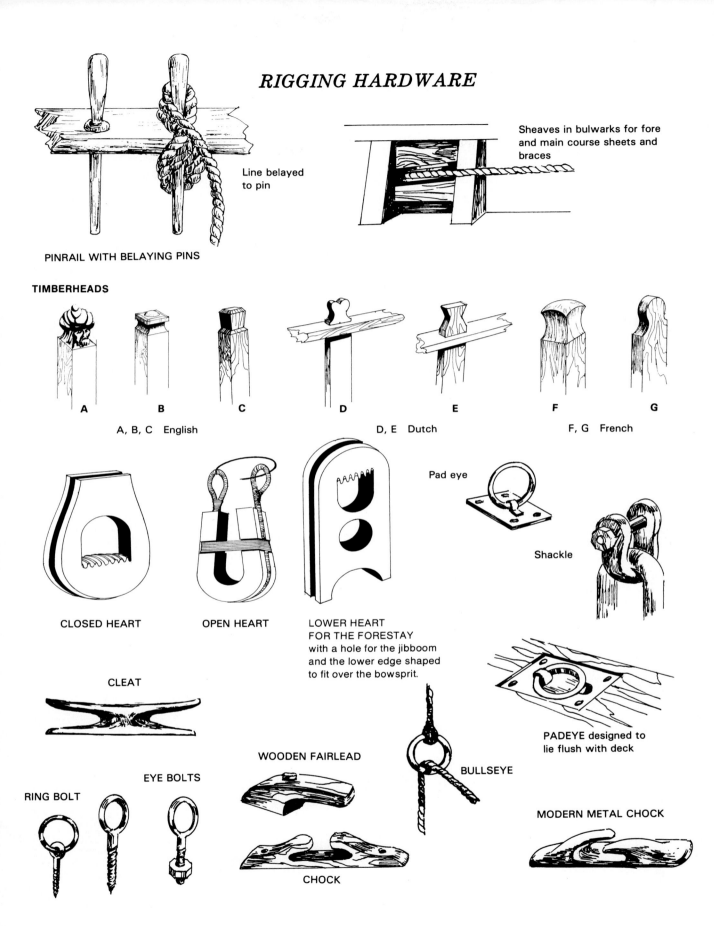

Line belayed to pin

PINRAIL WITH BELAYING PINS

Sheaves in bulwarks for fore and main course sheets and braces

TIMBERHEADS

A   B   C   D   E   F   G

A, B, C   English   D, E   Dutch   F, G   French

CLOSED HEART   OPEN HEART

LOWER HEART
FOR THE FORESTAY
with a hole for the jibboom
and the lower edge shaped
to fit over the bowsprit.

Pad eye

Shackle

CLEAT

PADEYE designed to lie flush with deck

WOODEN FAIRLEAD

BULLSEYE

RING BOLT   EYE BOLTS

CHOCK

MODERN METAL CHOCK

Chapter Ten
Standing Rigging

STANDING RIGGING

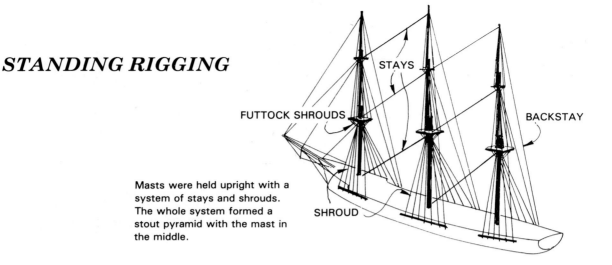

Masts were held upright with a system of stays and shrouds. The whole system formed a stout pyramid with the mast in the middle.

FUTTOCK SHROUDS

STAYS

BACKSTAY

SHROUD

The common elements in the rigging of ships of all ages depend on the fact that masts must be held upright, spars must be attached so they can be maneuvered, and sails fitted out so they can be raised, lowered, set or furled, and otherwise be manipulated to catch the wind just right. In principle, the techniques and nomenclature for doing all these things have not changed significantly in 500 years.

A ship's rigging breaks into two parts — the *standing rigging,* and the *running rigging.*

Standing rigging was that which held up the spars. This rigging was more or less permanently installed and was much heavier than the running rigging. Hemp standing rigging was preserved with a treatment of tar, while many lengths of the lines were wormed, parcelled, and served, as discussed above. By 1850, many elements of standing rigging were made from chain and wire cable.

Standing rigging consisted mainly of a system of shrouds and stays. The lower end of a stay was attached along the center line of the ship, forward of the mast it supported. The upper end was attached to the mast near the top.

Shrouds ran aft from the mast top down to the shipsides to the *channels* or "chain wales."

The whole setup formed a stout, three-sided pyramid, with the mast in the middle.

The higher masts were supported the same way, except that the shrouds led to the edge of the lower mast's top, and *futtock shrouds* under the top took on the job of the chain plates. The stays of the higher masts led forward along the center line of the ship, as did the lower stays, and tied off on a head spar, or at points around the cap of a more forward, lower mast. Upper masts often were fitted with *backstays* that came down to the shipside like shrouds, but farther aft.

SAILING SHIP RIGS

BRIG

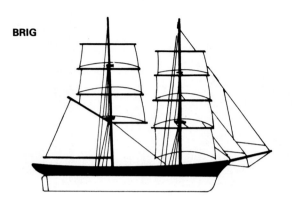

BRIGANTINE

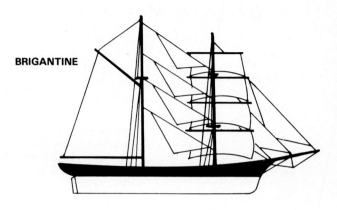

FULL RIGGED SHIP

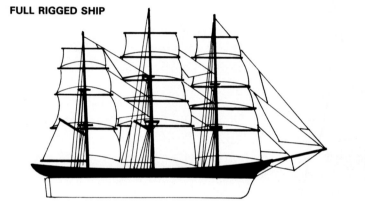

BARK

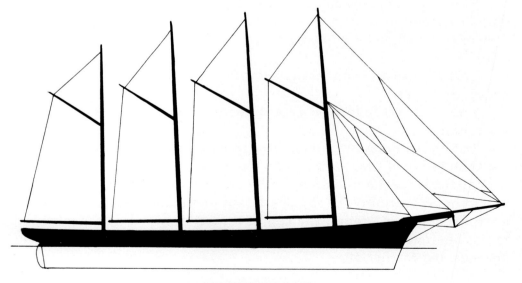

FOUR MASTED SCHOONER

RIGGING AT THE TOP
OF AN EIGHTEENTH CENTURY VESSEL

1 Topmast
2 Cap
3 Masthead
4 Top
5 Topmast shrouds
6 Upper deadeyes
7 Lower deadeyes
8 Laniards
9 Crow's foot
10 Euphroe
11 Main or fore stay
12 Preventer stay
13 Lower yard
14 Futtock shroud
15 Futtock stave
16 Lower shroud
17 Main or mizzen topmast stay
18 Main or mizzen topgallant stay
19 Lower yard lift
20 Jeers
21 Jeer block
22 Buntlines
23 Lower mast

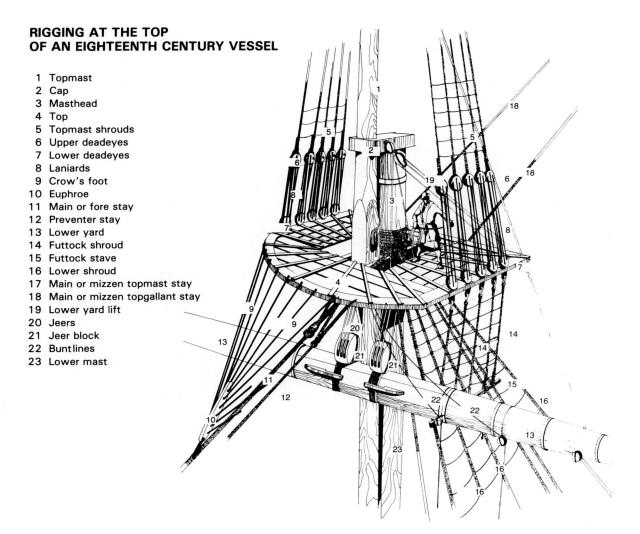

Rigging lines, particularly those made of hemp, stretched and shrunk with changes in the weather. It was necessary therefore to be able to adjust the tension on them. Tension on the shrouds was adjusted through a system of *deadeyes* and *laniards*. Deadeyes were oval blocks of hardwood with three holes drilled through them. A deadeye was fastened to the lower end of the shroud and another to the channel with an extension to the shipside called the chain plate. The two deadeyes were laced together with a laniard, a comparatively thin rope. Shroud tension was adjusted by slacking or tightening up the laniards.

To set up a shroud, purchase was applied to it above the deadeye while the laniard was rove and tied off. When the tackle was removed, the shroud and laniard stretched taut. A similar procedure followed with stays.

In the seventeenth century the techniques described above held for most of the shrouds and the lower stays. The upper stays, however, were set up with built-in tackle. For example, the main topmast stay led to a block on the head of the foremast, then down to a *fiddle block* which formed the running block of a four part tackle hooked into the deck.

The seventeenth century mizzen topmast stay illustrates another practice of the period that deviates from later principles. The stay

Deadeyes and lanyards were used to set up shrouds

divided in the middle and led to the mainmast shrouds. To spread the load over a length of the shrouds elaborate systems of *crow's feet* stretched on either side from a point near the middle of the stay.

The practice of tying off one stay on another in this fashion was applied to spritsail topmast shrouds, the main topgallant stays and other lines.

Another feature of seventeenth and eighteenth century standing rigging was the use of crow's feet leading fan-like from a high point on the stays up to the forward edge of the tops. The crow's feet here protected the lower edges of topsails from chafing against the tops.

In general, seventeenth century rigging was more complex than that of later eras, yet, in principle eighteenth and nineteenth century rigging was no different than that of the seventeenth. The distinctions were in the details. More deadeyes and hearts were applied to the upper

mast rigging, crow's feet became less elaborate, and the number of shrouds per mast decreased.

When a ship was being fitted out, the *mast tackles* were the first rigging to go over the masthead and worked to keep the mast aligned while the rest of the shrouds were setup. Thus, they were a kind of preliminary shroud.

Mast tackles were four to six part tackles variously rigged with whips or runners on their hauling ends with the standing blocks hooked to the channels.

In the seventeenth century, the main and foremast often had a pair of mast tackles on each side, and additional tackles on the mainstay. The latter were the garnet and winding (pronounced wynding) tackles. These were used for cargo handling and similar chores.

Yard tackles at the yardarms worked with the more inboard tackles in hefting gear or cargo over the sides. The yard tackles were frequently employed in the launching of boats.

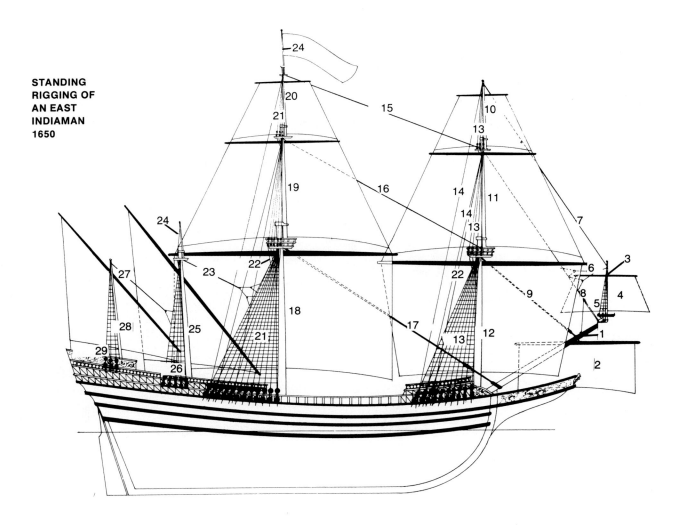

STANDING
RIGGING OF
AN EAST
INDIAMAN
1650

1 Bowsprit	11 Fore topsail and fore topmast	21 Main shrouds (named for their masts)
2 Spritsail	12 Fore course and foremast	22 Futtock shrouds
3 Sprit topmast	13 Fore shrouds (named for their masts)	23 Mizzen stay
4 Sprit topsail	14 Backstays (named for their masts)	24 Flagstaffs (named for their masts)
5 Sprit topmast shrouds	15 Main topgallant stay	25 Lateen mizzen sail and mast
6 Sprit topmast backstay	16 Main topmast stay	26 Mizzen shrouds
7 Fore topgallant stay	17 Main stay	27 Bonaventure mizzen stay
8 Fore topmast stay	18 Main course and mainmast	28 Bonaventure mizzen sail and mast
9 Forestay	19 Main topsail and topmast	29 Bonaventure mizzen shrouds
10 Fore topgallant sail and mast	20 Main topgallant sail and mast	

NUMBER OF SHROUDS

The number of shrouds per mast of a given size diminished through the centuries. The numbers given below are representative of the trend and are applicable to a mid-size ship. Larger or smaller ships might have one or two, more or less, than are shown. In general, upper masts carried about one-half as many shrouds as the mast just below it.

The number of mizzen shrouds remained fairly constant because the load on the mizzen increased at the same time that fewer shrouds were being used elsewhere.

MASTS	17th	18th	19th
Foremast	9	7	6
Main mast	10	8	7
Mizzen mast	5	5	5
Fore topmast	4	4	3
Main topmast	5	4	4
Mizzen topmast	3	3	3

**STANDING RIGGING OF
THE BRIG *SWIFT* - 1778**

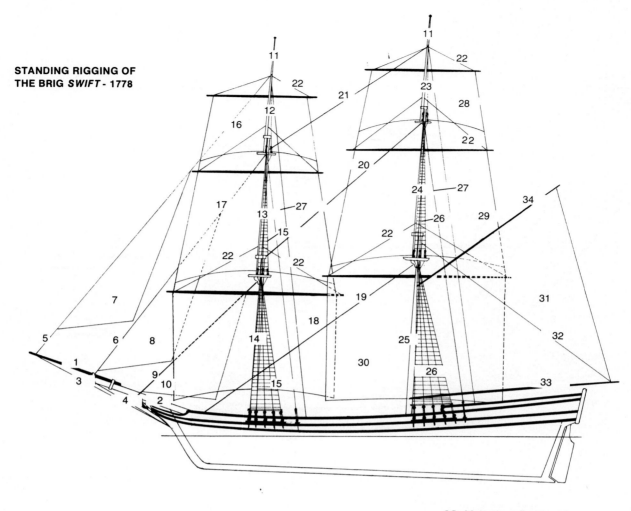

1 Jibboom	12 Fore topgallant mast	23 Main topgallant mast
2 Bowsprit	13 Fore topmast	24 Main topmast
3 Martingale	14 Foremast	25 Mainmast
4 Bobstay	15 Fore shrouds (named for their masts)	26 Main shrouds (named for their masts)
5 Fore topgallant stay	16 Fore topgallant sail	27 Backstays (named for their masts)
6 Fore topmast stay	17 Fore topsail	28 Main topgallant sail
7 Outer jib	18 Foresail	29 Main topsail
8 Inner jib	19 Main stay	30 Main course
9 Forestay	20 Main topmast stay	31 Main gaff sail
10 Fore staysail	21 Main topgallant stay	32 Topping lift
11 Flagstaff	22 Lift (named for their sails)	33 Main boom
		34 Main gaff

RATLINES

The *ratlines* formed ladders in the shrouds by which crewmen climbed aloft. For most of sailing ship history, the ratlines consisted of tarred rope rungs spaced about 15 inches apart. Each rung had eyes at both ends. Lashings bound it to the outermost shrouds, while clove hitches tied it to the intermediate ones. The lowest rung of the ladder, called the *sheer pole*, was wooden and mounted just above the deadeyes. The wooden sheer pole provided a stiff spreader for the shrouds, which otherwise might have sagged together in the fore and aft direction. Occasionally, wooden spreader rungs would be fitted higher up as well, particularly on high-masted ships.

214

STANDING RIGGING OF THE TEA CLIPPER *CUTTY SARK* - 1869

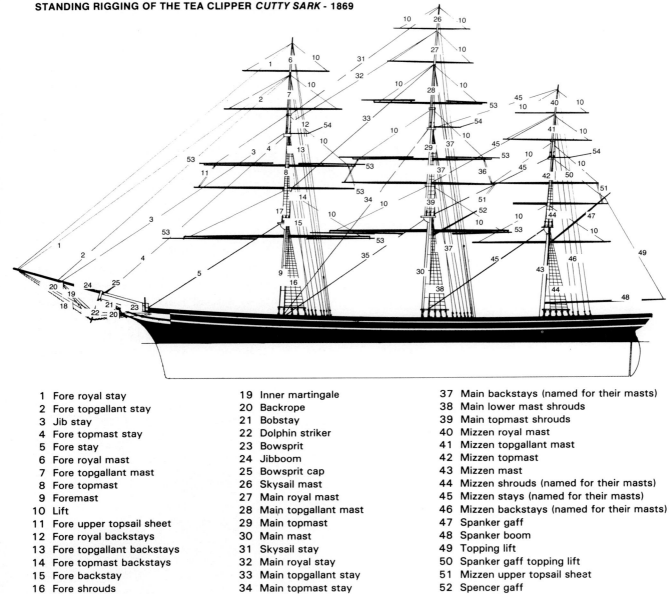

1 Fore royal stay	19 Inner martingale	37 Main backstays (named for their masts)
2 Fore topgallant stay	20 Backrope	38 Main lower mast shrouds
3 Jib stay	21 Bobstay	39 Main topmast shrouds
4 Fore topmast stay	22 Dolphin striker	40 Mizzen royal mast
5 Fore stay	23 Bowsprit	41 Mizzen topgallant mast
6 Fore royal mast	24 Jibboom	42 Mizzen topmast
7 Fore topgallant mast	25 Bowsprit cap	43 Mizzen mast
8 Fore topmast	26 Skysail mast	44 Mizzen shrouds (named for their masts)
9 Foremast	27 Main royal mast	45 Mizzen stays (named for their masts)
10 Lift	28 Main topgallant mast	46 Mizzen backstays (named for their masts)
11 Fore upper topsail sheet	29 Main topmast	47 Spanker gaff
12 Fore royal backstays	30 Main mast	48 Spanker boom
13 Fore topgallant backstays	31 Skysail stay	49 Topping lift
14 Fore topmast backstays	32 Main royal stay	50 Spanker gaff topping lift
15 Fore backstay	33 Main topgallant stay	51 Mizzen upper topsail sheet
16 Fore shrouds	34 Main topmast stay	52 Spencer gaff
17 Fore topmast shrouds	35 Main stay	53 Stunsail booms
18 Outer martingale	36 Main upper topsail sheet	54 Swifters (backstay spreaders)

It was not always necessary to rattle down all of a ship's shrouds. Usually, the older navy ships with their huge crews rattled everything, but the smaller crews of the later merchantmen required fewer ladderways.

Rope remained the standard ratline material throughout the days of sail because long lengths of hemp suffered extreme ratios of expansion and contraction, which would have cracked or distorted rigid materials. Wire shrouds, however, permitted wooden rung ratlines from top to bottom in some vessels, such as the *Star of India*.

FUTTOCK SHROUDS, CATHARPINS, BENTICK SHROUDS

The shrouds of topmasts and higher masts led to the top of the next lower mast which functioned for them as the channels on the hull functioned for the lower mast shrouds. The deadeye strops of the higher shrouds connected to futtock plates which went down through holes in the edge of the top, below which the plates hooked to another set of shrouds, called *futtock shrouds*. The futtock shrouds carried the thrust of the higher shrouds inboard and down several feet to a bar, the *futtock stave*, lashed to the lower shrouds. In this way the tension forces of all the higher masts were transmitted to the lower shrouds and ultimately down to the hull.

Since the futtock shrouds pulled the upper ends of the lower shrouds outward, the futtock staves on either side of the mast were bound together to counter the pull. The bindings were called *catharpins* (cat harpings).

Shrouds and stays expanded and contracted with changes in the weather. The circumstance obliged seamen to engage continuously in the task of keeping the rigging taut. Without almost daily attention to the laniards of a ship's standing rigging, the latter could become dangerously slack. Sometimes at sea slack rigging called for emergency measures and *swifters* were rigged from side to side crisscross between the shrouds to bowse them up tight long enough for the job to be done properly at the laniards. Swifters were rather like temporary catharpins.

Sometimes the futtock shrouds did not end on the staves, but continued diagonally past the mast and down to the opposite shipsides where they were setup with pairs of deadeyes. Such extensions of the futtock shrouds were called *Bentick shrouds*. A second method for rigging *Bentick* shrouds had them leading to a thimble aft of the mast and then straight down to the deck. After 1850 iron rod futtock shrouds connected to the mast.

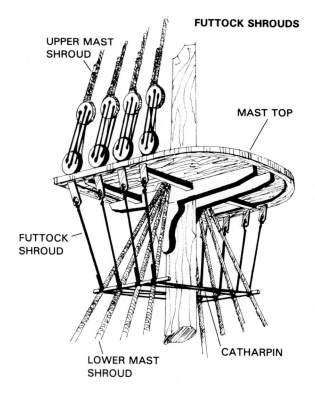

FUTTOCK SHROUDS

UPPER MAST SHROUD

MAST TOP

FUTTOCK SHROUD

LOWER MAST SHROUD

CATHARPIN

The Star's futtock shrouds lead to the mast

216

CATHARPINS

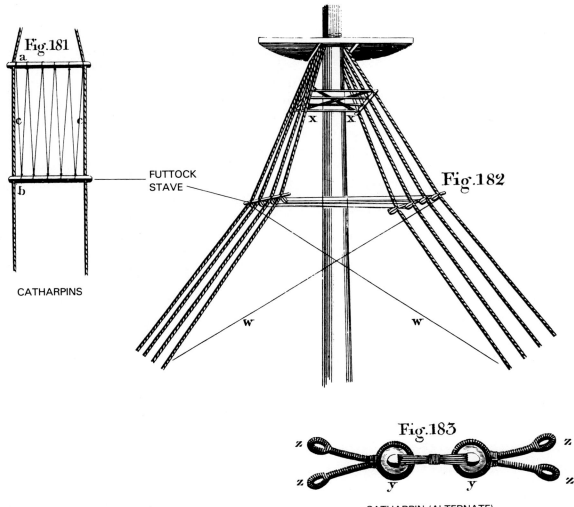

Fig. 181

FUTTOCK STAVE

CATHARPINS

Fig. 182

Fig. 183

CATHARPIN (ALTERNATE)

From Darcy Lever

The CATHARPINS are variously formed. Some go thus: They have an Eye spliced in each end (t), and are either wormed, parcelled and served, or else, wormed and leathered. Previously to these being fixed, a Spar is seized across the Shrouds on each side, Fig. 182: and Tail-blocks are made fast round the Spar, and each Shroud, that is to be catharpined in. A rope, called a Swifter (w), has its ends reeved through the middle Blocks on each side; then through the others, alternately, and the fall leads across the Deck: open end being through the foremost Block on one side, and the other through the aftermost one opposite. The Shrouds are then bowsed in: and the Catharpin legs (x), are seized to their respective Shrouds, and Futtock Stave. The foremost Shroud formerly, was never catharpined in, on account of its being so much abreast of the Mast, that the leg would chafe it; but it is now customary, in the Merchant Service, to have both the formost, and aftermost Shrouds catharpined. This is done by an additional leg on each side, (as may be seen in the Figure): one Eye is seized to the aftermost Shroud on one side, and the other to the foremost one opposite, above the other legs. These are called CROSS CATHARPINS: and are of great use in keeping the lee-rigging well in, when the Ship rolls.

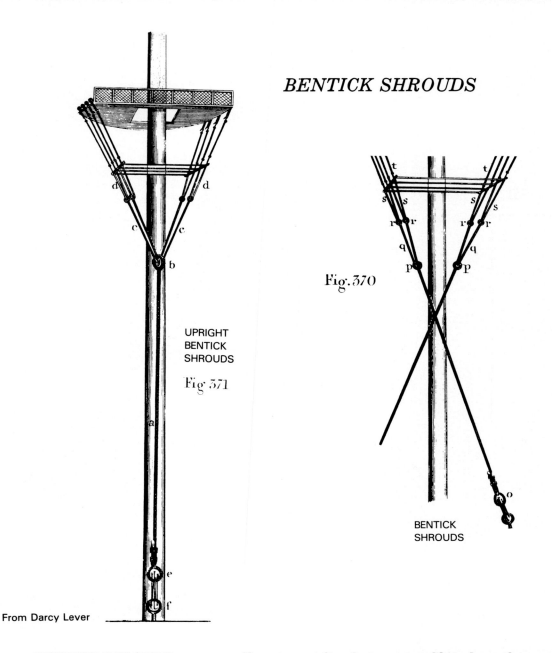

BENTICK SHROUDS

UPRIGHT
BENTICK
SHROUDS

Fig. 371

Fig. 370

BENTICK
SHROUDS

From Darcy Lever

BENTICK SHROUDS *are generally set up at Sea; but as some Ships have them constantly rigged, particularly when they lead like Fig. 371, it will be proper to describe them in this page.*

The Bentick Shrouds do not lead down on the Side they are meant to act upon; but they are taken across, the upper end being on the starboard, and the lower end on the larboard Side, and vice versa.

In the upper end of the Bentick Shroud, Fig. 370, a large Thimble (p). is spliced: through this, a Span (q), is reeved, which has also a Thimble spliced in each end (r): and through each of these Thimbles, another Span (2), is reeved, having a Thimble in each Leg. These Legs are seized to the Futtock Stave and lower Shroud, each one opposite to a Futtock Shroud (t).

In the other end of the BENTICK Shroud a Dead-eye (o), is turned, which is set up by a Laniard to another Dead-eye in the Channel. Another is led across in the same Manner, on the opposite Side.

An UPRIGHT BENTICK, Fig. 371, has only one Shroud or Pendent, and acts by its Legs on each Side, as before. The Shroud (a), has a large Thimble (b), spliced in as before, with two Spans (c), and Thimbles, leading on each Side. Two other Spans (d), with their Thimbles, are reeved through these, and seized to the Shrouds and Futtock Staves, as in the former Figure. The Dead-eye (e), in the lower end of the Shroud, is set up with a Laniard to another (f), which is strapped in an Iron Bolt in the Deck, abaft the lower Mast.

FOOTROPES, STIRRUPS AND HORSES

Each of a ship's yards except, perhaps, the high royal and skysail yards were rigged with *footropes* so that crewmen could man their whole lengths. The footropes were suspended on the after side of the yards running from the outboard extremity into a point a few feet beyond the mast on the opposite side of the yard. The sagging rope was further suspended at three or four intermediate points with *stirrups*, short lengths of line with eyes at their lower ends through which the footrope rove.

A second small footrope, called a *Flemish horse* or *horse*, often draped under the most extreme outboard end of the yardarm to provide extra footing in this important but dangerous locale.

The work for the men in the horses demanded an extra measure of seamanship since to them fell the task of "passing the earring" during sail bending or reefing operations. In passing the earring, the head of the sail was stretched as taut as possible along the length of the yard. The earring worked rather like a deadeye laniard between the clew of the sail and some turns of rope wrapped around the yardarm outboard of the yardarm cleats.

Footropes often appeared under the booms of fore and aft riggers, bowsprits and jib-booms, as well.

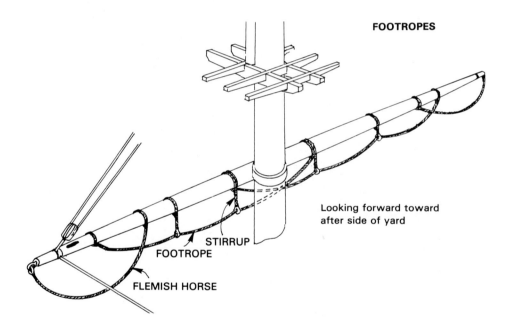

FOOTROPES

Looking forward toward
after side of yard

STIRRUP
FOOTROPE
FLEMISH HORSE

View of the *Star's* fore topgallant yard shows wire footropes, stirrups, and Flemish horses.

STAYS

The stays of a vessel were the heaviest of her many lines. Just how heavy may be appreciated from the fact that the diameter of the mainstay of a seventeenth century ship was about one-sixth the diameter of the mast it supported. Typically the mainmast of a 120 foot ship of this era had a diameter of three feet. Hence the diameter of the mainstay measured a hefty six inches.

Later as hemp cable improved in quality, the diameter of stays diminished, but by no means did the loads the stays supported become less.

The parting of a ship's mainstay was a disaster of the first order since its loss would collapse all the rigging aboard. In naval warfare it was a prime target. Seamen everywhere took special care that the mainstay was in perfect condition. The concern gave rise to the rigging of backup stays called *preventers*.

The stays were named for the masts they supported. Thus there were the *forestay, fore topmast stay, main topgallant stay* and so on.

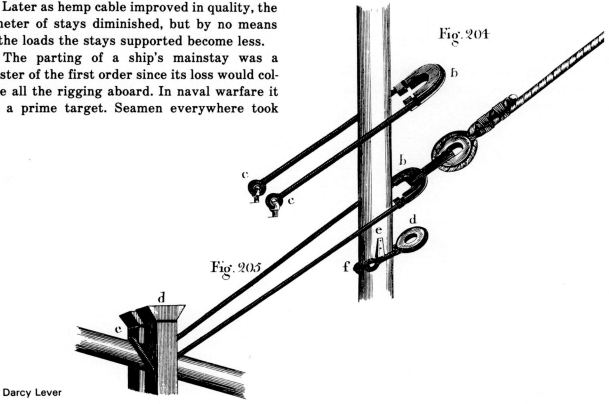

Fig. 204

Fig. 205

From Darcy Lever

In some Vessels, the Heart of the Main-stay Collar lays abaft the Foremast, Fig. 204, the Collar being made sufficiently long, for that purpose: and the Heart (b), is seized in the Bight. The Collar is served, and leathered, in the wake of the Mast: the ends (c), are spliced, or turned round Thimbles in Eye-bolts, one on each side of the Bows.

When the Collar goes abaft the Foremast, it is sometimes of one piece, middled: the Bight (c), Fig. 205, is laid over the Bowsprit without board, and the ends are reeved through holes bored for the purpose in the Knight-heads (d), then spliced, and the Heart (b), seized in as before: the Seizings are snaked in the Grooves of the Heart. This Collar acts as a preventer Gammoning to the Bowsprit. Sometimes it is laid over the Bowsprit within board, and led through holes in the Breast-Hook.

The Collar for the MAIN SPRING STAY has two Legs, with an Eye in each end. The Heart is seized in the Bight (d), laying abaft the Foremast (e): and a Seizing secures the two Eyes (f) together, before the Mast. It is set up with a Laniard to the Heart in the Stay as before, with Luff upon Luff.

BOWSPRIT STANDING RIGGING

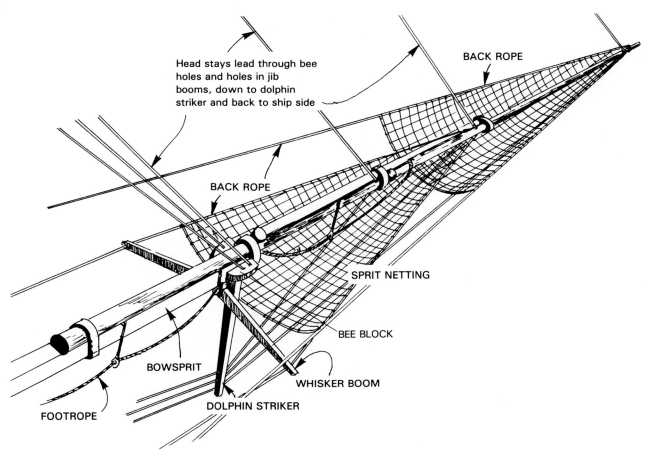

Head stays lead through bee holes and holes in jib booms, down to dolphin striker and back to ship side

BACK ROPE

BACK ROPE

SPRIT NETTING

BEE BLOCK

BOWSPRIT

WHISKER BOOM

FOOTROPE

DOLPHIN STRIKER

The bowsprit presented a set of problems to the rigger somewhat different from those of the masts, in that the spar was more horizontal. However, if one visualizes the bowsprit raised to a vertical position, the rigging will present a pyramid pattern quite similar to that of the masts. But, instead of three-sided, the pyramid is four-sided.

The "mainstay" of the bowsprit is the *bobstay*, which holds the spar down and forward, while up and after thrust is exerted by the forestays. Sprit shrouds and backropes hold the sprit steady in the lateral plane.

The jibboom is to the bowsprit as a topmast is to a lower mast. The *dolphin striker*, dropping as a short spar below the bowsprit cap, performs essentially the same task as the mast top, spreading the jibboom *martingales* as they haul down and aft.

Sprit shrouds, martingales, and backropes

on some ships were further spread by the *sprit yard* and *whisker booms*.

The setting of head sails required seamen to climb out to the end of the jibboom, hefting canvas as they went. To ease the hazard of the job, nettings were rigged between the backropes, which functioned as sail carriers.

The up and aft force on the bowsprit called for added reinforcements near its inboard end. A *gammoning* secured the sprit down to the beakhead just forward of the *knightheads*, which worked as the sprit's "partners" in the lateral direction.

The sprit gammoning on Seventeenth and Eighteenth Century vessels consisted of six or eight turns of heavy rope lashing. In the Nineteenth Century, rope lashings gave way to bolted iron straps, and the nomenclature switched from gammoning to *gammon iron*.

The bowsprits of the anchor hoys were retractable, so that the head rigging could be hauled inboard out of the way when the boat was hefting large anchors. Other ships also featured retractable head spars. The hoy also illustrates the practice of stepping the bowsprit off-center. The latter often occurred on seventeenth century ships where the heel end of the bowsprit passes to one side of the foremast.

Chapter Eleven
Running Rigging

RUNNING RIGGING

The ropes of a ship's rigging are called *lines*, which fall into three functional classes:

1. *Lines that hoist spars and other loads.* This group includes *top ropes*, *halliards*, *jeers,* and *mast* and *yard tackles. Ties, slings,* and *trusses* may also be classed in this group, though they support the spars rather than hoist them up.

2. *Lines that maneuver yards and sails while the ship is underway.* The *braces* hauled the yards fore and aft; the *lifts* tilted them up and down. The *clew line* hauled the lower outboard corner of a square sail up to the yard. The *sheet* pulled the same corner down and aft. The *tack* pulled the corner forward. A *bowline* hauled the windward edge of the sail forward.

3. *Lines that furled (rolled up and stored) sails. Buntlines* hauled up the lower edge (the foot) of a square sail. *Leech lines* hauled up the outer edges (the leeches). This group might also include the *reefing gear*, which was used to reduce a sail's working area in strong winds. Reefing tackle, attached to a *cringle* part way down the sail's leech hauled the cringle up to the end of the yard. The sail then was tied all along the yard on a line starting at that point with short reefing ropes run through the sail on the *reef band.*

Finally, some yards and sails were equipped with *downhauls, inhauls,* and *outhauls.* Their names declare their function.

Besides these standard lines, a given vessel would have dozens of supplementary lines designed to satisfy one or another of its peculiar requirements. Some of these lines would only be rigged if the ship were on a particular point of sail, or some other special circumstance. Their uses could vary from a need to prevent other rigging lines from fouling, to securing life and gear in battle or heavy weather.

SAILOR USES A HALLIARD TO HOIST A JIB

Some sails required multiple halliards.

THROAT HALLIARD

PEAK HALLIARD

TOPPING LIFT

SHEET

The *Franklin's* main and main topsail yards carried stunsail booms, rigged and ready to run out. Higher stunsail booms, as well as the yards themselves, were brought down when not in use. In heavy weather, the topgallant masts themselves might be brought down. Stunsails were rigged on the fore and main masts, though seldom on the mizzen.

1 Topmast
2 Cap
3 Top
4 Bunt block
5 Buntlines
6 Buntline monkey blocks
7 Leechline monkey block
8 Leechline
9 Lift
10 Reefing tackle
11 Footrope
12 Stirrup
13 Brace pendant
14 Brace
15 Clew garnet
16 Clew garnet block
17 Quarter block for topsail sheet
18 Topsail sheet block (sheet line not shown)
19 Lift block
20 Robands (rope bands)
21 Reef points
22 Jeers
23 Jeer ties
24 Slings
25 Sling cleat
26 Reef band
27 Cringle
28 Clew of sail
29 Clew block
30 Tack block
31 Sheet block

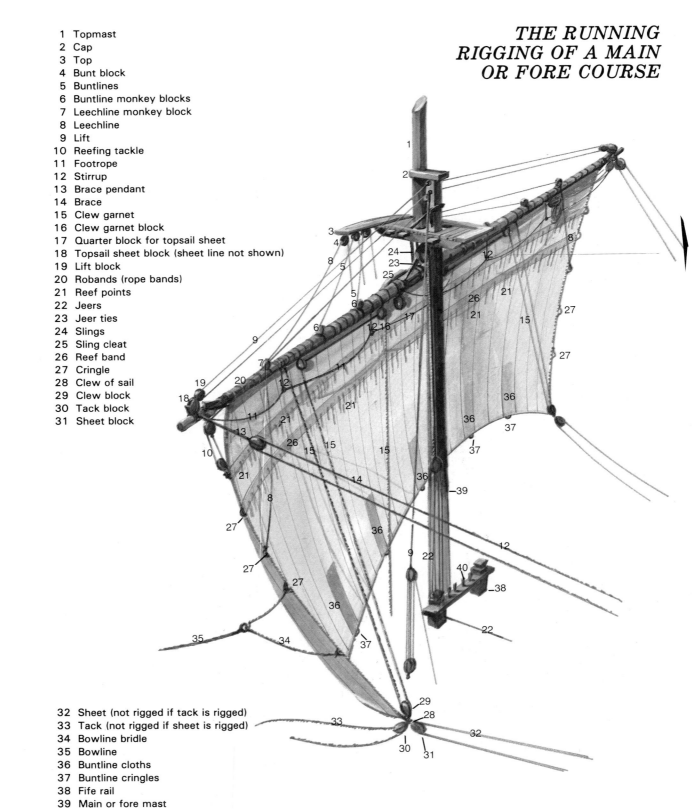

32 Sheet (not rigged if tack is rigged)
33 Tack (not rigged if sheet is rigged)
34 Bowline bridle
35 Bowline
36 Buntline cloths
37 Buntline cringles
38 Fife rail
39 Main or fore mast
40 Belaying pin

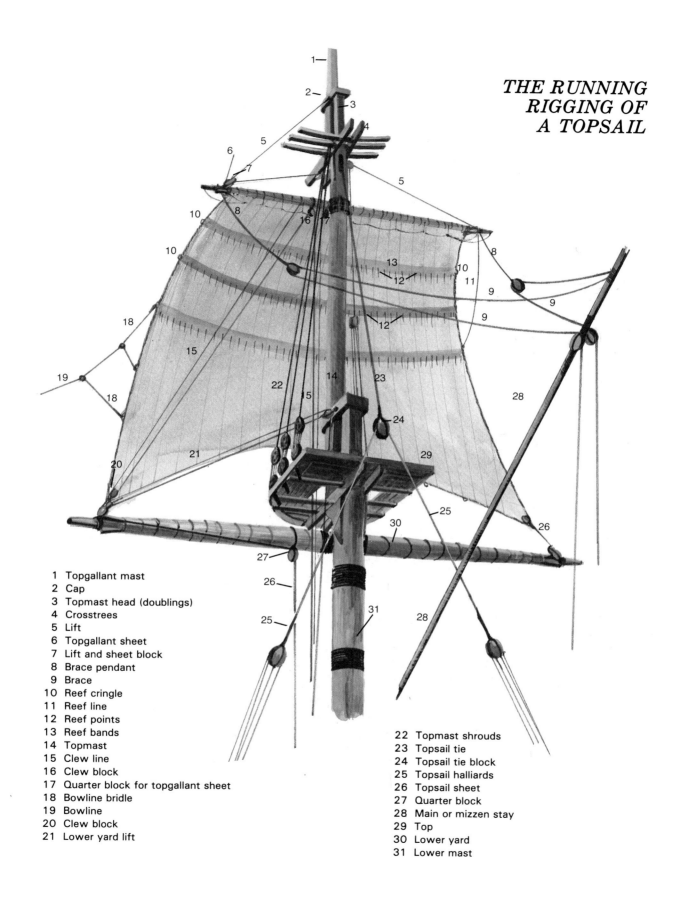

THE RUNNING RIGGING OF A TOPSAIL

1 Topgallant mast
2 Cap
3 Topmast head (doublings)
4 Crosstrees
5 Lift
6 Topgallant sheet
7 Lift and sheet block
8 Brace pendant
9 Brace
10 Reef cringle
11 Reef line
12 Reef points
13 Reef bands
14 Topmast
15 Clew line
16 Clew block
17 Quarter block for topgallant sheet
18 Bowline bridle
19 Bowline
20 Clew block
21 Lower yard lift

22 Topmast shrouds
23 Topsail tie
24 Topsail tie block
25 Topsail halliards
26 Topsail sheet
27 Quarter block
28 Main or mizzen stay
29 Top
30 Lower yard
31 Lower mast

THE RIGGING
OF BUNTLINES

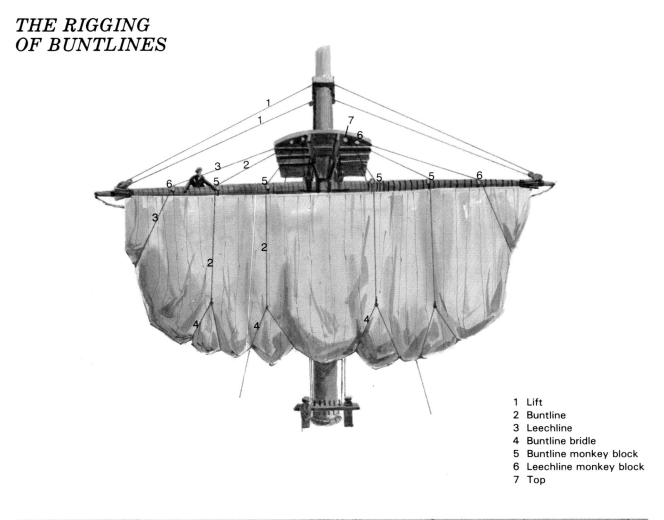

1 Lift
2 Buntline
3 Leechline
4 Buntline bridle
5 Buntline monkey block
6 Leechline monkey block
7 Top

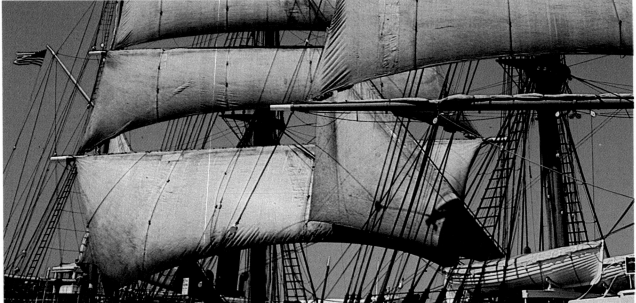

Buntlines stripe the *Star of India's* sails. Only the lower courses were equipped with leechlines because the narrow upper sails of the "split topsail" rigs did not require them.

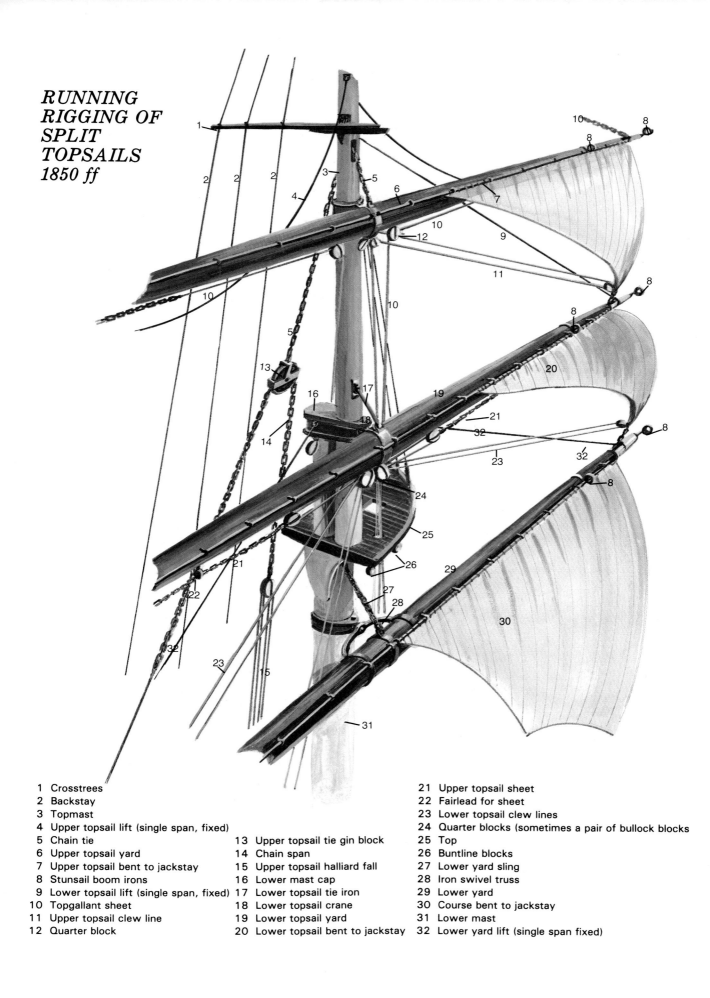

RUNNING
RIGGING OF
SPLIT
TOPSAILS
1850 ff

1 Crosstrees
2 Backstay
3 Topmast
4 Upper topsail lift (single span, fixed)
5 Chain tie
6 Upper topsail yard
7 Upper topsail bent to jackstay
8 Stunsail boom irons
9 Lower topsail lift (single span, fixed)
10 Topgallant sheet
11 Upper topsail clew line
12 Quarter block

13 Upper topsail tie gin block
14 Chain span
15 Upper topsail halliard fall
16 Lower mast cap
17 Lower topsail tie iron
18 Lower topsail crane
19 Lower topsail yard
20 Lower topsail bent to jackstay

21 Upper topsail sheet
22 Fairlead for sheet
23 Lower topsail clew lines
24 Quarter blocks (sometimes a pair of bullock blocks
25 Top
26 Buntline blocks
27 Lower yard sling
28 Iron swivel truss
29 Lower yard
30 Course bent to jackstay
31 Lower mast
32 Lower yard lift (single span fixed)

The *Star of India* puts to sea under full plain sail during the
1976 Bicentennial Celebrations, 112 years after
her launching in 1864.

Opposite: the *Star of India's* split topsails, typical of later Nineteenth Century ships, saved crewmen the heavy job of hoisting the huge full topsails of earler vessels. The rig also eliminated the need for reefing, since sail could be shortened by simply lowering the upper topsail.

Right: a view of the *Star's* masts from the starboard quarter.

Below left: a flagstaff extends from the end of the *Star's* spanker gaff. The line leading to the right from the mizzen truck is the main royal brace.

Below right: the mainsail and yard braced to the wind reveals the structure of the *Star's* main top, the lower yard crane in action, and the lower shroud wooden rung ratlines.

A. Looking forward toward the after side of the Star's foremast crosstrees shows many details of later nineteenth century rigging practice. Below the crosstrees, the upper topsail chain tie emerges from its sheave in the mast and shackles to the tie gin block with the halliard chain span rove through it. The "beehive" of heavy rigging above the trestletrees is comprised of the topmast shrouds. A unique feature is the use of fiddle blocks as quarter blocks under the topgallant yard.

B. The after side of the foremast cap shows the upper topsail parrel, wooden topmast ratlines, and the topsail halliard chain span.

C. The yardarms of the upper and lower topsail yards. The upper topsail downhaul leads from the upper yard down to the small block on top of the lower yard. The chain link is the upper topsail sheet. Under the lower yardarm is the lower topsail clew block with the chain sheet shackled to it. The latter is a variation from earlier rigging practice where the clew blocks were fitted inboard on the yard.

A.   B. C.

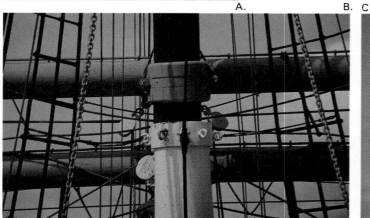

D. The forward side of the main top showing the main lower yard chain sling and the main stay doubled and seized around the mast.

E. The main topgallant yard swung on a fixed cranse iron at the topmast cap. Fiddle blocks serve as the quarter blocks for the royal sheets.

E

SPENCER GAFF SAIL

Later full-rigged ships featured "spanker-like" fore and aft sails on the mainmast called *spencer gaff sails.* This view of the *Cutty Sark's* spencer gaff shows the gooseneck attachment at the mast and the iron jackstay for the sail mounted on the afterside of the mast.

THE RUNNING RIGGING OF A SPANKER - 1800

One of several rig variations in use around 1800

1   Mizzen mast
2   Cap
3   Peak tie
4   Throat tie
5   Throat or nock halliard
6   Outer halliard
7   Middle halliard
8   Inner halliard
9   Spanker yard
10 Topping lift
11 Tack
12 Sheet rope
13 Horse or foot rope
14 Sheet
15 Traveller
16 Gooseneck

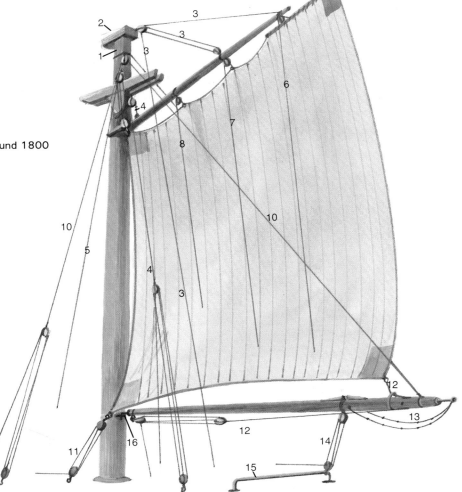

1 Fore topgallant stay
2 Lift
3 Shrouds
4 Sprit topsail yard
5 Brace pendant
6 Brace
7 Sheet pendant
8 Sheet
9 Halliard
10 Fore topmast stay
11 Forestay
12 Spritsail topmast backstay
13 Clew line
14 Spritsail lift
15 Spritsail yard
16 Bowsprit
17 Woolding

Between 1620 and 1700, ships carried a sprit topmast with a square sail on it. Securing the mast upright on the end of the bowsprit led to an awkward and complicated system of shrouds and stays set up with blocks and crow's feet to the fore or topmast stays. Braces, lifts, clews and the like led from the sail and spar aft and upward through leading blocks on the forestays then to the forecastle deck. The plan was to keep the lines clear of the bow gun line of fire.

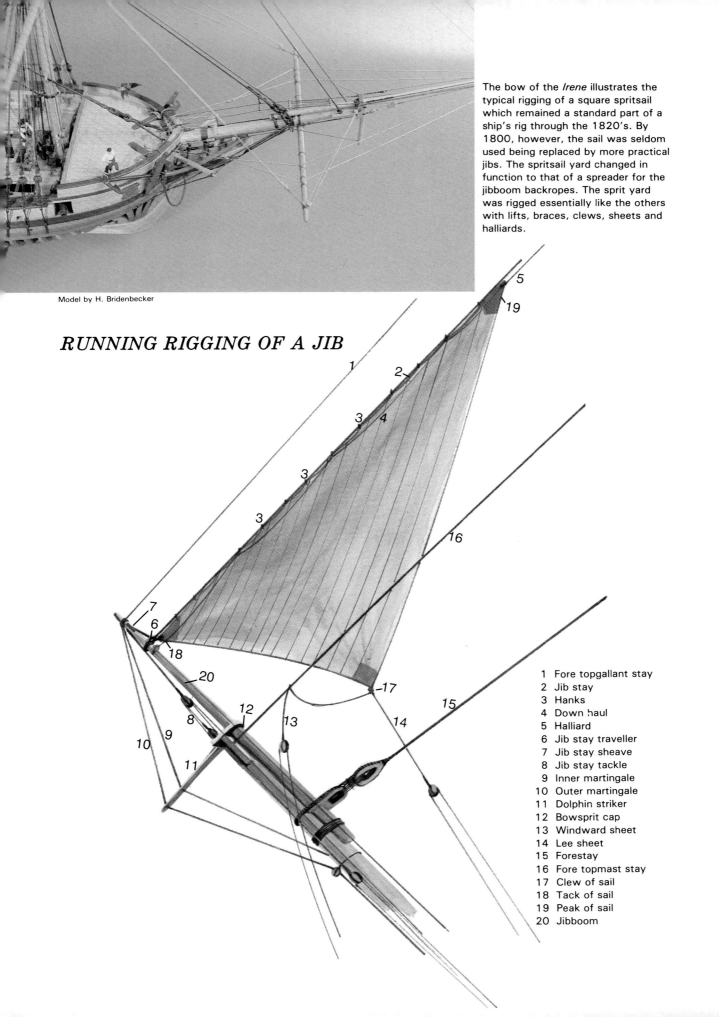

The bow of the *Irene* illustrates the typical rigging of a square spritsail which remained a standard part of a ship's rig through the 1820's. By 1800, however, the sail was seldom used being replaced by more practical jibs. The spritsail yard changed in function to that of a spreader for the jibboom backropes. The sprit yard was rigged essentially like the others with lifts, braces, clews, sheets and halliards.

Model by H. Bridenbecker

RUNNING RIGGING OF A JIB

1 Fore topgallant stay
2 Jib stay
3 Hanks
4 Down haul
5 Halliard
6 Jib stay traveller
7 Jib stay sheave
8 Jib stay tackle
9 Inner martingale
10 Outer martingale
11 Dolphin striker
12 Bowsprit cap
13 Windward sheet
14 Lee sheet
15 Forestay
16 Fore topmast stay
17 Clew of sail
18 Tack of sail
19 Peak of sail
20 Jibboom

The *Sovereign's* sprit topmast exhibits the elaborate rigging required to keep the comparatively flimsy spar supported. Here, euphroes and crow's feet were essential.

Model by R. van der Walker

Model by J. Dupray

Lateen mizzen sails were adapted from the Mediterranean lateen (Latin) rigs exemplified in the Barbary pirate chebecs.

THE RUNNING RIGGING OF A LATEEN MIZZEN SAIL - 1700

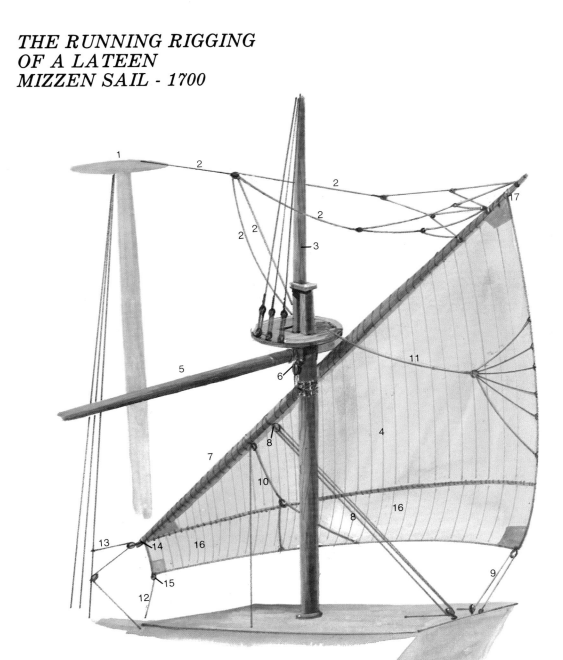

1 Main top
2 Mizzen lift
3 Mizzen topmast
4 Mizzen
5 Crossjack
6 Jeers
7 Mizzen yard
8 Sheet when sail is furled
9 Sheet when sail is set
10 Martnet and brail
11 Martnet (both sides of sail
12 Tack line
13 Bowline
14 Nock of sail
15 Tack of sail
16 Bonnet
17 Peak

THE RUNNING RIGGING OF STUNSAILS

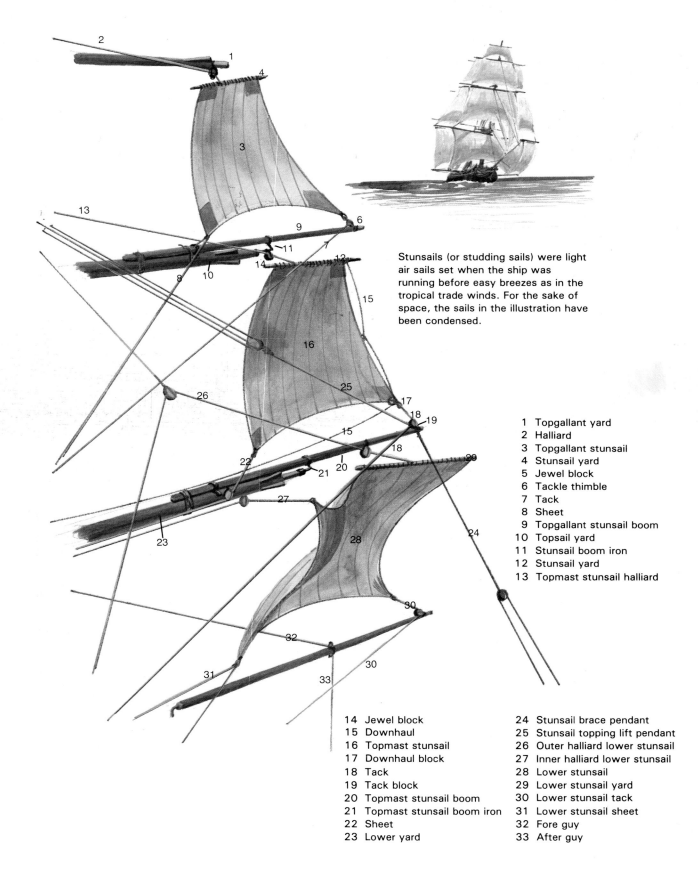

Stunsails (or studding sails) were light air sails set when the ship was running before easy breezes as in the tropical trade winds. For the sake of space, the sails in the illustration have been condensed.

1   Topgallant yard
2   Halliard
3   Topgallant stunsail
4   Stunsail yard
5   Jewel block
6   Tackle thimble
7   Tack
8   Sheet
9   Topgallant stunsail boom
10 Topsail yard
11 Stunsail boom iron
12 Stunsail yard
13 Topmast stunsail halliard

14 Jewel block
15 Downhaul
16 Topmast stunsail
17 Downhaul block
18 Tack
19 Tack block
20 Topmast stunsail boom
21 Topmast stunsail boom iron
22 Sheet
23 Lower yard

24 Stunsail brace pendant
25 Stunsail topping lift pendant
26 Outer halliard lower stunsail
27 Inner halliard lower stunsail
28 Lower stunsail
29 Lower stunsail yard
30 Lower stunsail tack
31 Lower stunsail sheet
32 Fore guy
33 After guy

TIES AND JEERS

Ties and jeers were two different methods of swaying up and supporting the heavy lower yards. *Jeers* were commonly used up to the latter half of the eighteenth century, after which *ties* came to be preferred.

Jeers consisted of a tackle system where a single or multi-sheaved block was fastened to the yard at mid-point, and other blocks or sheaves mounted at the mast hounds. The falls passed up and down before the mast, while one or two hauling ends led finally to the deck on the after side.

A *tie* consisted of a single, stout line fastened at the yard mid-point which passed up through a single sheave in the mast and down toward the deck abaft the mast. The tie ended in a multi-sheaved block which became the running block of the halliard tackles. The standing sheaves of the tackle were mounted in the stanchions of the fife rail or in extra heavy knights at the foot of the mast.

From Darcy Lever

An alternate form of jeers mounts blocks at mast cap, no block on yard.

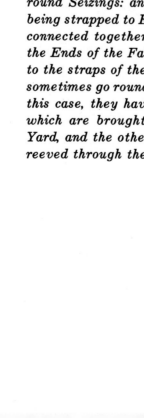

Fig. 227

For the JEAR TYES, Fig. 227, two Straps similar to the Sling Strap are sometimes put over the Yard, one on each side, within the Cleats, like (a). The Tyes are then led through the single Blocks (z), at the Masthead, (lashed in the same manner over the Cleats that the treble Blocks were): the Ends are bent to the Straps with a Sheet Bend, and seized to the standing Part (b), with a round Seizing. In the other End treble or double Blocks (c), are turned with a Throat, and round Seizings: and treble or four-fold ones (d), being strapped to Eye-bolts in the Deck, they are connected together by the Jear Falls as before: the Ends of the Falls are, in this case, made fast to the straps of the upper Blocks. The Jear Tyes sometimes go round the Yards, without straps. In this case, they have Eyes spliced in their Ends, which are brought up on the after side of the Yard, and the other Ends before it: the latter is reeved through the former (f).

PARRELS, TRUSSES AND SLINGS

From Darcy Lever

Are sometimes made thus: Fig 228. An Eye is spliced in one End: they are then wormed, parcelled, and served, the whole Length: a large Thimble (g), is seized in with a round Seizing, so as to make a long and short Leg: the Thimble hangs before the Mast: the long Leg goes round the Mast above the Rigging, and the End is reeved through the short one: it is then seized back to the standing Part (h). When the Slings go in this manner, either the Seizing at the Thimbles (g), or the Seizing (h), should be a Throat one. A Laniard (i), is then spliced into the Thimble (g), which is reeved alternately through it, and the Thimble (w), in the Strap on the Yard. When sufficient Turns are taken, the End-part is frapped round the whole, and stopped. The Jears or Tackles, are then eased off, and the Yard hangs by the Slings. It is kept in a horizontal Direction by the Lifts, which are hauled taught, and squared by the Braces...

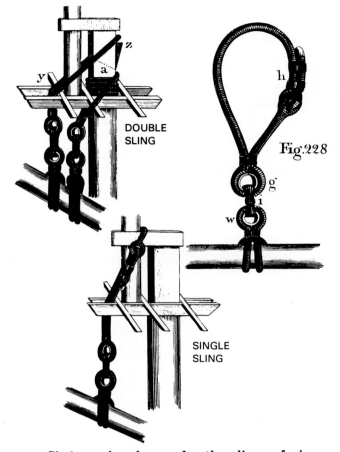

DOUBLE SLING

Fig. 228

SINGLE SLING

Parrels, trusses and slings held yards against the masts at their points of rotation.

Parrels allowed for yards to be raised and lowered and so were reserved for the topsail and higher yards, while *slings* applied to lower "fixed" yards. Early parrels consisted of a system of wooden ball-bearings strung together with spacer blocks. Later nineteenth century parrels were simply leather lined iron bands that fit loosely around the masts and called *tub parrels*. The parrels of the high, light, royal and skysail yards were seldom more than semicircular iron bands closing the half circles made by wooden yokes bolted to the after side of the spars.

Slings bore the weight of the lower yards along with the jeers or ties. They amounted to short lengths of heavy line running from the yard up through holes in the top to fastenings near the mast cap. The idea was to effect a more or less perpendicular suspension for the yard immediately forward of the lower mast.

Chain replaced rope for the slings of nineteenth century vessels. In this later period the sling would be shackled to the mast at about the level of the top, and led diagonally down to a similar fastening on the sling yard band. Specially devised cranes held the yard a foot or so forward of the mast at the point of rotation. These irons, comparable to universal joints, allowed the yard to swing fore and aft, and up and down.

Trusses performed the same mission as slings except that they amounted to comparatively light and adjustable lashings rigged to the lighter yards. A truss bound the lateen mizzen yard to its place on the mast because of the lateen yard's unique diagonal position, and the need to tilt it from side to side around the mast.

In the nineteenth century the term "truss" attached generally to chain rod and iron fittings rigged to help support spars of all varieties.

SUPPLEMENTARY LINES

Among the supplementary lines that might be employed aloft were *pasarees, slab lines, spilling lines, smiting lines, timenoggies, knave lines, fancy lines* and *gill guys*.

A *pasaree* ran from the outboard end of the lower stunsail boom down to the sheet clew of a main or fore course. Its purpose was to maximize the spread of the foot of the course when sailing before the wind in light airs.

Slab lines lifted the foot of a course so the helmsman could see ahead when steering in sensitive waters.

Spilling lines were rigged down and around sails to help spill the wind from them prior to furling. They worked as extra buntlines in strong winds.

A *smiting line* consisted of a chain of slip knots at the gaskets of a lateen mizzen sail or at bonnet lacings such that a single haul would quickly undo the fastenings. Thus one hears, "Smite the mizzen", as the command to set that sail.

When a square-rigger sailed close hauled, the windward edge of the courses were bowsed forward with *tacklines*. The fore tack often came aboard in the vicinity of the catheads and anchor, and a *timenoggy* would be rigged. The timenoggy led from the fore yardarm to the tack holding it up and clear of the anchor.

Timenoggies might also be rigged to sheets and other lines to keep them up and clear of gunports, channels, or other gear likely to be fouled.

Knave lines were light tackles rigged to the after side of old parrels to keep them from binding as the yard was heaved up.

Fancy lines occurred on fore and aft, boom-footed sails such as spankers. The outer ends of the booms of these sails were held up by the windward half of a pair of topping lifts. The lee half of the topping lifts were slacked off and held forward out of the way with a fancy line.

Gill guys were short lines with eyes in their ends seized to shrouds or stays which worked as fairleads. Sometimes gill guys were made with wooden shanks.

The Star's main staysail downhaul is kept under control with a gill guy

Chapter Twelve
Sails

SAILS

The crew of every ship included a sailmaker who, along with the carpenter and cook, enjoyed noncommissioned officer status. "Sails," as he was called, was continually at work creating and repairing his ship's store of usable canvas.

The word "canvas" derives from *cannabis sativa*, the Latin name for "hemp," from which canvas was originally woven. The term, however, came to apply to any heavy, treated cloth variously used for tents, awnings and, of course, sails.

The Egyptians, among others whose countries abound in flax, made linen canvas. But cotton, at least by Renaissance times, had become the most economical fiber for sailmaking. Cotton duck remained the standard shipboard canvas until the introduction of artificial fibers in our own century.

Sailcloth was woven in widths from about eighteen to thirty inches wide. The widths were widest in the Seventeenth Century, gradually becoming narrower in the years afterward. Sails consisted of parallel strips of this material sewn together along seams about two inches wide.

The stitching in the seams was of two sorts. The first, known as a *flat stitch*, joined the cloths of lighter sails, while the second, the *round stitch*, was used in the larger, heavier sails likely to need extra strength.

In the flat stitch, the cloths simply overlapped one another, and two rows of stitches, spaced about three to the inch, bound the two selvedge edges to the seam lines of the opposite cloth.

The round stitch involved the doubling back of the selvedge in both cloths, so that the stitch passed through four layers of the material. The two rows of stitches were spaced closer at about four to the inch.

The assembled cloths were then reinforced with additional bands of canvas called *tablings*. Especially stout tablings, penetrated with reinforced holes called *grommets*, were sewn into the heads of square sails to accept the robands, which bound it to the yard. Fore and aft sails featured similar tablings to accept hanks, or other means of attaching the sail to a mast, boom or stay. Other tablings occurred as *reef bands*, and at the foot of square sails, where the buntlines offered the threat of chafing. Extra tabling was built into the corners of sails to counter the stress of the attachments at these points.

TYPES OF SAILS

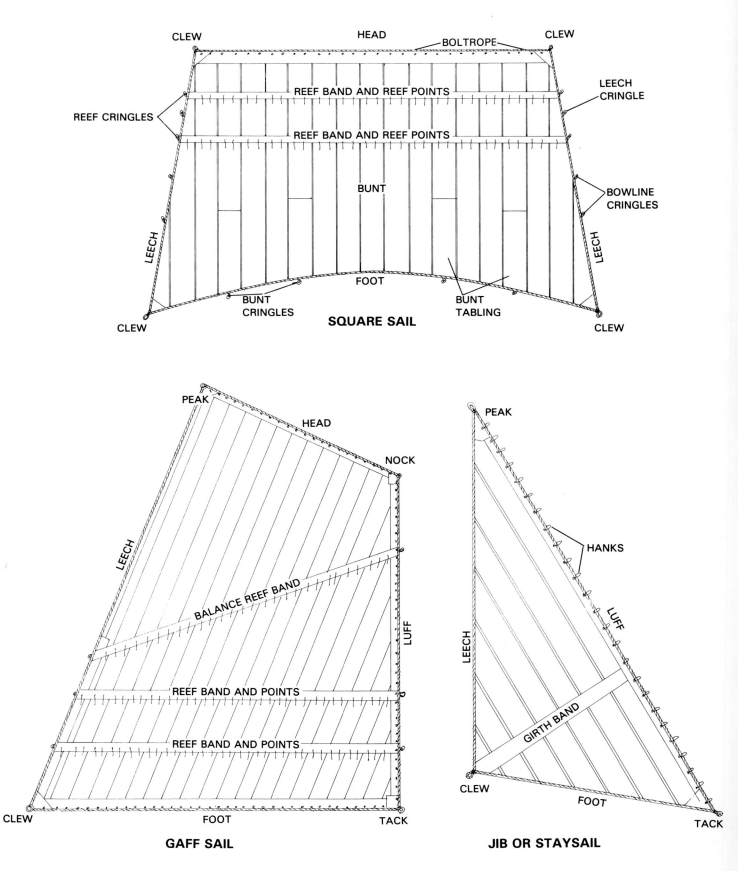

SQUARE SAIL

CLEW — HEAD — BOLTROPE — CLEW

REEF BAND AND REEF POINTS

LEECH CRINGLE

REEF CRINGLES

REEF BAND AND REEF POINTS

BOWLINE CRINGLES

BUNT

LEECH — LEECH

FOOT

BUNT CRINGLES — BUNT TABLING

CLEW — CLEW

GAFF SAIL

PEAK — HEAD — NOCK

LEECH

BALANCE REEF BAND

LUFF

REEF BAND AND POINTS

REEF BAND AND POINTS

CLEW — FOOT — TACK

JIB OR STAYSAIL

PEAK

HANKS

LUFF

LEECH

GIRTH BAND

CLEW — FOOT — TACK

246

Triangular staysails featured *girth bands* intended to reinforce the sail in line with the haul of the sheet.

The outer edges of a sail were finished with a *bolt rope*. The bolt rope protected the sail edge, provided the material for various cringles, and helped create the sail's aerodynamic shape. A square sail was found more efficient if it bellied like a parachute. To effect such a shape the bolt rope was made somewhat shorter than the edge of the cloths to which it was sewn. The shape of other kinds of sail were similarly adjusted.

The remarkably efficient sails of modern racing yachts employ similar principles. Certain racers, such as those which compete in the *America's Cup* races, use thin adjustable "bolt ropes" on the leech of their mainsails so that the sail can be precisely shaped for maximum lift with every subtle change in wind.

As we have said, sails included tablings called reef bands. Along these bands occurred short lengths of line called *reef points* which were, in effect, built-in robands for use when the sail was reefed, or shortened, in heavy winds. Each cloth of the sail was fitted with two reef points at each reef band.

Ships carried sail as the situation required. When the wind was light a ship would bloom with dozens of sails never seen in a stiff gale. Yet a ship's ability to pack on sail in strong winds was a key measure of her speed. The dazzling speeds of the clipper ships were due precisely to the huge spreads of sail they could set when other ships were forced to heave to under bare poles.

The captains of the American clippers, and before them, the captains of the Atlantic packet ships, gloried in their reputations as "drivers." That is, they drove their ships and crews to the point of hazard and exhaustion. The logs of these drivers vividly portray their mania for speed and the incredible workloads their crews endured in quest of record-breaking passages.

SAILMAKER'S STITCHES

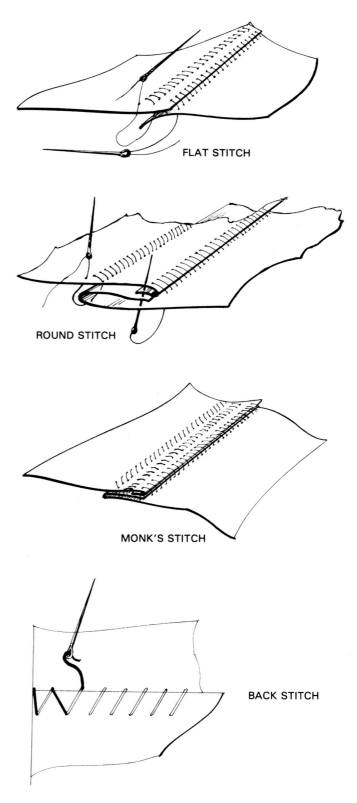

FLAT STITCH

ROUND STITCH

MONK'S STITCH

BACK STITCH

Greg Smith inspects the clew of an old staysail. Note the spacing of the bolt rope stitches.

248

BENDING SAILS

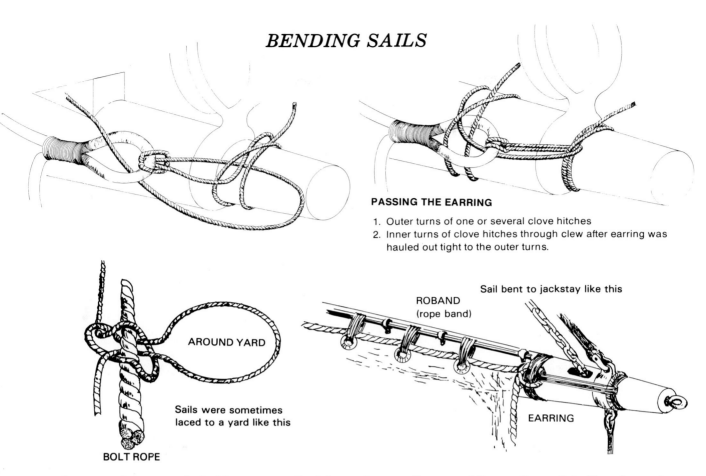

PASSING THE EARRING

1. Outer turns of one or several clove hitches
2. Inner turns of clove hitches through clew after earring was hauled out tight to the outer turns.

AROUND YARD

Sails were sometimes laced to a yard like this

BOLT ROPE

Sail bent to jackstay like this

ROBAND (rope band)

EARRING

Among the record holders was Josiah Cressy, who drove the clipper *Flying Cloud* from New York to San Francisco around Cape Horn in 89 days and 21 hours. His voyage ended April 20, 1854. He was in the vicinity of Cape Horn in July, the heart of the Antarctic winter. His log reads, *July 20 Lat. 54.25 Lon. 65.00...Winds cloudy, 3 hours 30 minutes set Lauboard Studding Sails, at 10 in studding sails, weather Rainy with sleet & Squally Mid(night) in topgallant sails, at 4 AM close reefed Topsails & furled Courses & snow, at 11 PM obliged to ware ship & haul off to Northward Cape St. Diego bearing by Estimate S 9 degrees W 16 miles, no observations.*
July 24 Lt. 55.43 Lon. 72.57...Gentle breezes light snow Squalls...all sail set.
July 27...Sent up Main topgallant & Royal Yards. set all possible sail.
July 30...Fresh breezes fine weather. Latter part unsteady all studding sails set.
July 31 Lat. 36.58 Lon. 95.46 SE...Fresh breezes fine weather 2 PM wind SE, at 6 squally, in lower

& topgallant studding sails at 7 in Royals, at 2 AM in Fore topmast studding sails, Latter part High sea running ship very wet, fore & aft, Distance Run this day by observation 374 miles, an average of 15 7/12 knots per hour, during the Squalls 18 knots of line was not sufficient to measure her rate of speed,...
August 1 Lat. 31.28 Lon. 96.25...Strong Gales & Squally at 6 PM in Topgallant sails, Double Reefed Fore & Mizen Topsails, bad sea Running at 4 AM made sail again Ends all Lauboard studding sails set...

Captain Cressy's men scrambled up and down the rigging several times a day in a relentless routine of setting, reefing and furling sails. The temperature, never mind Captain Cressy's "Fine Weather", was at least freezing, if not below zero.

The routine aboard the *Flying Cloud* was typical of all clippers, while life aboard some of them was twice as grueling.

The mainsail of H. Bridenbecker's model of a Tancook whaler is bent with spiral lacing on the boom, and sail hoops on the mast. Small portion of the foresail shows the bonnet lacing.

An older furling technique employed the use of brails as shown here on the *Yassi Ada* ship.

Chapter Thirteen
Fore and Aft Rigs

FORE AND AFT RIGS

Sails set along a line parallel with the keel of a vessel are classed as fore and aft sails to distinguish them from square sails set on yards athwartship. Staysails, jibs and spankers are among the fore and aft sails set on otherwise square-rigged ships.

A large class of vessels were exclusively fore and aft rigged. For the most part, these vessels were smaller than their square rigged cousins, finding their greatest usefulness in the navigation of inshore waterways, where frequent tacking and upwind sailing had to be managed.

The earliest form of fore and aft rig was the lateen rig which, as we have seen, originated in the Mediterranean in the first centuries of the Christian Era. The diagonal yards of lateen sails, however, displayed characteristics more akin to the square rig, than true fore and aft principles. It was not until 1400 or so when the Dutch popularized the *sprit rig*, that fore and aft sailing as we know it came into being. The sprit rig consisted of a loose footed main attached to the mast along its forward (luff) edge. Then a pole (the sprit) was rigged diagonally from a "snotter" at the base of the mast, upward to the peak of the sail aft. The arrangement was wonderfully simple and efficient.

The sprit sail had a drawback, however, in that the sprit itself was a long and cumbersome spar. The inconvenience led to the development of the gaff. The gaff did the same job as the sprit, except that the entire head of the sail, not just the peak clew, was laced to the spar, and both sail and spar were hoisted up the mast. The gaff pivoted on the mast in a pair of jaws.

Loose footed gaff sails never lost their place, but in a large number of cases, a boom was added to the foot so that the sail could be stretched on spars along three of its four sides. The gaff stretched the head; the boom, the foot; and the mast, the luff. Thus evolved the traditional "gaff-headed" rigs nigh universal in fishing fleets, among coastal vessels, yachts, and dozens of other classes of ships, large and small.

The lug rig developed as a variation of the fore and aft theme, along in the Seventeenth Century. The rig was used exclusively on small craft. The dipping lug consisted of a yard set similar to a lateen yard, but with a sail shaped like a gaff sail. Coming about was a matter of slacking off the lug halliards, and dipping the spar around the mast to the new lee side. The procedure was similar to that with a lateen rig.

The standard lug differed in that less of the lug was set forward of the mast, and so approximated the operating characteristics of a gaff.

The Gunter rig was a standing lug where the lug was set almost straight up, parallel with the mast.

The last refinement of fore and aft rigs came with the development of the Marconi, or Bermuda sails, typical of modern yachts and sailboats. The rig consists of triangular sails set on high masts. It originated in Bermuda about 1800, and rapidly gained favor among West Indian island-hoppers. Later, yachtsmen adopted the rig, and since have brought it to a penultimate level of aerodynamic efficiency.

FORE AND AFT RIGS

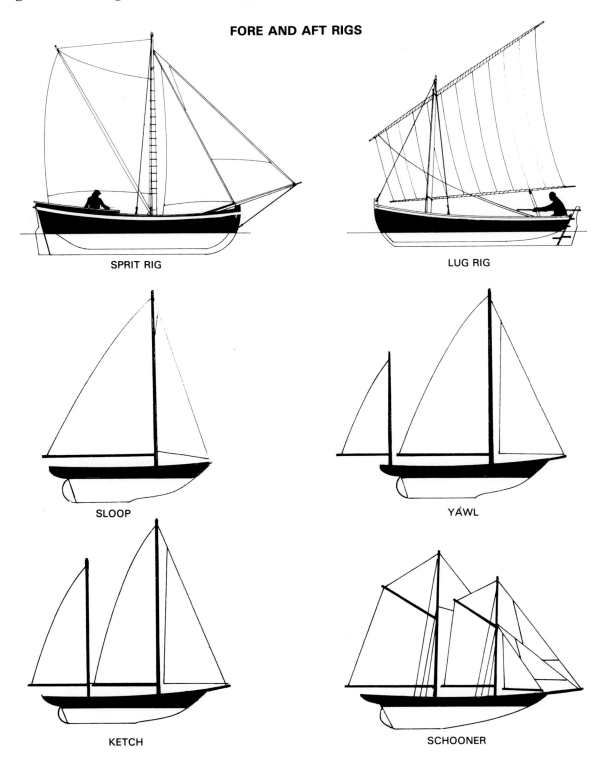

SPRIT RIG

LUG RIG

SLOOP

YAWL

KETCH

SCHOONER

H. Bridenbecker's model of the *Virginia*, 1640, the first ship built in the American Colonies, is sprit rigged. The sprit rig originated in the Netherlands as the first practical fore and aft rig designed for inland waterways and offshore sailing.

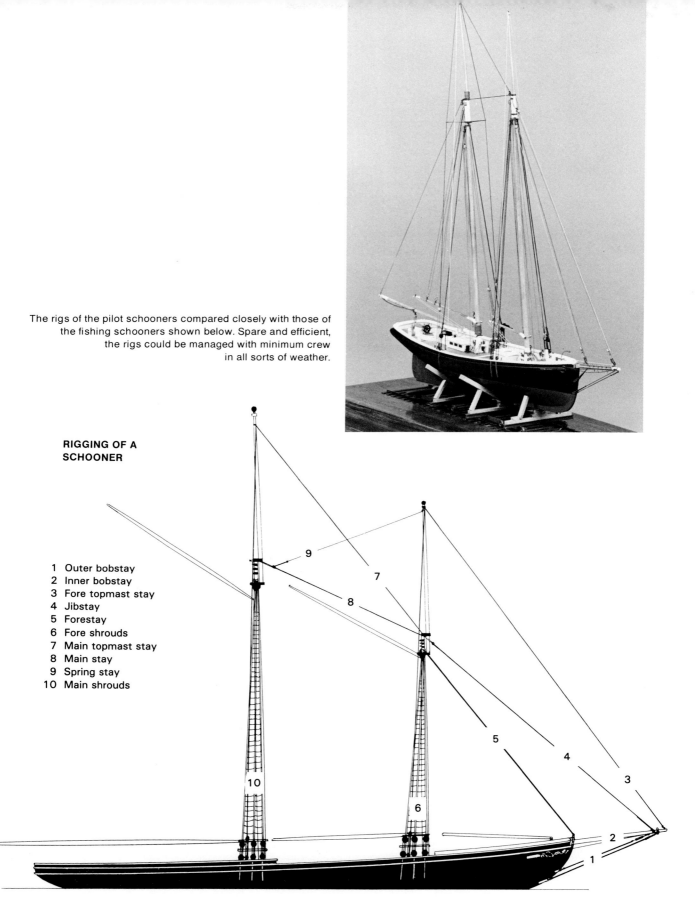

The rigs of the pilot schooners compared closely with those of the fishing schooners shown below. Spare and efficient, the rigs could be managed with minimum crew in all sorts of weather.

RIGGING OF A SCHOONER

1 Outer bobstay
2 Inner bobstay
3 Fore topmast stay
4 Jibstay
5 Forestay
6 Fore shrouds
7 Main topmast stay
8 Main stay
9 Spring stay
10 Main shrouds

The standing rigging of the fishing schooner was remarkably simple and efficient.

NAMES OF MASTS ON SHIPS WITH MORE THAN THREE MASTS

In the latter half of the nineteenth century some large 2000 or 3000 ton sailing ships were rigged with four, five, six, and in one case, seven masts. These masts from fore to aft were designated *fore, main, mizzen, jigger, driver, pusher,* and *spanker*.

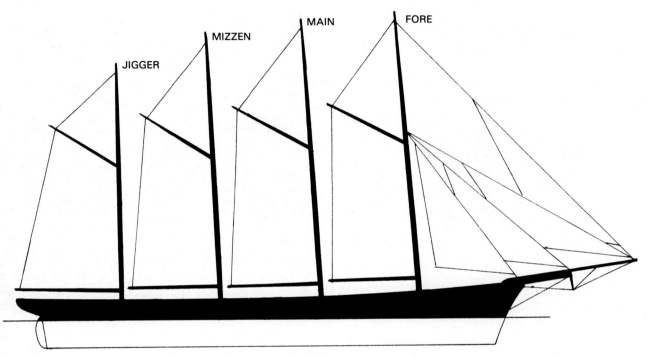

FOUR MASTED SCHOONER

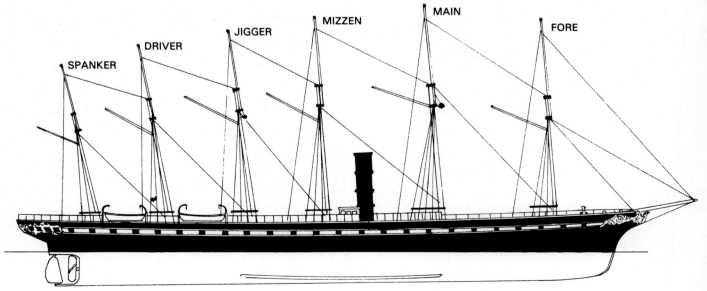

GREAT BRITAIN

Model by D. Dressel

FAIR AMERICAN - 1776   1/4″ = 1′0″

Among several ships of the period christened *Fair American* was this 14-gun brig, thought to be the ship captured by the British during the American Revolution. Sharp, and wide of beam, the hull lines of the vessel anticipate the design ideas to be incorporated later in the famed Baltimore clippers. The ship was 80′8″ in overall length, 24′0″ in beam, and 9′0″ in depth.

MALEK ADHEL - 1840   1/4″ = 1′0″

Model by H. Bridenbecker

William Webb of New York figured as one of the greatest of American ship designers and builders of his era. The *Malek Adhel* was one of the many ships from his yard built for the China trade. She was one of Webb's smaller efforts, measuring 80′0″ on deck, 20′0″ in beam, and 7′9″ depth of hold. Strongly rising floors and sharp entry and run recall the "fast ship" design ideas of the period between 1810 and 1845.

RACEHORSE - 1750 3/16" = 1'0"
The *Racehorse* was originally a 385 ton
French privateer christened *Marquis de
Vaudreuil. The British captured her during
the Seven Years Wars (1756-1763). Later,
in 1773, she and a consort, the Carcass,
sailed on an Arctic expedition in an
unsuccessful attempt to find a Northeast
passage from Europe to China over the
top of Russia. The Americans captured her
during the Revolution, after which the
British blew her apart during a 1777
engagement in Delaware Bay.*

Model by L. Whomsley

The *Star of India's* mizzen staysail
exemplifies the fore and aft rigging that
occurred on square riggers. The slack line
along the luff is the downhaul, supported
in the middle with a gill guy.

The rest of this color section is devoted to
models of fore and aft rigged vessels.

Model by R. Roos

PINKY SCHOONER - ca 1850   1/4″ = 1′0″

Among the earlier U.S. fore and aft riggers were the pinky schooners like this one. They were the common "poor man's" fishing boat of the New England coasts between 1800 and 1850. Their unique features were the strong sheer, broad buoyant bow, slender, double-ender stern and entry, and deep-dragging keel. For their time, the pinks were fast and weatherly sailers. They were the forerunners of the great New England fishing schooners built between 1860 and 1920.

Model by R. Van der Walker

NINETEENTH CENTURY CHEBEC (XEBEC) ca 1800   1/4″ = 1′1″
The chebec's lateen rig represents the earliest form of fore and aft sail arrangement. The rig demanded heavy labor because often two complete sets of sails and yards were carried — one set for each tack. Coming about entailed lowering the windward set and raising the leeward one. The Barbary Pirates, defeated by the U.S. Marines on "the shores of Tripoli," in 1806, terrorized the Mediterranean in chebecs.

Model by A. Robinson

PHANTOM - 1868 1/8″ = 1′0″

The harbors of the world employed specialized seamen, known as pilots, whose job it was to con the larger seagoing vessels in and out of local waters. They met incoming ships offshore in vessels like this New York pilot schooner. Captains reckoned the length of their passages from port to port from the time they dropped their pilots to the time they picked them up.

THE *HANNAH* TOPSAIL SCHOONER - 1775 1/4″ = 1′0″

Model by H. Bridenbecker

The *Hannah* enjoyed a mottled career as the first ship commissioned by the Continental Army in July, 1775.
Her mission was to capture gunpowder from British ships. What she actually accomplished was to recapture
an American vessel, for which no prize money was offered. The crew mutinied. A second crew managed to
get the ship chased ashore by a British sloop. Grounded and helpless, the *Hannah* was decommissioned
October 10, 1775, three months after being sworn in.

Model by H. Bridenbecker

TANCOOK WHALER — ca 1900   3/8″ = 1′0″

The Tancook Islanders, whose habitat lay off Nova Scotia, built an industry supplying whale boats to the New England whaling fleet. They also used their boat building skills to make fine, seaworthy fishing craft like this one for their own use. Their lightweight construction, and pink sterns made fast sailers, and especially good in following seas. This boat, built about 1900, was 40′0″ overall; 9′8″ beam, with a 4′2″ draft with her centerboard down.

AMERICAN FISHING SCHOONER - ca 1900

Among the most famous and romantic of fore and aft craft were the American New England fishing schooners that plied the North Atlantic between 1850 and 1925. Since the first ship in to port with a load of fish earned a premium price, these schooners were built as much for speed as for carrying capacity. The annual races to market gave rise in the 1920's and 30's to the legendary ''Fisherman Races'' of *Bluenose, Columbia, Gertrude Thebault, Elsie,* and others. These great vessels were upwards of 130 feet in length, though most of the work-a-day schooners, like the one in this painting were in the 60 to 100 foot range.

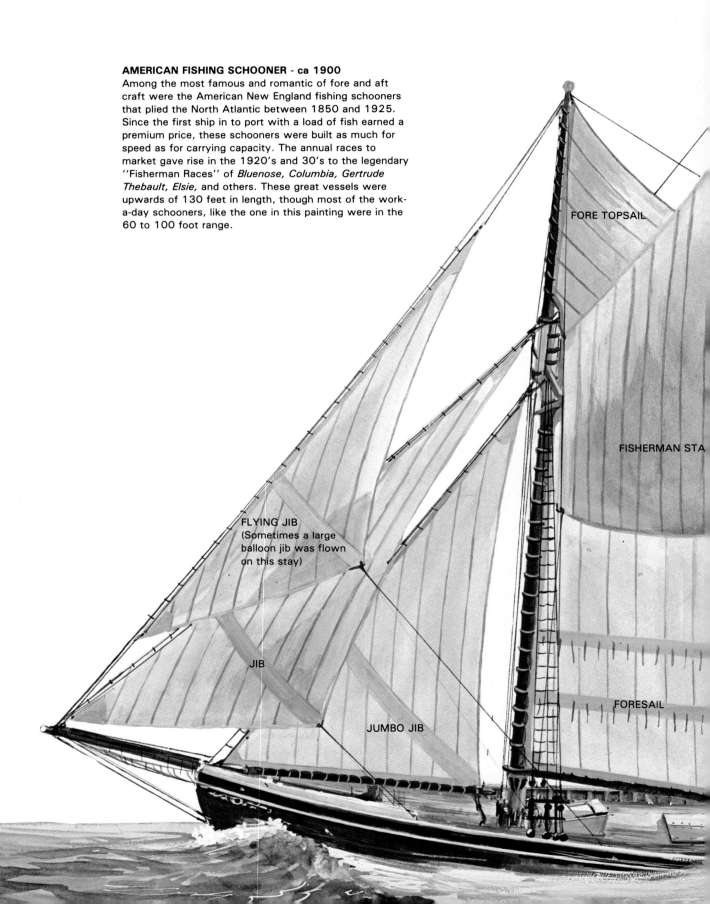

FORE TOPSAIL

FISHERMAN STA

FLYING JIB
(Sometimes a large balloon jib was flown on this stay)

JIB

JUMBO JIB

FORESAIL

MAIN TOPSAIL

MAINSAIL

FANCY LINE

MAIN TOPPING LIFT

267

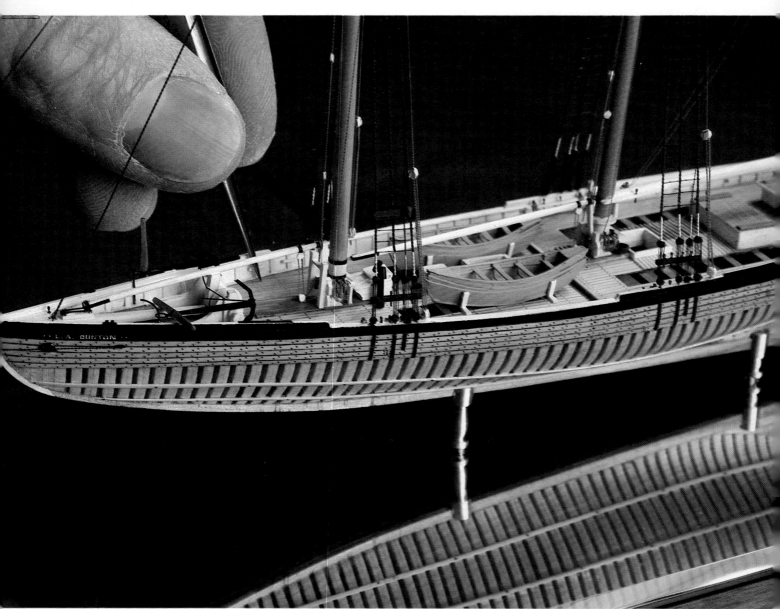

L. A. DUNTON - 1921 1/16″ - 1′-0″

Model by L. McCaffery

Length 123′-0″, beam 24′-11″, maximum draft 13′-6″

The *Dunton* exemplifies the final stages in the evolution of the American fishing schooner. She was designed by Thomas F. McManus, an architect who played a major role in the evolution in the years around 1900. The hull design of the *Dunton* was among the early solutions to the problems associated with auxiliary engines on sailing craft.

Model by D. Dressel

***ELIZABETH* ca 1815**   1:48
Length 90'0", beam 24'0", depth in hold 9'0"
Elizabeth is a model representative of the type of ship knowns as "Baltimore Clippers." She was rigged as a
topsail schooner, so called because, in addition to her regular fore and aft schooner sails, she also carried
square sails on her foremast. A subtle difference distinguishes the topsail schooner rig from that of the
brigantine — the latter carries no gaff foresail.

Model by H. Bridenbecker

***SPRAY* ca 1890**   3/8″ = 1′0″
Length 37′0″, beam 14′0″
Captain Joshua Slocum bought the sad and neglected hull of an old sloop from a friend in 1892, and rebuilt
her into the sturdy little ship shown here. In 1895, he set off in her by himself to circumnavigate the globe. He
completed his great voyage in 1898, after which he published his classic work *Sailing Alone Around the
World*, in 1900. Sir Joshua sailed again in *Spray*, in 1909, never to be heard from again.

Sir Joshua built and rigged *Spray* for his comfort and convenience. Sheets led aft to the cockpit; plenty of fresh water was carried in scuttlebutts near at hand; he cooked good food for himself in his miniature galley, and he could sleep without fear as his unique "self-steering" apparatus held his ship on course. Sir Joshua invented the precedents for seagoing enjoyment that are taken for granted on modern-day cruising yachts.

Spray carried a small boat cut down from a fishing dory, so Sir Joshua could visit beaches through waters too shallow for the yawl.

***EAGLE* - ca 1935**   1/4″ = 1′0″

Twentieth Century yachtsmen, extending the ideas of Slocum, McManus, and others, turned life at sea under sail into a luxurious pastime. Ocean sailboat racing, which had been steadily growing in popularity through the latter half of the Nineteenth Century, inspired a new tradition in marine architecture — that of yacht designers. Among the great names in yacht design were Olin James Stephens of the firm of Sparkman and Stephens, who designed the 50 foot *Eagle*, shown here. Also dear in the memory of yachtsmen are Nathaniel Herreschoff and John G. Alden. The rigs of most modern yachts are of the gaffless "Bermuda," or "Marconi," types, where tall, triangular sails replaced the four-sided gaff sails of earlier periods.

Model by A. Weiss

Chapter Fourteen
Ship Modeler's Art

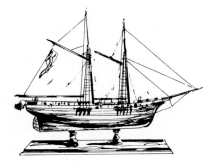

THE
SHIP MODELER'S
ART

The artists who engage in ship modeling employ the same variety of techniques as artists in other areas. Tools, materials, method, and approach differ with the individual. Yet, all share some common ground. This section deals largely with the latter, though we have presented a few of the "tricks" individual modelers have used in some of the more mysterious corners of the craft.

MODEL PLANS

Since ship models require thousands of hours of work, those who undertake to build them want the finished product to be worth the effort. Hence, they go to great lengths to be sure their plans are as accurate as possible.

Howard Chapelle, the distinguished maritime historian at the Smithsonian Institution, once chastised that group of ship modelers who insist on building "reconstructions" of vessels about which little more is known than their overall dimensions. Says he,

"In view of the huge quantity of plan material available it does not seem to me that there is little excuse other than obstinancy for 'reconstructed' models.

". . . If you are going to spend a lot of time and effort on a model, at least be certain your plans are authentic and that the portions reconstructed are known to you and are understood. One ought to remember that accuracy in a model is of far more importance in giving a model value than fine workmanship alone."

Mr. Chapelle's position unquestionably applies to latter day ships and, in principle, to any ship model project regardless of era. Yet the farther back in history one goes, the less complete authentic plans for a given ship are likely to be.

For example, the *Mayflower* is a ship known to every American school child yet the records contain little more than her raw dimensions to tell us what she looked like. Several years ago the marine architect and historian, W.A. Baker, worked out a reasonable guess about the *Mayflower* based on what is known of seventeenth century shipbuilding practice in general. The result was *Mayflower II* currently on exhibit in Plymouth, Massachusetts.

Similar educated guesses lay behind the reconstruction of Sir Francis Drake's *Golden Hind* in San Francisco, and Raymond Aker, a preeminent authority on Drake and his ship, has taken strong issue with some of the guesses made in this reconstruction. In any case, no one pretends that these otherwise very scholarly efforts are actual "replicas" of the ships in question.

After 1736, more or less, the British Admiralty began to file drafts of the major ships in His Majesty's fleet so reasonably complete plans exist for these vessels. But here certain details of rig and furniture are obscure because they were not considered important enough to document.

The same situation occurs with even the most fully documented vessels of later periods. Mr. Chapelle's comprehensive study of American fishing schooners illustrates the point. He says, *"Documents and publications relating to the building of fishing schooners were found to be very scarce, and usually unreliable when found. Old marine catalogs were of some assistance, but a very great part of the fishing schooner hardware was made to 'fit the work' by the local shipsmiths. It was rare, then, to find a fitting that could be described by a catalog listing . . ."*

A *". . . fairly complete specification of a 75-ton clipper schooner, probably a fishing schooner, built about 1875 . . . had little on hardware and fittings . . . Fragments of blueprints showing some fittings for the 1891 rigging of 'Grampus' were found, but these were suspect as not being typical of fishing schooners of this date . . ."*

We must add to the problem of incomplete documentation of historical vessels, the fact that most of them underwent continuous modification from the time of launching to the day they were retired. Thus even the most thorough set of plans can only represent a vessel at a certain point in her history. Today a number of maritime museums around the world feature restorations of actual historical ships. Without question these ships yield the most detailed plans presently available to modelers, and thousands of hobbyists as well as kit manufacturers have been drawn to them. Among these popular modeling projects are the *Cutty Sark*, and Nelson's *Victory* in England, The *Charles W. Morgan*, the whale ship in Mystic Connecticut; the *USS Constitution* in Boston, Massachusetts; and the *USS Constellation* in Baltimore, Maryland. Of these, the *Constitution* is probably the pet of American modelers, and particularly illustrates a vessel that underwent substantial modification during her lifetime.

The *Constitution* was launched in 1797 as one of the first six frigates of the brand new U.S. Navy. She subsequently suffered combat damage, was rerigged several times, carried various numbers of guns, was twice decommissioned and recommissioned, and finally in 1871 was hauled out and completely rebuilt. Little of her present restored condition reflects her appearance at the date of her launch. Model plans most always describe her as she looks today.

Thus, in spite of Mr. Chapelle's indictment of "reconstructions", all models are to some extent dependent on informed guesswork. The best models are those where the modeler has backed his decisions with intensive research and historical perception.

The plans included with ship model kits are often simplified though the good ones represent accurate scholarship as far as they go. No kit plans are intended to be used for plank-on-frame construction so they declare nothing about the ship's internal structure, though some lines drawings are sufficient to allow for the lofting of frame timbers if the modeler should wish to do so. Generally, however, kit plans are insufficient for a plank-on-frame project.

SCALE

Successful ship models have one outstanding characteristic in common. All of their parts are made to precise scale. Experienced modelers wrangle about thousandths of inches in the size of rigging lines, belaying pins, and trennels which in scale represent a one or two inch difference in the full size ship. The question arises as to why such infinitesimal detail is important in a model when the unaided human eye is incapable of discerning such small increments of space. The answer lies partly with the modeler's pride in craftsmanship and passion for accuracy, and partly in the fact that a model built with such precision exudes an uncanny aura of reality a viewer more feels than sees. The effect is rather like the subtle distinction one senses between a portrait by Rembrandt and a portrait by a lesser light. Newcomers to the craft therefore are advised to adjust their standard of craftsmanship accordingly.

Ship models are built to any scale the modeler finds convenient, though 1/96, 1/64 and 1/48 are popular in English speaking countries. Commercially prepared wood strips and fittings often are sized to accommodate these scales.

Dick Roos' *Pinky* is an example of a solid hull model planked over.

TYPES OF SHIP MODEL HULLS

A modeler comes to a particular project with a distinct idea of what he intends to accomplish with it. His purpose declares his approach.

Many times his purpose is to document to the last detail exactly how a given vessel was built. At other times, his concern is how a ship looked at a certain point in her history. At still others, he wants to show his subject in action, show only the hull shape, or create a working model.

A model built to the last trennel is classed a true "plank-on-frame" effort. Such models are often left partly unplanked so that the hull's internal timbers can be seen. A variation of true plank-on-frame is the *dockyard model* which employs a stylized treatment of the frames. Dockyard models hold interest in that they are of the sort Phineas Pett devised to sell Charles I on his concept for the *Sovereign of the Seas*. The framing convention of dockyard construction typifies models built as sales tools by many of

the old shipwrights. The technique showed a proposed ship in substantial detail, yet was simpler and less costly to create than an exact miniature.

Portrait models, intended only to show the outside of a ship, are often solid hull models. Solid hulls may be carved from a single block of wood, or from a series of boards laminated together in the horizontal or vertical plane. Solid hulls built-up from horizontal laminations are said to be "bread and butter" models.

Bread and butter models also play an important role in real ship construction. It is common practice for shipwrights to use models of this sort in lieu of drawings in the yard. Normally, they represent but one half of the hull, while the individual boards, or *lifts*, come apart, revealing the waterlines from which the ship's timbers are lofted. Such builder's *half models* are used today, particularly in the building of yachts.

The uninitiated may be surprised to learn that a solid hull carved from a single piece is among the more challenging approaches. With it the modeler is required to carve the hull, more or less blindly, to the correct curves at the various stations of the body plan. As he carves to a point where the hull begins to look about right, he must continually match specific contours to templates else he will carve off too much and ruin his work. At the same time both sides of the hull must match.

Some commercially available kits include machine formed solid hulls which remarkably simplifies the hull carving job. Many experienced, as well as beginning hobbyists, start with kits of this sort with excellent results.

PREFORMED SOLID HULL

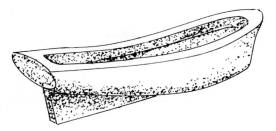

Kit manufacturers often provide hulls machine formed to the ships lines.

CARVING A HULL FROM A BLOCK

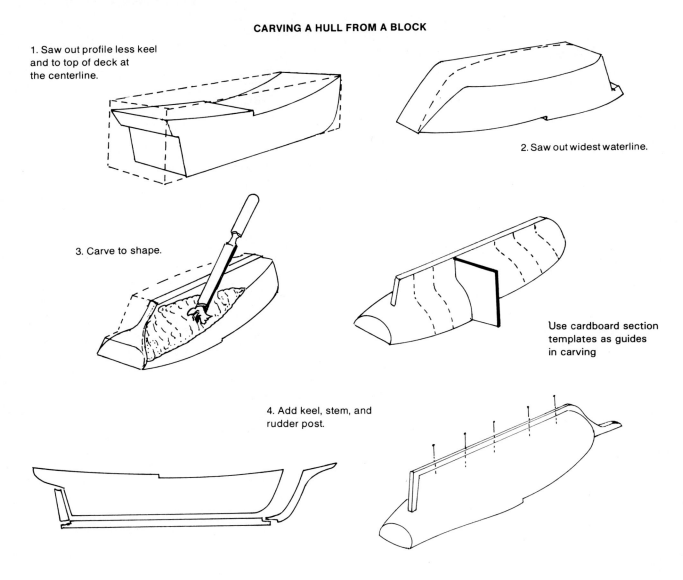

1. Saw out profile less keel and to top of deck at the centerline.

2. Saw out widest waterline.

3. Carve to shape.

Use cardboard section templates as guides in carving

4. Add keel, stem, and rudder post.

BREAD AND BUTTER
HULL CONSTRUCTION

Solid hulls made "bread and butter" fashion are built as a series of boards or "lifts" laminated together. The technique calls for each lift to be precisely cut to waterlines or buttocks transferred from the lines drawings. After the lifts are fastened together, the curves are carved in, using the seams between the lifts as guides.

The technique provides a handy means for achieving perfect symmetry and accuracy in the rendering of a set of lines.

Precise cutting and registration of the lifts provide a symmetrical and accurate guide to carving.

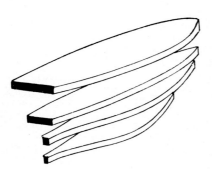

BOARDS CUT TO WATERLINES

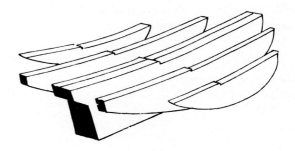

BOARDS CUT TO BUTTOCKS

GLUE AND CLAMP

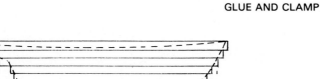

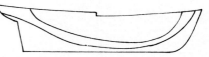

CARVE AS WITH SOLID BLOCK
USING BOARD SEAMS AS GUIDES

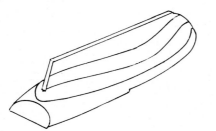

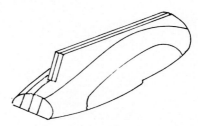

PLANK-ON-BULKHEAD

The most popular, and perhaps easiest, hull construction method among hobbyists today is the plank-on-bulkhead method. Many fine ship model kits are packaged around it.

The approach calls for the ship's frames to be simulated with a number of transverse panels (bulkheads) notched into a keel piece. The keel piece in some cases may be so wide as to extend right up to the underside of the deck. The bulkheads usually are direct translations of the body sections shown in the lines drawings,

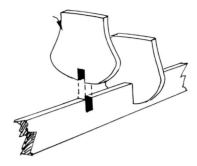

BULKHEADS HALF NOTCHED TO KEEL

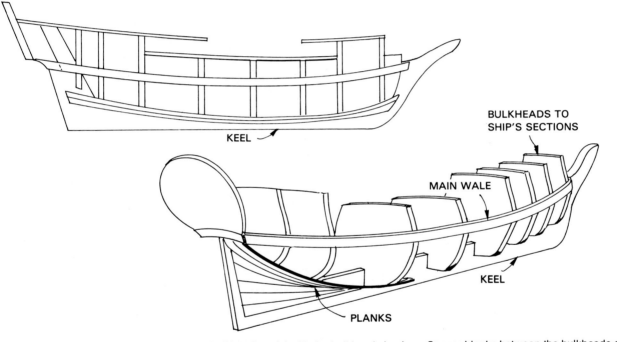

KEEL

BULKHEADS TO SHIP'S SECTIONS

MAIN WALE

KEEL

PLANKS

A plank-on-bulkhead model with the bulkheads in place. Spacer blocks between the bulkheads assure accurate alignment in both the transverse and vertical planes. Note the carefully carved rabbet in keel and posts.

Model by D. Kachmarsky

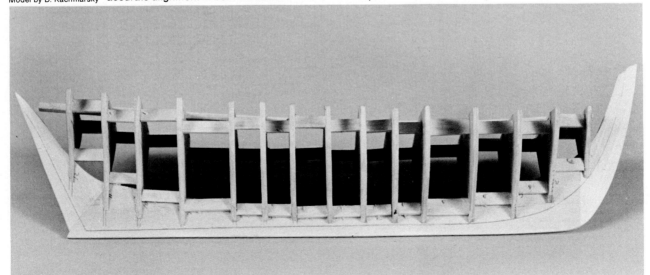

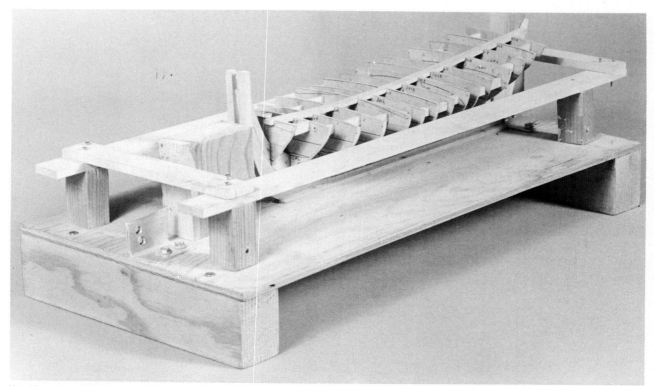

Workboard and jig are used to assure that bulkheads are mounted to the correct height. A deck "carling" piece has been fitted to notches in the bulkheads for the same purpose.

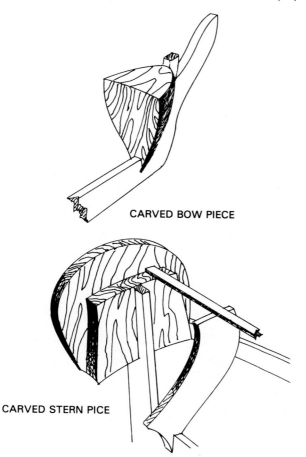

CARVED BOW PIECE

CARVED STERN PICE

not necessarily representing any of the ship's frames, as they would be lofted in full-scale practice. The intention is to simplify the construction of the hull below decks since none of the internal structure will be seen in the final work.

The technique assures a high degree of symmetry and adherence to the prescribed shape of the vessel, since each bulkhead can be easily and perfectly matched to its plan before installation. Comparable accuracy in a solid hull requires a tedious routine of shaping and comparing the hull to body section templates.

Many plank-on-bulkhead models have simplified bow and stern structures. They are carved from solid blocks, and thus provide firm footing for the planks that end on them.

The bulkheads need not be cut from material of any particular thickness, though it must be thick enough to provide a firm support for the planks. In many kits, 1/8" thick material is used.

Once the bulkheads have been fastened to the keel, the edges are bevelled to the run of the planks with sandpaper or a file.

DOCKYARD MODEL

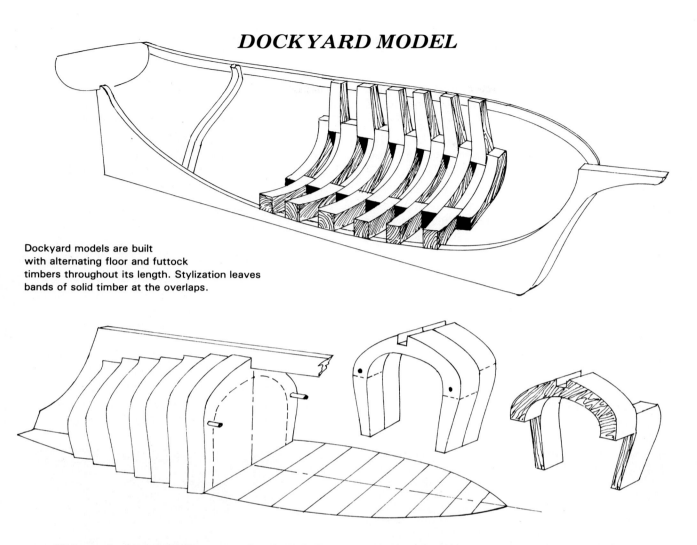

Dockyard models are built
with alternating floor and futtock
timbers throughout its length. Stylization leaves
bands of solid timber at the overlaps.

This technique, while not reflecting full scale shipbuilding practice, is nonetheless of real interest to modelers and historians.

The shipwrights of the Seventeenth and Eighteenth Centuries built dockyard style models as sales presentations to their customers, much as architects today build scale models of proposed buildings. A number of these old models have survived, and may be seen in museums around the world. They are considered invaluable collector's items, and often provide us all the information there is about the appearance and construction of certain ships. Modern modelers employ the dockyard stylization to maintain the tradition as much as to enjoy the beauty of such works.

Among the oldest dockyard style models, sometimes called "Navy Board" models" after the agency to which they were submitted, date

from the 1650's. One of them was taken to Sweden from England in 1659 by the famous shipwright Francis Sheldon. Presumably, the model helped Mr. Sheldon establish the business in Sweden which grew into a significant family of shipwrights there.

The procedure for building a dockyard style hull is akin to the bread and butter technique, except that the lifts are cut to the shapes of the body sections instead of waterlines or buttocks. The lifts are carved first to the outside surfaces of the frames while assembled into a solid mass. Then the lifts are disassembled and the insides are cutaway, as well as the unwanted portions of floor or futtock on alternate lifts. Finally, the parts are reassembled into the finished hull.

Most always, the modeler will build a jig or mold to assist him in the final assembly process.

BUILDING OVER MOLDS

Excellent fully-framed models, particularly small open boats, can be built over molds. In general, the technique is to carve from a block of wood, a mold to the shape of the hull *inside* the frames. A slot is carved (or otherwise contrived) along the bottom of the mold to accept the keelson. The frames then are shaped over the mold and secured to the keelson from the bottom up. Planking is added and the mold removed at such time as the hull structure becomes rigid enough to hold its shape on its own.

To avoid gluing the structure to the mold, the mold is shallacked and well rubbed out with wax.

The mold for a decked ship is built in sections. The first section provides a form for the bottom of the ship up to her main or lowest deck as well as a form for the deck itself. Additional sections carry the shape of the ship sides up to the various higher decks.

The decks are framed first, starting with the lowest deck. When a deck is completed, the next higher mold section is screwed into the lower mold sandwiching temporarily the deck between them. After all the decks and mold sections have been assembled, the bottom and side framing begins, starting as before, with the mold upside down and the fitting of the keelson.

One must, of course, allow for the removal of the molds once the structure is complete. Therefore, the decks are not fastened to the outside framing while the molds are in place. Furthermore, a vessel's *tumblehome* (a narrowing of the ship's beam from the waterline upward) may require that part of the mold be split vertically in two places as well as divided along the decks.

With the outside structure brought to a sufficient state of completion, the mold is disassembled and removed leaving the hull and the several decks as separate components ready to be snugly and neatly joined together into the finished piece.

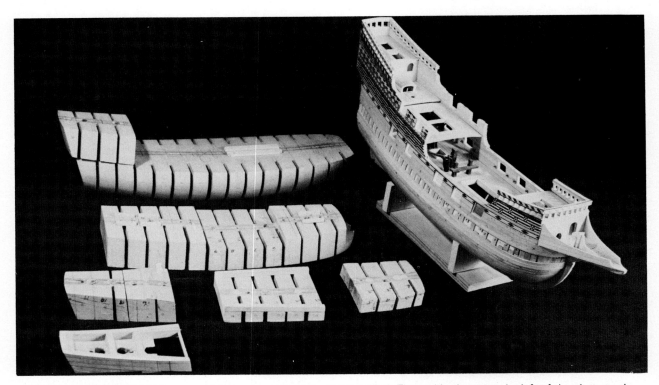

Model of the Golden Hind built over molds can be completely disassembled. The molds shown to the left of the photograph allow the model to be built up to the deck levels. The assembled hull reveals the interlocks between the upper and lower sections. This area will be planked over in the finished work. The model is by Howard Judson.

OPEN MOLD

Kryenia is an example of a model whose hull might be built over an open mold. The actual ship was built shell first, and the comparatively light reinforcing timbers added afterwards.

Open mold model hull construction is a miniature version of full scale boat building practice. Bulkhead molds are fixed to a workboard, keel-side up, and the planks formed over them. Once the shell of the hull is completed, it is removed from the mold, and ribs, knees, thwarts, and stringers are added.

The method is usually reserved for models of craft whose construction followed similar procedures. Whaleboats, launches, longboats, and gigs are of this sort.

The technique is also applied in modeling clinker-built Viking vessels, ancient ships such as *Kyrenia*, shown above, and other ships whose full scale construction followed procedures different from those of conventional plank-on-frame shipbuilding.

Building a model over an open mold, while conforming to full scale practice, can be challenging because the shell of the hull must be removed from the mold before internal reinforcement is in place. Extreme care must be taken during the installation of the reinforcing structures, however, lest the hull be distorted out of shape.

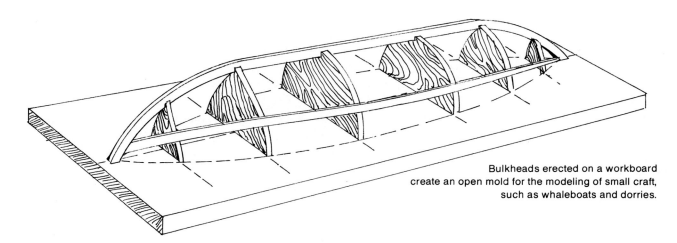

Bulkheads erected on a workboard create an open mold for the modeling of small craft, such as whaleboats and dories.

PLANK-ON-FRAME CONSTRUCTION

Joe Seela's *Leon* is a superb example of a true plank-on-frame model. She is shown on the ways, partially planked, revealing the ship's internal structure.

A true plank-on-frame model represents the epitome of the ship modeler's art. The objective is to duplicate, in miniature, every structural detail of the actual ship. While some compromise with this objective might be necessary, due to the physical limitations of materials, some of the best examples of plank-on-frame models contain scale parts so small they cannot be seen with an unaided human eye.

One might wonder why a modeler would go to the trouble of creating parts that no one can see. Part of the answer to the question, no doubt, lies simply in his pride of craftsmanship. But beyond this, models built with such precision exude an uncanny air of authenticity that the viewer feels more than sees.

The pages that follow describe some of the considerations and procedures plank-on-frame ship modelers employ.

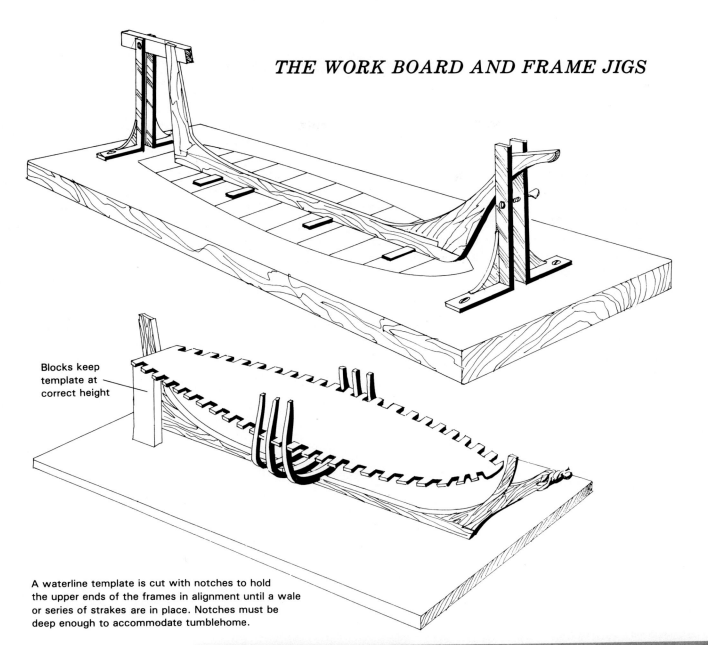

Blocks keep template at correct height

A waterline template is cut with notches to hold the upper ends of the frames in alignment until a wale or series of strakes are in place. Notches must be deep enough to accommodate tumblehome.

Bill Wicks uses a construction method advanced by Harold M. Hahn in which the basic hull framing is assembled upside down. The top timbers of the frames are initially cut to extended lengths referenced to a flat plane above the rails, and corresponding with the plane of the workboard.

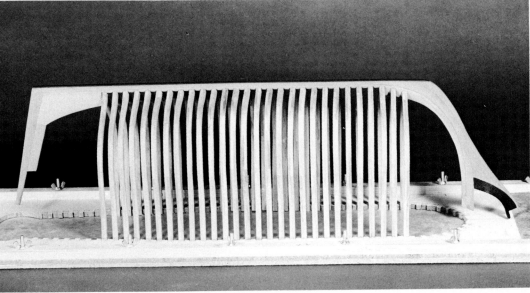

KEEL, STEM AND STERNPOST

The keel, stem, and sternpost of a model may be pieced together exactly as the real ship, though just as often these parts are simplified into as few as three pieces of wood perhaps scribed to simulate the joints of the scarfings.

In making these components the modeler is especially required to attend to their *rabbets* and *bearding lines* for these account for the clean joining of the planks to them. We may observe that a plank's edge is 90 degrees or square with its surface, yet the garboard strake of a vessel meets the keel, stem, and sternpost at various angles ranging from somewhat less than 90 degrees at midships to very acute angles in the deadwood. Thus, in a given section of a keel, one will find a 90 degree notch oriented more or less perpendicular to its vertical axis. The outboard edge of the notch corresponds to the rabbet line; the inboard edge to the bearding line.

A full rendering of the rabbet to the bearding in small scale models is not always attempted since the garboard seams are more easily faked without loss of effect. Nonetheless the outboard rabbet line must be defined with precision if the clean joint of a well-made ship is to be properly simulated. Some modelers prefer to carve the rabbet which is true to actual shipbuilding practice. Others prefer to simulate the notch with a lamination of fine wood to the outer portions of the keel. The keel's boot completely obscures this subterfuge.

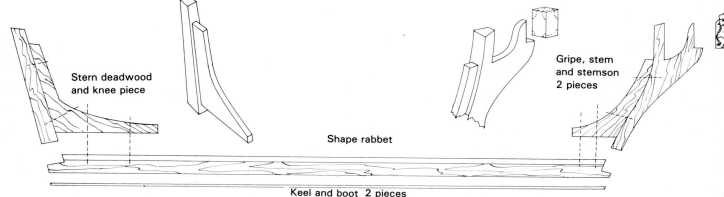

Stern deadwood and knee piece

Shape rabbet

Gripe, stem and stemson 2 pieces

Keel and boot 2 pieces

The rabbet of the stem, keel, and sternpost was carefully carved before the frames were installed.

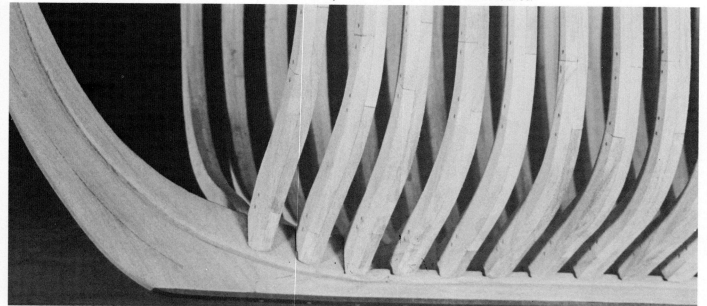

FRAMES

In real ship construction, care was taken that the grain of the wood followed the curves of the frame as closely as possible. Modelers also follow the principle, making each frame of from three to six floor and futtock pieces.

One procedure is to trace the shape of each frame on tracing paper and glue the frame material to this pattern with the butts of the pieces cleanly joined. After all the rough cut material is treenailed and glued, the frame is cut out to the tracing paper pattern. The frames are cut slightly oversize to allow for faring up once all are in place on the keel. The futtocks and floors of each frame are treenailed together with bamboo dowels. Metal nails interfere with the final shaping and finishing. The tracing paper patterns, of course, are removed before the frames are set up.

The keel is notched to accept a corresponding notch at the center of each full frame. Grooves are cut in the deadwood to accept the half frames fore and aft.

The two top timbers (upper futtocks) on each side of a frame rise to different levels. One is designed to form a seat for the deck beam; the other, higher one, rises to the caprail.

The inside of each frame must be bevelled and finished also. Occasionally a modeler will include a few ceiling or clamp strakes on the inner face of the frames requiring that he take as much pains faring up the flow of these strakes as he does with the outer ones. But normally, the inner faces of the frames are left uncovered and only have to look reasonably accurate from an outer perspective.

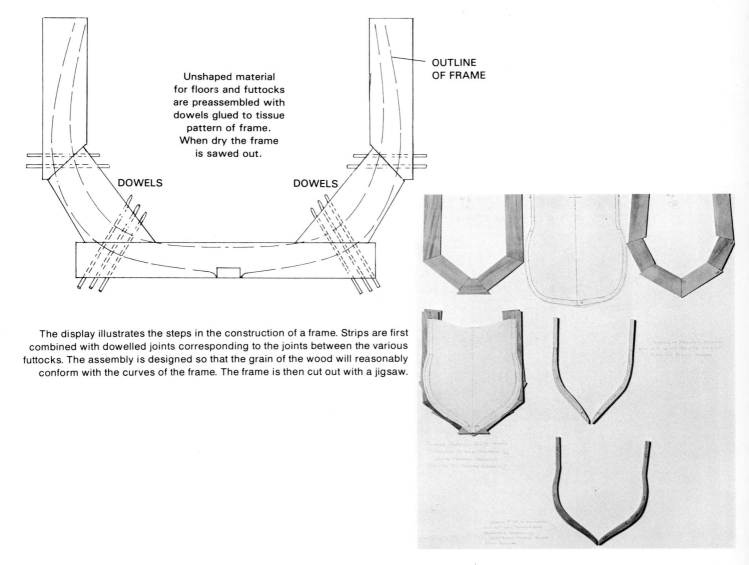

Unshaped material for floors and futtocks are preassembled with dowels glued to tissue pattern of frame. When dry the frame is sawed out.

DOWELS   DOWELS

OUTLINE OF FRAME

The display illustrates the steps in the construction of a frame. Strips are first combined with dowelled joints corresponding to the joints between the various futtocks. The assembly is designed so that the grain of the wood will reasonably conform with the curves of the frame. The frame is then cut out with a jigsaw.

CANT FRAMES - FRAMING THE BOW

The shapes of the cant frames are derived from the lines drawings by carrying out a procedure somewhat different than that for the full frames. The key to it is to perceive that the true shape of the cant frames do not show up in the body plan. To plot their true shape, one must adjust his point of view to one at right angles with them. The center line of each cant frame, as seen in the top view, angles out from the keel, intersecting the waterlines at distances other than a line perpendicular to the keel. These distances give us the true x's for the 'xy' plot of the cant frame contours, the y's remaining the waterline heights as before. The important thing is to measure the x distances along the center line of the frame and not on a line perpendicular to the keel.

The cant frames, like the half frames, are fitted to the keel in grooves cut into the deadwood to receive them.

The shape of a cant fram is plotted from the waterlines and buttocks from the distances struck out by the plane of the cant frame, as shown in the half-breadth plan.

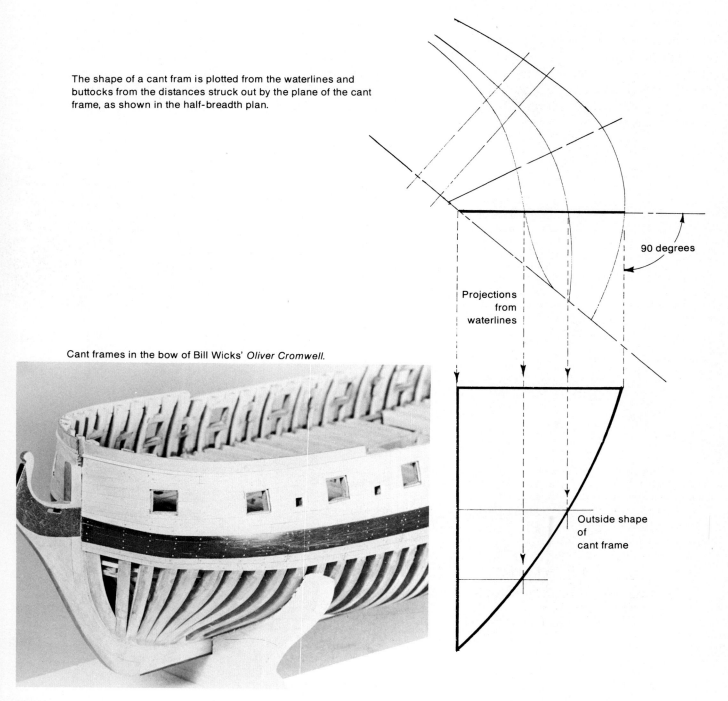

Cant frames in the bow of Bill Wicks' *Oliver Cromwell.*

90 degrees

Projections from waterlines

Outside shape of cant frame

FRAMING THE STERN

Modeling the frames of the stern as actually constructed in the shipyard is a challenge to even the most experienced modeler, because of the tricky joinery and shaping required for a fair number of small timbers. Often as not, modelers will simply forego the task in favor of carving this section out of a block of wood, since planking, even in models with some frames exposed, usually covers the areas around the counter. Purists, however, frown upon such expedients.

A common approach to the problem of stern framing is to build it over a mold formed to the inside of the planking, and matched on its forward face to the shape of the fashion frame. This mold is then grooved with saw cuts to accommodate the framing material in such a way as it may be held rigidly while working it down, flush with the mold. Once the outer contours of the frame members have been formed, they are removed from the mold, and the inside contours are shaped.

Mr. Underhill suggests a dockyard model approach. Boards of appropriate thickness are sandwiched together, then shaped, solid-hull fashion, into the shape of the stern inside the planking. The boards have opposing grains. When the sandwich is disassembled after forming, one half of the boards become part of the frames above the knuckle timber; the other half becomes the part below. The unused part of each half is cut away, as well as the inside shapes of all. Then the two halves of the frames are sandwiched together again, their ends overlapping where the knuckle timber would otherwise have been.

Mr. Underhill's "boards" initially face the fashion frame , so that no problem occurs while shaping the outside contours of the frames. A jig, however, is required to keep the parts in line during assembly, and the parts must be fitted, one at a time, to the model itself.

With the mold, assembly is somewhat easier, since the mold will hold all of the parts positively in line until the glue dries, after which the assembly is fitted to the rest of the hull.

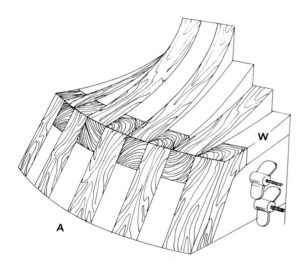

Underhill suggests a dockyard approach to stern framing.
A. Boards cut to the buttocks are bolted together with the grain alternating. The stern is then shaped as in carving a solid hull. Disassembled the individual parts are then cutaway and reassembled into the structure B.

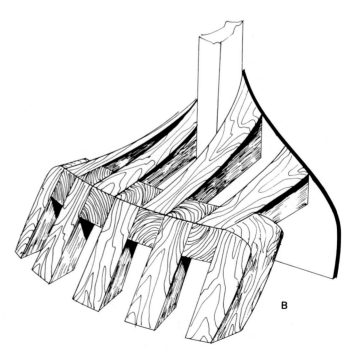

ASSEMBLY

None of the frames are attached to the keel until all are ready. Numerous trial fittings, remakes, and adjustments of the frames may be required before the decision to fasten things together is taken, but once all the parts are thought to be as perfect as possible, the frames are each keyed with a pencil mark to the waterline template described above. The midship frame is the first to be glued and treenailed through the floor timber into the keel. Then the template is put in place and the cant and half frame fastenings are drilled from the outside faces of the frames into the keel. The template does not interfere with the fastenings of these frames.

The opposite is the case with the full frames so temporary plank battens on the outside are rigged at an appropriate waterline level to guide the placement of the full frames when the template is removed. The full frames are installed working alternately fore and aft from the midship frame.

After all the frames have been fastened, the template is replaced and the frames fared down sufficiently to allow for installation of the main wale, a component capable of giving the structure some rigidity.

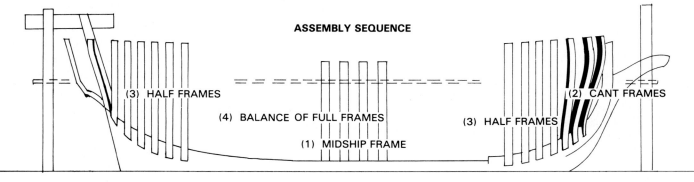

ASSEMBLY SEQUENCE

(3) HALF FRAMES

(4) BALANCE OF FULL FRAMES

(1) MIDSHIP FRAME

(3) HALF FRAMES

(2) CANT FRAMES

THE KEELSON AND BELOW DECKS DETAILS

With the essential hull structure reasonably rigid, the modeler attends to the rest of the internal, below decks framing which, of course, includes the keelson, stem, and stern knees. The keelson might be laid flat on the floors, with no attempt to notch and fit the component, though such a procedure can lead to akeelson that waves up and down through its length, or one with gaps between it and a certain number of floors. To avoid this, the modeler has a choice of either faring off the tops of the floor timbers, or slightly notching the bottom side of the keelson. The latter is probably the easier and safer of the two because an unattached part is remedied by making a new part. Once a component is fastened in, unfastening it is a formidable nuisance. This bit of philosophy is perhaps the hear of the

ship modeler's religion which, tersely stated, comes out, "Fasten nothing together until all the parts are finished!" Beginning modelers, lacking the discipline of this injunction, tend to "assemble" themselves into impossible corners, where all chance of installing an important part is lost.

The issue is particularly applicable at the stage of construction when the keelson is being fitted, because any details to be built into the lower inside of the hull must be considered before the decks make the space inaccessible.

A check list of such details for a particular model could include rudder rigging, hawse pipes, attachments for stays, doublings, plank reinforcement timbers for chain plat attachments and the like, ladders, limber chains, and mast steps.

DECK FRAMING

Deck beams are formed from a single board shaped to the correct camber. Then beams are sliced off like bread from a loaf.

The sliced bread principle holds for many duplicate or partially duplicate parts such as knees.

Deck beams for a given deck in a model are often fabricated from a single board shaped first to the largest deck beam mouldings. Since the camber of a deck's beams remains the same regardless of their individual lengths, slices to appropriate sidings, rip-sawn from this single board provide perfectly matched timbers for the length of the deck. The more lightly moulded beams are formed from the same material by carving away the less critical concave under surfaces.

In theory, as will be remembered, half of the top timbers of the frames have been cut to the precise height required to provide a footing for the ends of the deck beams. In practice such precision is rarely to be expected. If the beams are mounted accordingly, the deck planks will look like roller coasters. The clamp strakes and shelf timbers provide the even heights required for the fitting of the deck beams. These are the next parts to be installed followed by the eking at the bow and a cross seam timber on the inner face of the wing transom aft.

Most decks require a formidable number of knees which are most easily made by the same principle as the deck beams. A single piece of stock is formed along its length so that its cross section will match the curvilinear outer contour of the knees. Then the blanks for the individual knees are sliced off and trimmed to fit particular joints.

The heavy full width deck beams such as those fore and aft of the main hatch are the first to be fitted. After being cut to length and the ends trimmed to a snug fit on the shelves and top timbers, stiff paper patterns are traced off the joint to obtain the facing shapes of the knees.

When all the parts have been cut and matched to their final positions, the beam is set in place on the model and the knees are glued and treenailed to the beam only. One has to be able to remove each beam while the rest are under construction because otherwise there would soon be no way to access the lower areas.

Main deck framing of the *Oliver Cromwell* was built without bosom and lodging knees.

As the full width deck beams are completed, various pairs of them may be preassembled into units. For example, the mast partners may be fastened between the two beams that usually go fore and aft of them. Then these deck sections are fitted up with the half beams, carlings, lodging knees, bosom knees, and the like. So long as such deck units can be removed from the model they can be developed independently on the bench. All of the details that attach to the deck framing are installed at this point. The check list might include hatch coamings, deckhouse coamings, capstan barrels, bitts, the mortice for the heel of the bowsprit, hatch covers and gratings, booby hatches, galley components, and fastenings for the stays.

When this is done the parts are set aside unassembled while work goes on in the fabrication of other individual bits of equipment. Boats, guns, masts, other spars, the steering wheel, and so on may all be finished completely before the modeler returns to the hull for the final fastening of the deck beams and planking because the odds are very good that he has overlooked something which needs doing below decks. In leaving the hull open as long as possible he gives himself the opportunity to discover and rectify mistakes before it is too late.

The planking on Bill Wicks' *Oliver Cromwell* accurately reflects full-scale shipbuilding practice. Double treenail fastenings for each plank at each frame show up clearly, while extra fastenings appear at the butts. The butts correctly stagger from strake to strake.

PLANKING

The time has come to plank the ship. Whether one starts with the deck, or the sides and bottom, is a matter of inclination, but we shall deal with the latter first. Most plank-on-frame models are left partly unplanked below the wales because one wants to see the internal structure. But, in spite of this, some modelers do, indeed, first build-up every futtock and floor, only to hide from view, forever, the hours of effort thus spent, with full planking. They have, after all, set themselves to build a model like the real thing. Besides, what is a ship without her planking?

The modeler comes to the job of planking in the same way as the full-scale shipwright. He will first compute the number of strakes he will have on each side by dividing the width of his planking material into the distance around the midship section. He will then plot the taper of each strake by computing the various widths required to come out with the same number of strakes at each of the smaller frames.

He will then place several temporary battens (strips of wood or tape) along the frames to identify two or three "belts" of planking, the curves of which will be followed as each belt with its share of strakes is laid.

Most commonly, the belts are laid out from the sheer or wale, down to just above the turn of the bilge, and the second belt from there down to the keel. Depending on the hull, a third belt may be assigned to the area around the bilge.

Some modelers cut their planks to scale lengths. Others use a single strip to run almost the whole length of the strake, and then scribe in the scale butt seams after the fact. However, it is done, though, the position of the butts is carefully worked out, because the model must simulate full-scale practice.

A SPILING AND PLANKING PROCEDURE

1. Use masking tape to mark the position of the main wale or sheer strake.

2. Use tape again to mark the separation between the upper and lower planking belts. The upper belt should run from the joint of the wing transom, with the sternpost over the turn of the bilge, and up to the bow in a smooth curve.

3. Place the length of tape along the edge of the midship frame or bulkhead. Cut the tape into two pieces representing the exact width of the planking belts at miships.

4. Remove the midship tapes and lay them flat. Subdivide the length of each tape by the width of the planking material, marking the tapes accordingly.

5. Tape the edge of the frame that represents the *shortest* linear distance from wale to keel. Often, this frame will occur near the bow. Cut the tapes as before to correspond with the two planking belts.

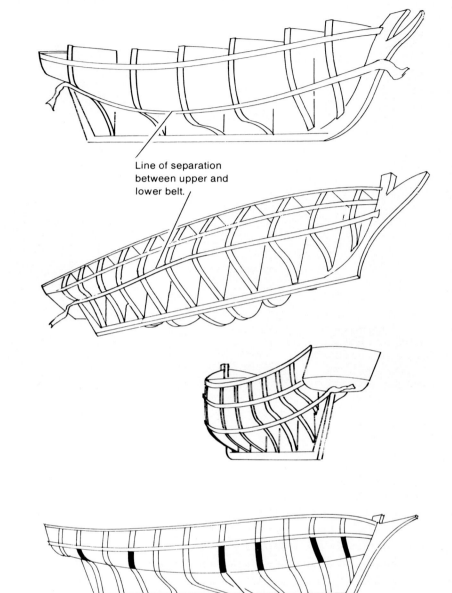

Line of separation between upper and lower belt.

6. Draw a pair of parallel lines with a T-square on the drawing board spaced apart a distance equal to a "shortest frame" planking belt. Place the tape from step 5 for an exact perpendicular measure.

7. Place midship tape diagonally between the parallel lines so that its length precisely fits between the parallels.

8. Prepare tape lengths for six or eight other frames, and place them diagonally between the parallels, as in step 7.

9. With a T-square, draw parallel lines across all of the tapes, using the plank widths marked off on the midship tape. Use a very sharp pencil.

Length at midship frame marked off in widths of planking material.

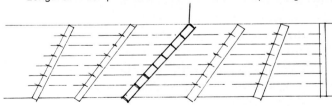

Tapes replaced reveal planking pattern.

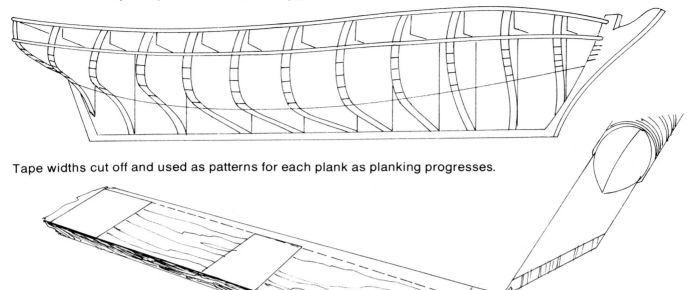

Tape widths cut off and used as patterns for each plank as planking progresses.

10. Replace the tapes on the edges of the frames. The pencil marks on the tapes will provide the exact plank widths required at each frame. Since most of the pencil marks will run diagonally across the widths of tapes, one must refer to the correct edge of the tape to obtain the appropriate plank width.

The procedure outlined above provides the means for laying out the key planking pattern on the face of the frames. As planking progresses, the tapes are cut off at the various widths, and the small bits placed on the planking stock to provide a pattern for the shaping of the pieces.

JOINTS

The flow of a line of planks from one end of the ship to the other is called a strake. Seldom was a strake made of a single plank. Rather, it consisted of several planks, twenty or so feet in length, joined end to end.

Sometimes the joints between the plank ends were simple butt joints; at other times, they were scarfed, so that the plank ends overlapped one another across a pair of frames. From the outside, both of these joints appear the same, so modelers normally save themselves the trouble of cutting in scarfs.

The particular frames on which the joints of a strake occur are most important. Admiralties and insurance companies laid out strict rules concerning such positioning.

The joints of a given strake would be at least five feet from the joints on either side of its immediately adjacent strakes. They would be at least four feet from the joints in the strakes next farther away, and at least three strakes had to separate any joints occurring on the same frame.

Modelers, therefore, carefully plan the location of each joint before laying wood. One such planning procedure is outlined here in which a vessel of 100 feet in length is presumed to be planked with 24 foot lengths of timber.

1. Divide the length of the strake by the length of the plank stock. If one is planking a 100 foot vessel with 24 foot planks, one will require four full lengths and one short length for each strake.

2. Assign an arbitrary dimension for the "short" lengths. Say 20 feet in our example.

3. Beginning with the sheer strake, locate a "short" length at midships and mark the butts.

4. Locate the next lower short length on a pair of frames five feet aft of the first.

5. Locate the third short length so that its after end is on a frame five feet from the forward end of the one above.

6. Locate the fourth short length five feet aft of the third.

7. Repeat the sequence to assign the positions of the "short" lengths in the rest of the hull. Thus, the butts of strake 5 will occur on the same frames as strake one; strake 6, the same as 2, and so on.

8. The rest of the butts in the planking follow from the positions of the "short" planks, with full plank lengths lying fore and aft of them out to the ends of the ship. The actual lengths of the ending planks will vary.

The location of the short planks around midships can vary from exact center to somewhat forward, depending on the hull. Bluff-bowed ships with strongly tapered joggle planks require that butts occur close to the bow. More forward placement of the short plank pattern satisfies this requirement.

Joggle planks at the bow of a bluff-bowed ship maintain correct flow and taper of planks.

Toward the bow, the pattern may show planking tapering away to points, a circumstance which would be disallowed in a real ship. Where this occurs, one plank is fitted to do the job of two widths. Such a plank, called a *joggle plank*, runs from the place on the hull where two planks diminish to the width of one forward (or aft) to the bow or stern.

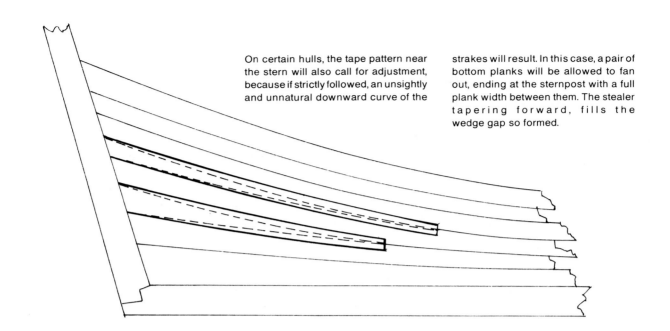

On certain hulls, the tape pattern near the stern will also call for adjustment, because if strictly followed, an unsightly and unnatural downward curve of the strakes will result. In this case, a pair of bottom planks will be allowed to fan out, ending at the sternpost with a full plank width between them. The stealer tapering forward, fills the wedge gap so formed.

The natural flow of the planks near the sternpost often fan out, requiring the installation of "stealers."

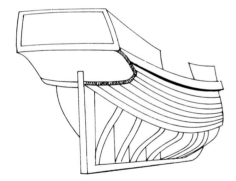

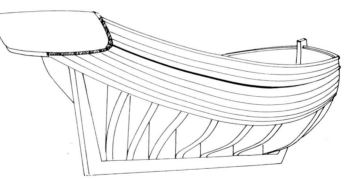

Upper planking belt in place on stern of ship where planks end on the wing transom.

Lower planking belt in place.

Upper planking belt in place on a ship with an overhanging counter. Planks aft of the sternpost might mesh herringbone style or be nibbled to a central king plank.

Lower planking belt in place.

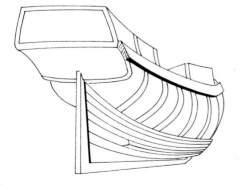

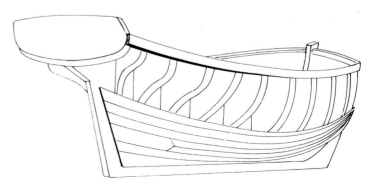

BENDING PLANKS

The planking on some models requires strong bends as at the bows of eighteenth century vessels, and the wood needs special treatment to be made to conform to the shapes. A number of treatments work. One way is to soak the planks in ordinary household ammonia until saturated, after which the wood bends easily and dries to the shape formed.

Another is to stick the plank in the nozzle of a teakettle of boiling water.

Moderately bent planks can be formed dry by rolling the inner face of the stock as one would roll out pie dough.

Make a "rolling pin" with a bolt and a length of tubing. Roll the inside face of the plank to shape it to the correct curve.

SHAPING PLANKS

Shaving a curving taper to a long thin strip of springy wood is a bit of a trick unless one clamps it securely along its length between two larger and more rigid strips with just the part to be removed exposed. Then a file or small plane can be used to shape the strake very handsomely.

The same job can be accomplished with a small disc sander and a holding block. One rabbets the holding block to a depth slightly less than the strake is thick and about half as wide. With the block, the strake can be held firmly against the sander without danger to the finger tips.

FINISHING AND PAINTING

As we have described the old wooden ships were finished with "tar" and tallow, and a minimum of paint. Modelers simulate these finishes with a variety of commercially available materials. Fast drying acrylic paints and varnishes are popular.

However, it is just as possible, with materials available today, to successfully finish a model with genuine 'tar' using artists' oil painting mediums. Venice turpentine is a refined version of the very material known as pitch tar to the shipwrights. In itself, it is a thick, gummy, sticky substance which dries to a brittle varnish-like texture. To make a satisfactory finish from it, one

diluates it in ordinary turpentine then increases the volume of the mixture 25% with the addition of linseed oil, and finally about one drop per ounce of cobalt drier. The linseed oil softens the finish and makes the film more resilient. In time the Venice turpentine finish will darken as much as the tar on the old ships.

Artists oil colors of today include the same pigments used by our ancestors, while the 'tar' described above is a traditional medium for oil paints. A model finished with artist's oil paints therefore is probably the most authentic one within the modeler's reach.

CARVING FIGUREHEADS
AND OTHER DECORATIONS

A figurehead is a piece of wood sculpture, and the procedure for making one in miniature varies little from that used in the creation of its full-scale equivalent. There are no fixed rules as such, since we are dealing with an art form, but carvers often approach their business from one of two directions.

The first approach we can designate the "profile" method, since the first step is to sketch the profile of the sculpture on the appropriate side of the block and shape the whole width of the block to it. Care is taken to include both left and right profiles in the initial carving, especially if the two sides differ. The next step is to shape the sculpture in its frontal aspect, coming up with a shape curved in side and front views, but still square if viewed from the top. In the final step, the carver works in the intermediary curves and angles.

The profile method works best with more or less symetrical subjects. But it becomes awkward when dealing with more complex forms. The second approach to the problem helps in the latter cases. We can call this second technique the "dead reckoning" technique because it depends on measurements of direction and distance.

In dead reconing, one first models his subject in clay or wax. This prototype need not be of the same scale as the proposed finished piece and,

in fact, a miniature sculpture comes out better if a much larger prototype is worked out. The prototype is then placed in a box frame of the same proportions as the block from which the piece is to be carved. At the top of the box frame, one mounts a ruler, or pair of rulers, equipped with plumb lines which can be dropped from any point along their lengths. This apparatus allows one to specify the position of every point on the surface of the sculpture in terms of its distance from the faces of the block. A number of these points are plotted on the block, and holes are drilled to the measured depths. Care is taken to drill somewhat short of the distance measured on the prototype so that some working room remains on the roughed block. When enough holes are drilled from the top, bottom, and sides of the block, one starts carving away the material between the holes, thus producing a form from which the final sculpture follows with ease.

The "dead reckoning" procedure, as we have said, works when the subject matter is so complex as to defy simpler solutions. Ship modelers encounter such subject matter in the elaborate, baroque figureheads and quarter figures of seventeenth and early eighteenth century ships. Later, figureheads tend to be simpler and accessible to profile carving.

PROFILE METHOD

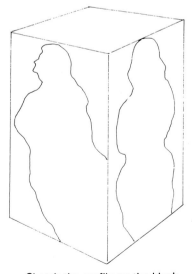

Sketch the profile on the block.

Cut profile full
width of block

Cut frontal
view full
width of block

Carve curves
and details

DEAD RECKONING METHOD

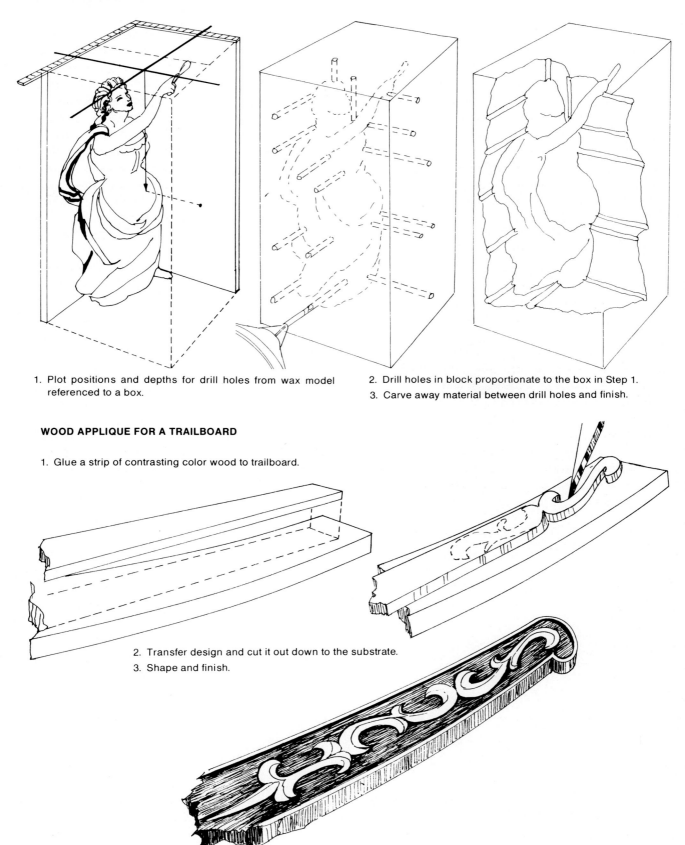

1. Plot positions and depths for drill holes from wax model referenced to a box.

2. Drill holes in block proportionate to the box in Step 1.
3. Carve away material between drill holes and finish.

WOOD APPLIQUE FOR A TRAILBOARD

1. Glue a strip of contrasting color wood to trailboard.

2. Transfer design and cut it out down to the substrate.
3. Shape and finish.

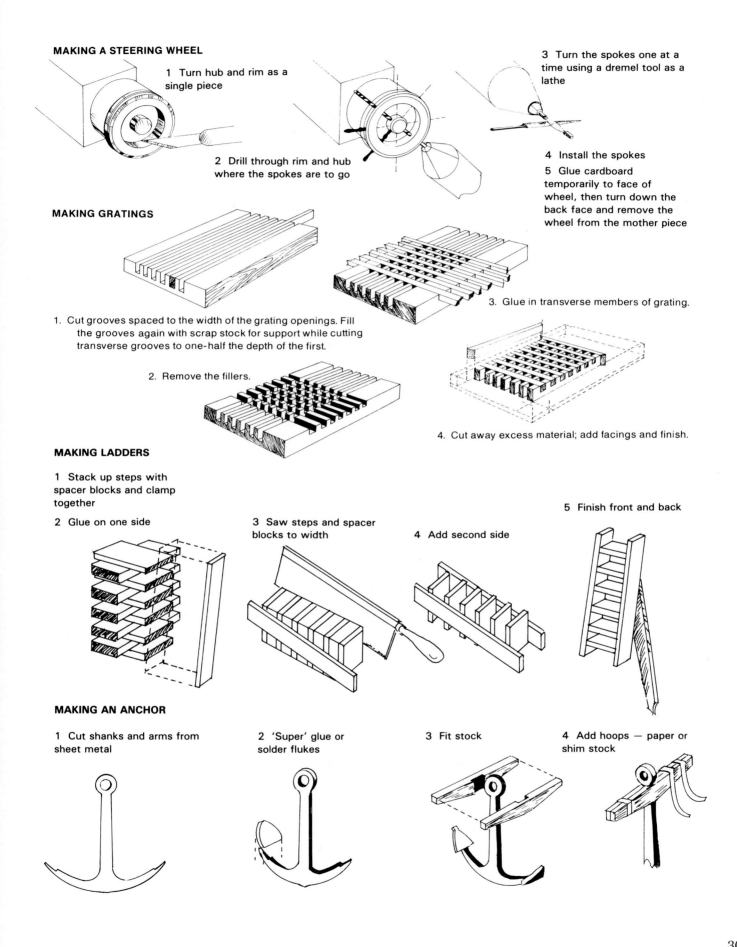

MAKING A STEERING WHEEL

1 Turn hub and rim as a single piece

2 Drill through rim and hub where the spokes are to go

3 Turn the spokes one at a time using a dremel tool as a lathe

4 Install the spokes

5 Glue cardboard temporarily to face of wheel, then turn down the back face and remove the wheel from the mother piece

MAKING GRATINGS

1. Cut grooves spaced to the width of the grating openings. Fill the grooves again with scrap stock for support while cutting transverse grooves to one-half the depth of the first.

2. Remove the fillers.

3. Glue in transverse members of grating.

4. Cut away excess material; add facings and finish.

MAKING LADDERS

1 Stack up steps with spacer blocks and clamp together

2 Glue on one side

3 Saw steps and spacer blocks to width

4 Add second side

5 Finish front and back

MAKING AN ANCHOR

1 Cut shanks and arms from sheet metal

2 'Super' glue or solder flukes

3 Fit stock

4 Add hoops — paper or shim stock

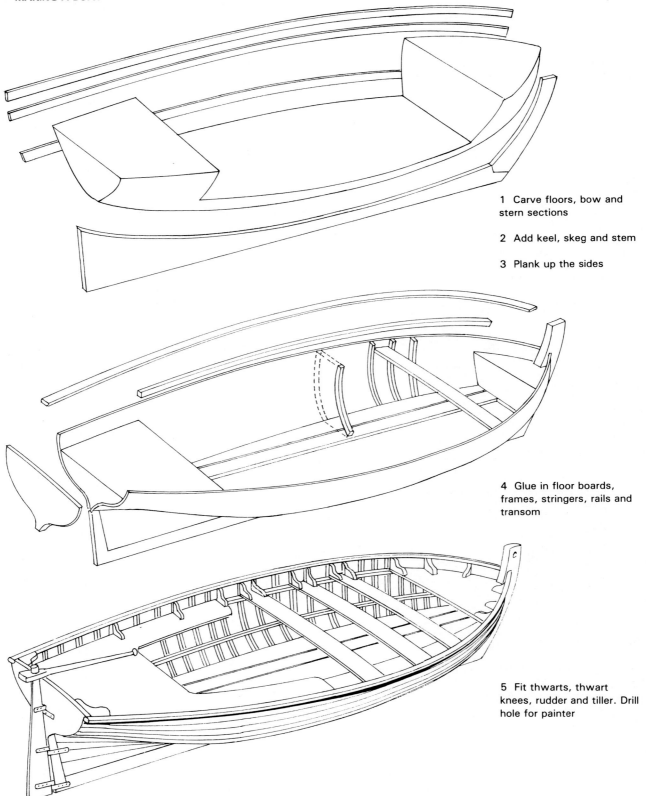

1 Carve floors, bow and
stern sections

2 Add keel, skeg and stem

3 Plank up the sides

4 Glue in floor boards,
frames, stringers, rails and
transom

5 Fit thwarts, thwart
knees, rudder and tiller. Drill
hole for painter

MAKING SPARS

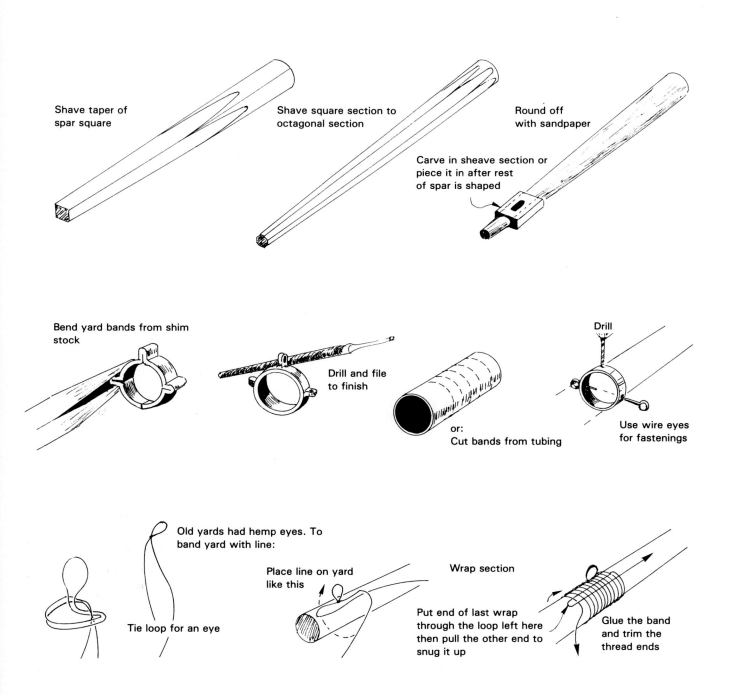

Shave taper of
spar square

Shave square section to
octagonal section

Round off
with sandpaper

Carve in sheave section or
piece it in after rest
of spar is shaped

Bend yard bands from shim
stock

Drill and file
to finish

or:
Cut bands from tubing

Drill

Use wire eyes
for fastenings

Old yards had hemp eyes. To
band yard with line:

Tie loop for an eye

Place line on yard
like this

Wrap section

Put end of last wrap
through the loop left here
then pull the other end to
snug it up

Glue the band
and trim the
thread ends

WOODS FOR SHIP MODELERS

Ship modelers employ a great many different types of wood and often spend considerable time researching possibilities. The general criteria for suitable woods can be stated briefly.

1) The wood should be dry and stable so as to minimize warping and buckling.
2) The grain should be fine so that the scale of the model can be retained.
3) The wood should readily accept gluing, staining, and finishing.

4) The wood should be hard enough to hold an edge during cutting and drilling, while limber enough to allow bending and twisting when cut to small dimensions.

A ship model of course has many different parts, each of which may be better made from one kind of material than another. The important consideration is selecting the right material for the right job with the recognition that no single material can fill the bill for everything.

Some well known woods used for furniture, full scale boat building and other kinds of construction are questionable for ship modeling though some craftsmen have used them very successfully. Teak, oak and Philippine mahogany, for example, are normally too open-grained to be effective in a model though pieces can be selected which are quite satisfactory.

Balsa wood fails on criteria four, while some exotic woods fail on criteria three. The latter, however, may be useful for small "color patch" details, since these woods can often provide color without staining.

The names of woods are sometimes confusing so it is important in specifying a type of wood that your name for it corresponds with that of your supplier. Lemonwood, for example, is also called degame, camaron, guayabo, palo blanco, pau mulato, and pau marfim. Note that lemonwood is not wood from a lemon tree. The easiest way around this problem is to obtain a sample of the wood you want and tell your supplier to match it.

The following list is a sample of some of the woods ship modelers have used successfully.

Most of them may be obtained through hardwood suppliers, some at hobby shops and some at cabinet shops. A few, traditionally popular with ship modelers such as holly and box are becoming scarce and may only be obtained (if at all) through specialized mail order distributors.

A local hardwood dealer is probably the best place to begin a search for suitable woods. What he may not have on hand, he may be able to obtain.

Basswood (limewood in England) — A light cream colored wood with a fine, uniform grain that is quite easy to work and usually available in hobby shops in many forms. Can be easily finished with stains or paint and is an excellent choice of beginners. It may be used for solid, built-up or plank-on-frame hulls.

Beech — A medium hard, light tan wood with small brown flecks that is easy to stain and finish. Universal application.

Birch — A light yellow brown to tan wood of medium hardness and fine grain. Resembles oak on a miniature scale and is very good for framing. Glues and stains easily.

Boxwood — A premium wood becoming difficult to obtain. A light yellow in color and very fine grained. Excellent for fine carving as well as planking, framing, deck equipment and blocks. Stains poorly because of fine grain. Glue works better if the wood is first wiped with solvent.

Cherry — A light red-tan which will darken with age to a warm reddish brown. Fine grained and of moderate hardness, this is a good choice for plank-on-frame construction. Glues and finishes nicely.

Degame or Lemonwood — A hard light yellow wood with a very fine grain. This wood is an excellent substitute for boxwood, though slightly more brittle. Degame glues and stains much more readily than boxwood.

Ebony — A very fine grained brown-black wood. Quite hard but not too difficult to work. Care should be taken when working ebony because the dust is like lamp black and gets into everything. Recommended for trim work, rails, deadeyes, and similar parts.

Holly — A moderately hard very fine grained wood, usually a uniform white in color. Excellent for planking because it bends well and accepts fastenings near the ends without splitting. Glues, stains and finishes very well. This is a premium wood and difficult to obtain.

Lignum Vitae — A very hard, fine grained wood, light to dark olive brown, sometimes with a greenish cast. An oily wood it is usually used only for blocks and deadeyes.

Mahogony — Honduras (Philippine mahogony is usually too coarse and soft) — A moderately hard, rich, reddish wood that is easily worked and finishes beautifully. Ideal for solid or built-up hulls; less so for planking though many have used it for this purpose.

Maple — A very hard, fine grained wood, light cream in color. Stains and glues well. Excellent for small parts, but also usable for plank-on-frame construction, although its hardness makes it less desirable than other woods.

Padauk — An exotic, moderately hardwood, with irregular grain. Color bright orange to blood red frequently with darker streaks. Used for trim and deckhouses to add color highlights.

Pear — A premium wood, moderately hard and very fine grained, varying in color from beige to a warm, chocolate brown. Very uniform in texture and color. Glues and stains readily, but is best with a natural finish. Used for plank-on-frame construction as well as deck fittings, carvings and trim.

Pernambuco — One of the most expensive of the exotics. Bright orange to orange-red. Fine texture, very hard, but works and carves well. Best used for trim and fittings.

Poplar — Soft, easy-to-work wood. Very light tan to light green to tan and usually uniform in grain. Glues, stains and finishes well. Is a favorite of many modelers. Good for solid, built-up hulls and plank-on-frame construction.

Purpleheart — A very hard and difficult wood to work, of fairly fine texture. Pinkish cinnamon with light brown streaks when fresh but oxidizes to a bright violet when exposed to light. Used only for trim and fittings not requiring too much detail or carving.

Redgum — A good, fine grained wood similar to pear but slightly darker. Glues and finishes very well. Used for plank-on-frame construction.

Rosewood — A light to dark purple wood with reddish tints. A fairly hardwood of medium texture that finishes well. Used mostly for trim and color variation. Makes beautiful mounting bases.

Sitka Spruce — A light cream to tan wood that is very straight grained and easy to work. Splits nicely into long scantlings. Considered by many to be the best for masts and spars.

Walnut — A popular, medium hardwood. Color varies from tan to very dark brown. Although quite open grained, pieces can be selected that will give pleasing results. Mostly used for planking, deckhouses and trim.

METAL

Brass, "white" metal, and Brittania metal are perhaps the three most commonly used metals in ship modeling.

Hobby shops carry brass in a variety of forms including wire, sheets of shim stock dimensions, tubing and other extrusions. Small brads and screws are also available.

Many brass ship model fittings are also available. Among these are anchors, steering wheels, capstans, cannon, belaying pins, propellers, cleats and yard irons. Since the fabrication of many of these small intricate parts is quite challenging and time consuming the beginner is probably best advised to use these prefabricated fittings.

The same array of fittings is also available in white metal, a rather brittle alloy of lead.

The modeler wishing to make his own metal fittings can find the needed technical information in many of the books available on jewelry making. These handbooks often contain detailed descriptions of turning, casting, drawing, soldering, forging and the like of small metal parts.

METAL WORK

Though many of the small metal parts necessary to a ship model may be obtained as prefabricated fittings, some modelers like to make them from scratch. There are hundreds of techniques that may be employed in such work which a craftsman may wish to investigate. A good place to start looking would be a handbook on jewelry making.

The suggestions below cover a few of the basics:

BASIC METAL WORKING TOOLS:
VISE(S)
HAND VISE(S)
PIN VISE(S)
MANDRELS
ANVIL(S)
MILL FILES - small in various cross sections
PLIERS - small, needle nose, round, semi-round and square
TWEEZERS - standard, self locking
DRILLS - #75 up
SNIPS OR SCISSORS
JEWELLER'S SAW
TUBE CUTTER
BALL AND PEEN HAMMER(S) - small
TORCH - Jeweller's breath operated alcohol type for hard solder, or;
PINPOINT SOLDERING IRON - for soft solder
EMERY CLOTH OR PAPER
SMALL BUFFING WHEEL
TRIPOLI - or automobile rubbing compound

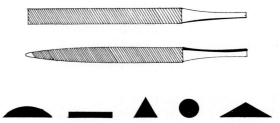

Sheet metal is most easily formed over mandrels. A jeweller's ring mandrel tapering to various diameters is a useful tool made for the purpose, but bolts, nuts or other hardware of the right size will work just as well.

Mill files are available in a variety of cross sections.

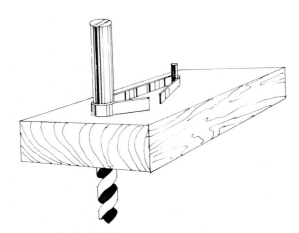

A link such as that in a chain plate may be formed to the correct diameter(s) by using the shank of a properly-sized twist drill sunk into a piece of wood.

Anvils may be made by sinking heavy carriage bolts into a block of hardwood.

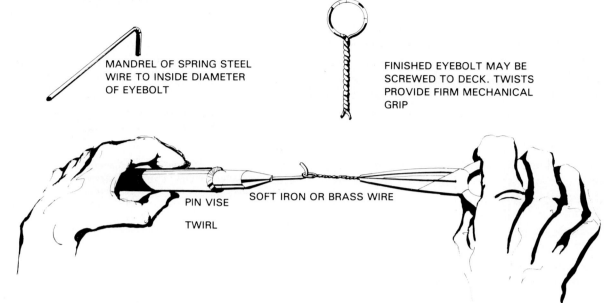

MANDREL OF SPRING STEEL
WIRE TO INSIDE DIAMETER
OF EYEBOLT

FINISHED EYEBOLT MAY BE
SCREWED TO DECK. TWISTS
PROVIDE FIRM MECHANICAL
GRIP

PIN VISE

SOFT IRON OR BRASS WIRE

TWIRL

Ship models require large number of eyebolts which while small in size, must be strong. Beginners frequently underestimate the tension that can be developed in the rigging of a model. Fife rails, pinrails, tops, channels, bobstays and so forth are remarkably prone to breaking if they are not built for maximum strength. Wherever possible, these fastenings should be provided solid mechanical joints with the hull such as bolts, dowels, screws, or mortice and tennon joints. Glue alone should remain suspect.

Commercially available eyebolts usually are bent so that one end of the ring simply butts up against the pin end leaving a real possibility that the bolt will unfold under tension. This is particularly true of soft iron or brass wire eyebolts. A better alternative is to twist a length of wire using a mandrel, pin vise and pair of pliers as shown. Mandrels of the correct diameter may be bent of spring steel wire. Larger diameter spring steel may have to be heated to be formed. If so, heat, form, then heat again and immediately douse the mandrel in cold water.

MAKING CHAIN

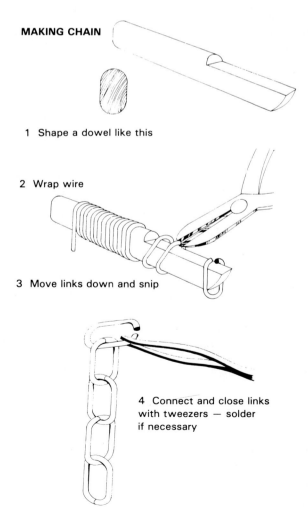

1 Shape a dowel like this

2 Wrap wire

3 Move links down and snip

4 Connect and close links
with tweezers — solder
if necessary

SOLDERING

Solder joins two pieces of metal together by becoming alloyed with them. Heat causes both the solder and adjoining metals to partly melt together into a kind of molecular bond.

There are two varieties of the technique; hard and soft, though both require that the metals to be joined have a higher melting point than the solder or filler itself.

Hard soldering (sometimes called brazing) employs a filler with a melting point above 800 degrees. The most common of these is silver solder which is an alloy of silver, copper and zinc.

Silver itself has a melting point of about 1761 degrees; copper 1981 degrees; and zinc 787 degrees. The proportions of these metals in a particular solder determine its melting point.

Soft soldering employs lead and tin alloy fillers which have melting points as low as 360 degrees.

Both hard and soft solder find their place in ship modeling. Each has its advantages. Hard solder is by far the stronger of the two and can be hammered and shaped with the same freedom as the original metal. But fittings must be made from iron or copper. Brass of the sort popular with modelers has too low a melting point to be workable at hard soldering temperatures.

Soft solder, because it requires less heat, may be employed with brass. It also requires no more than a conventional soldering iron while hard soldering requires a torch.

Soldering requires a flux which serves as a vehicle for carrying the molten alloy into and through the joint. The solder will flow where the paste or liquid flux lies. 20 Mule Team Borax in a water paste works with silver solder. Lead/tin solders might have a rosin or acid core as a built-in flux.

A wide variety of solders are available in hobby shops and hardware stores ranging from hard to soft. They differ in the proportion of metals in their alloys and in the type of flux.

There are also soft soldering pastes on the market. With the paste one can stick two pieces of metal together as he would glue wood, then heat them to obtain a fine soldered joint.

SILVER SOLDER COMES IN WIRE, RIBBON OR SHEET

SILVER SOLDERING PROCEDURE

1 PLACE PART TO BE SOLDERED ON A HEARTH OF FIRE BRICK OR CHARCOAL

2 APPLY FLUX (20 MULE TEAM BORAX PASTE) TO JOINT WITH TOOTHPICK

3 PLACE SMALL FLAKE OF SILVER SOLDER OVER JOINT WITH TWEEZERS

4 HEAT JOINT WITH BLUE TIP OF TORCH FLAME UNTIL SOLDER FLOWS. REMOVE HEAT IMMEDIATELY

5 COOL PART IN WATER AND FINISH JOINT WITH FILE

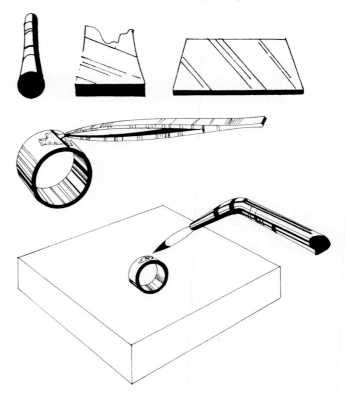

MAKING BLOCKS

Most scale model blocks are very small, some not much larger around than a pencil point. For this reason, few modelers try to make them with working sheaves. Most often, small blocks are single units of wood with holes through them to simulate the sheave.

Somewhat larger scale blocks are sometimes built up of three layers of stock corresponding to the shell and sheave.

Finally, there are cases where blocks of 1/8″ and smaller have fully functional sheaves turning on a pin.

A sailing ship model, of course, may have hundreds of blocks in her rigging, the making of which can be a formidable labor. Therefore, even the most pure in heart among modelers have been known to buy commercially manufactured blocks for their otherwise completely scratch built models.

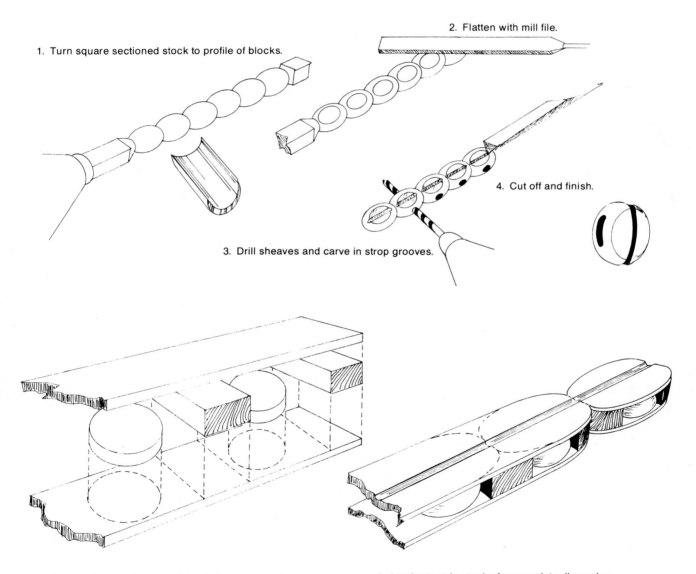

1. Turn square sectioned stock to profile of blocks.

2. Flatten with mill file.

3. Drill sheaves and carve in strop grooves.

4. Cut off and finish.

1. Punch sheaves from cardboard of correct thickness using sharpened length of tubing as a die.

2. Laminate strip stock of appropriate dimensions.

3. Groove for strop, shape, cut off, and finish.

STRAPPING

Press a channel into a piece of kneaded eraser (available in art supply stores) with a length of tube or screw driver. Press the strapping thread into the eraser athwart the channel, then press the block over it exactly in position. The eraser will hold the block and thread aligned while you tie the strap.

Use the same trick to support lines while clapping on seizings.

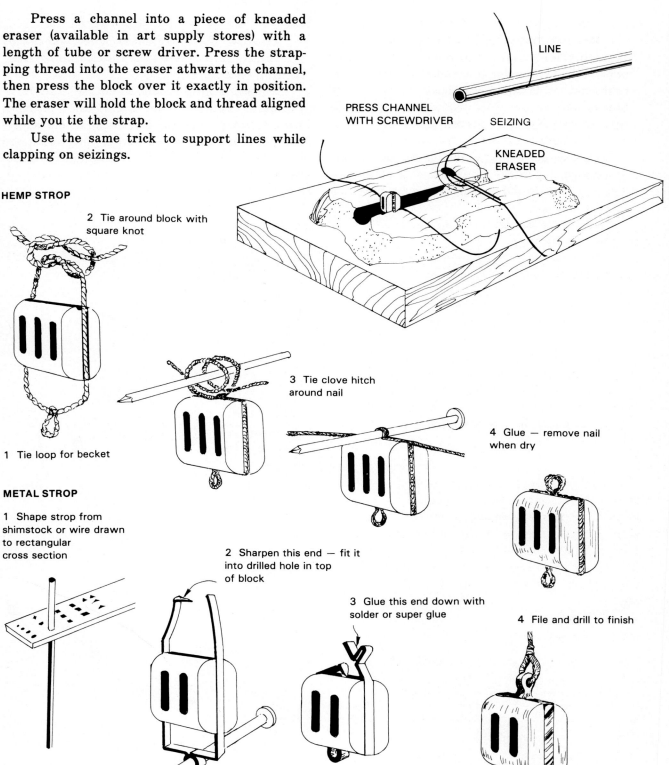

LINE

PRESS CHANNEL WITH SCREWDRIVER

SEIZING

KNEADED ERASER

HEMP STROP

2 Tie around block with square knot

1 Tie loop for becket

3 Tie clove hitch around nail

4 Glue — remove nail when dry

METAL STROP

1 Shape strop from shimstock or wire drawn to rectangular cross section

2 Sharpen this end — fit it into drilled hole in top of block

3 Glue this end down with solder or super glue

4 File and drill to finish

CORDAGE

Linen thread is the most popular and best recommended material for ship model rigging. Linen provides a clean hard rope-like finish and does not shrink or expand too much with changes in the weather. Cotton is less satisfactory though some modelers use it to good effect. Artificial fibers such as Nylon or Dacron, however, should be avoided because they are too elastic.

Linen rigging is available in hobby stores and through ship model mail order distributors in a variety of scale dimensions and with black or natural finishes.

Black is for tarred standing rigging; natural for the running rigging.

The "natural" colored linen is often too white to simulate hemp correctly so modelers often dye it slightly with shoe dye. Coffee or tea work, but may cause the line to deteriorate.

The thread looks better if it is "de-fuzzed" with a treatment of beeswax or a dilute clear acrylic wood finish such as Deft.

Linen rigging is available in sizes ranging from .25 to 1.75 millimeters in natural color and from .25 to 1 millimeter in black.

Surgical silk or a strand unravelled from a heavier line can work for thin lines, servings and the like.

Linen and other thread in small diameters exhibits a certain springiness, which can be a nuisance during such operations as tying ratlines. This problem can be relieved by soaking the thread in fabric softener.

SCALE CONVERSION

Ship modelers often work out scale conversion charts as a guide in selecting the right sized line for their particular model. Ship model kits and plans come in large number of different scales.

Many experienced modelers use a micrometer to measure line thickness and some go to the extreme in selecting or fabricating rigging line to precise scale dimensions. Most modelers, however, do not fuss over a few hundredths of a millimeter and simply use the standard model rigging line closest to the requirement.

The chart below will serve for the scales of 1/8" = 1'0"; 3/16" = 1'0"; and 1/4" = 1'0".

Size of Rope in real ship Diameter in inches	Size of Model Rope Dia. in Millimeters (1 Millimeter = .0393 inches)		
	1/8" - 1'0" 1/96	3/16" - 1'0" 1/64	1/4" - 1'0" 1/48
1/4"	.07	.10	.13
1/2"	.14	.20	.27
3/4"	.21	.30	.40
1"	.28	.40	.53
1½"	.42	.60	.80
2"	.56	.80	1.07
2½"	.70	1.00	1.34
3"	.84	1.20	1.61
3½"	.98	1.40	1.88
4"	1.12	1.60	2.15

MINIATURE ROPE WALK

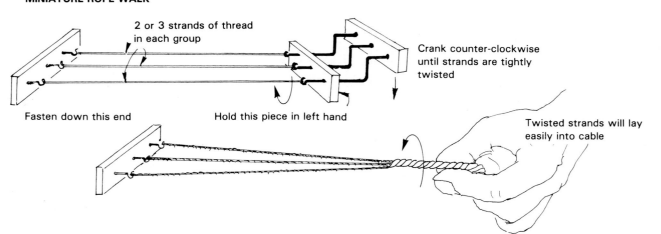

2 or 3 strands of thread in each group

Crank counter-clockwise until strands are tightly twisted

Fasten down this end

Hold this piece in left hand

Twisted strands will lay easily into cable

SETTING UP SHROUDS / REEVING DEADEYE LANYARDS

1 Set up the lower mast and plot the line of the shrouds past the channel to the hull side to determine the correct alignment of the chain plates.

2 Install the lower deadeyes and chain plates.

3 The shrouds will go around the masthead in pairs. The first pair begins at the foremost lower deadeye on the starboard side and goes up around the masthead and back down to the second deadeye on the starboard side. The bight is round seized where the two ends go around the masthead. The second pair repeats the process to port, while subsequent pairs alternate from starboard to port. If there is a remaining odd shroud, it will run from starboard to port and be fitted around the masthead with a "cut splice." Place the seizings on the pairs of shrouds before fitting them to the masthead, put them over and slide the seizings up. Make the cut splice by seizing a short length of material to the odd pair.

4 Make a deadeye spacer as shown in the illustration and turn in the upper deadeyes starting with the foremost on the starboard side, followed by the one to port. Keep the tension even from side to side being sure that the mast stays straight as you work aft. As each set of deadeyes is turned in and seized, secure the seizings with glue, then remove the spacer tool and let the turned in shrouds hang by the mast while you proceed to the next pair.

5 Reeve the laniards starting again with the foremost on either side. Make a "needle" out of the end of your laniard material by soaking a half inch of it in "super glue."

Remember in setting up standing rigging that the first lines to go around the masthead are the mast tackles, then the shrouds from forward-starboard to forward-port and so on aft; and finally the stays.

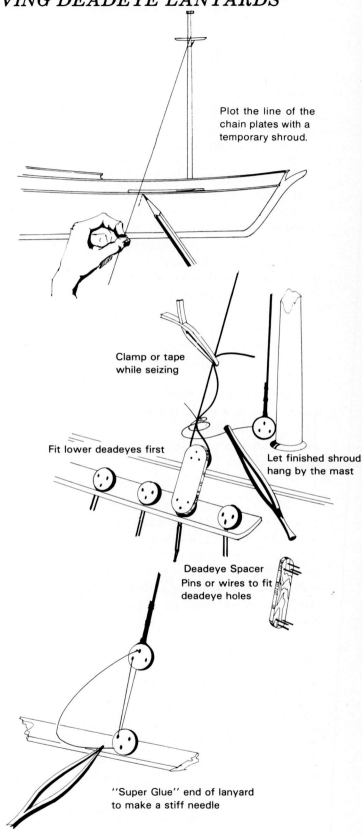

Plot the line of the chain plates with a temporary shroud.

Clamp or tape while seizing

Fit lower deadeyes first

Let finished shroud hang by the mast

Deadeye Spacer
Pins or wires to fit deadeye holes

"Super Glue" end of lanyard to make a stiff needle

REFERENCES

Abell, Sir Westcott
The Shipwright's Trade
Cambridge, MA, 1948

Anderson, R.C.
Seventeenth Century Rigging
London, 1955

Baker, W.A.
*The Development of
Wooden Ship Construction*
Quincy, MA, 1955

Bass, G.
*A History of Seafaring from
    Underwater Archaeology*
London, 1972

Botting, Douglas
The Pirates
Alexandria, VA, 1978

Bowen, John
Scale Model Sailing Ships
New York, 1978

Campbell, G.F.
Jackstay
Bogata, NJ, 1962

Chapelle, Howard I.
The American Fishing Schooners 1825-1935
New York, 1973

Charnock, J.
History of Marine Architecture
London, 1802

Cutler, Carl C.
Greyhounds of the Sea
Annapolis, 1930

Dana, Richard Henry
Two Years Before the Mast
London, 1912 from original of 1869

Davis, C.G.
The Built-Up Ship Model
New York, 1975 (reprint)
Ship Model Builder's Assistant
New York, 1970 (reprint)
Ships of the Past
New York, 1929

Durant, Will and Ariel
The Story of Civilization
Vols. 7, 8
New York, 1961, 1963

Edson, Merritt et al
Ship Modeler's Shop Notes
Washington, D.C., 1979

Grimwood, V.R.
*American Ship Models
and How to Build Them*
New York, 1942

Haws, D.
Ships and Sea
Gothenburg, 1975

Heyerdahl, Thor
Early Man and The Ocean
New York, 1978
Kon-Tiki
Chicago, 1950

Howard, F.
Sailing Ships of War 1400-1860
Greenwich, 1979

Johnson, Gene
Ship Model Building
Cambridge, MD, 1961

Kemp, P.
The History of Ships
London, 1978
*The Oxford Companion
to Ships & the Sea*
London, 1976

Kinney, Francis S.
*Skene's Elements of Yacht Design
Eighth Edition*
New York, 1981

La Fay, H.
The Vikings
Washington, D.C., 1972

Landstrom, B.
The Ship
Stockholm, 1961

Lever, Darcy
*The Young Sea Officer's Sheet Anchor
    or a Key to the Leading of Rigging*
London, 1819

Lubbock, Basil
The Western Ocean Packets
Glasgow, 1956

Mansir, A.R.
How to Build Ship Models, A Beginner's Guide
Dana Point, CA, 1979
A Modeler's Guide to Hull Construction
Dana Point, CA, 1980
A Modeler's Guide to Rigging
Dana Point, CA 1981

Melville, Herman
Moby Dick
New York, 1851

Millar, John F.
*American Ships of the Colonial
    & Revolutionary Periods*
New York, 1978

Morrison, Samuel Eliot
*The European Discovery of America
The Northern Voyages*
New York, 1971
*The European Discovery of America
The Southern Voyages*
New York, 1974
Admiral of the Ocean Sea
Boston, 1942

Nordbok, A.B. et al
The Lore of Ships
Gothenburg, 1975

Rogers, Woodes
A Cruising Voyage Around the World
New York, 1970 Republication of
    1928 & 1712 Editions

Ronnberg, E.A.R., Jr.
Benjamin W. Latham
Bogata, NJ, 1973

Underhill, Harold A.
*Plank-on-Frame Models and
    Scale Masting and Rigging*
Vols. 1 and 2
Glasgow, 1958

Webster, F.B.
Shipbuilding Cyklopedia
New York, 1920

Wiener, Philip O. and Noland Aaron
Roots of Scientific Thought
New York, 1957

Wilcox, L.A.
Mr. Pepy's Navy
New York, 1968

Wendt, Herbert
In Search of Adam
Boston, 1956

Periodicals:
    Model Shipwright
    Greenwich, England

    Nautical Research Journal
    Washington, D.C.

    Sea History
    New York

    Scale Ship Modeler
    Canoga Park, CA

    Ship Model Builder
    Menomenee Falls, WI

A

Aaron Manby, Iron
    steamship, 166
Achaens, 53
Agamemnon, 53
Aker, Raymond, 274
Akrotiri, city, 50
*Alaska Packers Assn. of
    San Francisco,* 168
anchor, 21, 127 ff, 148, 149;
    modeling, 301
anchor cable, 127, 130
anchor hoy, 131, 222
Anson, Commodore George,
    42, 43
apron, 88, 92, 103, 106
Arab dhow, 62, 70
Archimedes, 57 ff
area of lateral resistance, 33
armaments, 57 ff
Athens, Athenians, 52, 54

B

backrope, 95, 221
backstay, 95, 211, 213 ff, 229
Bacon, Roger, 58
Baker, Mathew, 25, 33
Baker, William A., 77, 274
ballast, 32
ballast keel, 32
balloon jib, 264
Baltimore Clipper, 34
barge, 164
bark, *Colonial,* 70, 113, 133,
    177
bark, *Star of India,* 7 passim
Bass, George, 8, 59, 69, 100
basswood (limewood), 309
beakhead, 93 ff
beam, 14 passim
bearing, relative, 14
beat, to point of sail, 15
becket, of a block, 200, 204
bed, of gun, 144
bee, bee block, bee holes, 186,
    205, 206, 221
before the wind, point of sail
    15
beitass, 61
belay, modeling, 308
belaying pin, 207, 226
belfry, 134, 145

bell, ship's, 134, 135
bending sails, 249
Benson, William D., 6, 10
bent frame construction, 112
bentick shroud, 216 ff
Bermuda sail, rig, 252, 272
bilge keelson, 106, 109, 168
bilge stringer, 106, 109, 168
billboard, 129, 145
binnacle, 21
bireme, 52
bitts, 20, 95, 130, 205
bitter end of anchor cable,
    22, 130
blackwall hitch, 198
blocks, 199 ff, modeling, 309
boarding ladder, 145
boarding port, 123,
boat, 14, 147, 164; modeling,
    302
bobstay, 95, 186, 214, 221
bobstay piece, 88, 103, 106
body plan, 24 ff
bollard, 205
boltrope, 246 ff
bonaventure mizzen mast
    and rigging, 174, 177,
    213
bonnet, 239, 250
boom, 191, 214, 250
boot (false keel), 88, 103
bosom knee, 103, 119
bow, 14, 21, 91 ff;
    modeling 288
bower anchor, 95, 127, 149
bowline, 19, 226, 227; knot,
    198; line of square sail,
    19, 224; line of lateen
    sail, 234
bowsprit, 21, 95, 109, 174 ff,
    186 ff, 191, 221
brace, 19, 224 ff
brail, 239, 250
brazing, 304
bread and butter model, 278
breast hook, 88, 92
Bridenbecker, Henry, 10,
    68 ff, 76 ff,
    89, 97, 104 ff, 117, 131,
    151, 250,
    254, 264 ff, 270 ff

brig, 94,110, 210, 214
brigantine, 210

British 3rd rate, 174
broach to, to, 22
broad off, point of sail, 15
broad on, point of relative
    bearing, 14
broad strake, 117
Brunel, Isambard Kingdom,
    166, 168
*Builder's Old Measurement
    (B. O. M.),* 29
bulkhead, 20
bulkhead model, 279 ff
bullock block, 181, 184, 189
bullseye, 205, 206, 207
bulwark, 106, 109, 123, 205,
    207
bumkin, 201, 205
bunt of sail, 246
buntline, 211, 224, 226, 228
buntline, monkey block, 226,
    228
buoyancy, 30
Burrell, William, 25
burton tackle, 20, 133, 201
buttocks, buttock lines, 24
*Byzantine Empire,
    Byzantium,* 58, 59, 69,
    100

C

cable, anchor, 128, 130 ff
cable-laid rope, 194
camber of decks, 120
cannon, 161 ff
cant frames, 92; modeling,
    288
canvas, 245
cap of mast, 171 ff
caprail, 21, 106, 119
capstan, 21, 95, 109, 133, 145,
    156
caravel, 81
caravella latina, 81
caravella redonda, 81
carling carline of deck, 86,
    103, 119 ff
carrack, 64, 76, 81, 180, 187
carrick bend, 198
carronade, 161 ff
carvel planking, 54, 64 101
cascabel of gun, 144
castle, forecastle, stern
    castle, mast castle, 63 ff

transom, 88, 96, 103, 113
traveller, 235, 237
treenail (trennel), 13, 86, 118
trestletree, 171 ff, 178
    190, 234
trireme, Greek battleship, 54
Trojan War, 53
Trotman's anchor, 129
truck of mast, 172, 233
trunnion of gun, 144
truss, 205, 224, 229, 242
tub parrel, 185
tumblehome, 282
turnbuckle, 205
tun (tun), 27
Two Years Before the Mast,
    20, 87

U

upper topsail, 181, 229

V

Van der Walker, Roger,
    238, 262
Venice, 62
venice turpentine, 169
Viking ships, 60 ff, 71, 98, 99
Virginia, the 254

W

wale, 21, 90, 100, 103, 118
waist, 20, 103, 145
waring (wearing) a square
    rigger, 15, 19
watches, sailors' work
    periods, 134
watch tackles, 204
water retting, 194
waterlines, 24 ff
waterway, 119
wave line theory, 34
Weiss, Allan, 272
whaleboat, 150 ff
wheel, drum, 140, 141
wheel, steering, 14, 21
    141 ff, 154 ff
whip, tackle, 204, 212
whipping of rope, 195
whipstaff, 140, 141
whisker boom, 95, 221
Whomsley, Luther, 259

Wicks, Bill, 10, 94, 113,
    285, 286
William the Conqueror, 63
winding tackle, 20, 204
wing transom, 88, 96, 113
wire rigging, 194, 215
wood for modeling, 304
wooden ship, 48, 82 ff, 103
woolding, 103, 145, 171 ff
worm gear, 140 ff
worming, 195

X

xebec (chebec), 235

Y

yacht, 252; *Eagle,* 272
yard iron, 205
yard tackle, 212, 224
yards, 183 ff; proportions of,
    190, 219
Yassi Ada, Island, and ship
    from, 59, 69, 100, 250
yaw, component of ship
    motion, 35
yawl, 164, 253

Z

z-laid rope, 194